Urumqi ■

Casablanca ■   Tehran-Karaj ■

■ Hefei

Hyderabad ■

Addis Ababa ■   ■ Ho Chi Minh City

Lima ■

Gauteng ■

YOUNG RESEARCH FORUM

Research Papers for Future Megacities on Governance, Water, Planning, and Mobility

Lukas Born (editor)

Book Series
Future Megacities
Additional Volume

SPONSORED BY THE

Federal Ministry
of Education
and Research

The Book Series "Research for the Sustainable Development of Megacities of Tomorrow" is sponsored by the German Federal Ministry of Education and Research (BMBF) through the funding priority "Research for the Sustainable Development of Megacities of Tomorrow". The authors would like to thank the Ministry for this initiative, for the financial support, and for the extraordinary opportunity to connect activity- and demand-oriented research with practical implementation in various pilot projects targeting the challenges of Future Megacities.

The book series "Future Megacities" is published by Elke-Pahl-Weber, Bernd Kochendörfer, Lukas Born, Jan Müller, and Ulrike Assmann, Technische Universität Berlin. The series contains the cross-cutting results of the nine projects. These results are the intellectual property of the authors.

This additional volume "Young Research Forum" is edited by Lukas Born, Technische Universität Berlin (cross-project programme support of the Future Megacities Programme). The editor would like to thank Francisco Aguilera S. and Lascha Sochadse for their support of the editing process.

Index

Preface and Introduction

Governance

Urban Resources: Water

Planning and Architecture

Mobility and Transportation

Appendix

PREFACE AND INTRODUCTION

CASABLANCA: Young trees planted in an act of "guerilla gardening" in Casablanca's suburbs [Lukas Born]

Elke Pahl-Weber, Bernd Kochendörfer, Irmgard Kasperek, Lukas Born, Carsten Zehner

The Future Megacities Programme— Framework and Contribution of Young Researchers

The Future Megacities Research Programme

The Global Urban Future

The development of future megacities describes a new quality of urban growth with today's unprecedented pace and dynamics of urbanisation. At the beginning of the twentieth century, only 20% of the world's population lived in cities. Since 2010, however, the share of urban dwellers has dramatically risen to over 50%. By 2050, world population is predicted to increase from 7.0 billion to 9.3 billion and by that time, 70% of the population will be living in urban areas, many of them in urban corridors, city- or mega-regions [UN-DESA 2012; UN-Habitat 2012].

Urban areas contribute disproportionately to national productivity and national GDP. Globally, they are responsible for 80% of economic output [UN-Habitat 2012; UNEP 2011]. Urban areas thus also are very relevant in terms of energy consumption. Although cities cover only a small percentage of the earth's surface,[1] they are responsible for around 60–80% of global energy consumption as well as approximately 75% of global greenhouse gas emissions [UNEP 2011]. In the future, this will increase for cities in so-called developing countries, as they will be responsible for about 80% of increases in global annual energy consumption between 2006 and 2030 [UN-Habitat 2011]. Hence, cities are significantly contributing to climate change while, at the same time having to deal with its devastating consequences because many are located close to rising sea levels, in flood-prone or in arid areas. Cities therefore must take action to increase energy and resource efficiency as well as towards climate change mitigation and adaptation.

Megacities, as a spreading phenomenon, do have a special role in this context and illustrate the urban challenges of the future. These urban centres are not only reaching new levels in terms of size, but are also confronted with new levels of complexity. They are facing multifaceted problems directly affecting the quality of life of their inhabitants. In many cases, indispensable assets, such as social and technical infrastructure, delivery of basic services, or access to affordable housing are lacking. Capacities for urban management and legal frameworks tend to be chronically weak and are often insufficient for dealing with rapid population and spatial growth. Moreover, excessive consumption of resources, such as energy or water, is further aggravating existing problems.

In many countries, medium-sized cities are especially experiencing extraordinary growth rates. These "Future Megacities" are to be taken into consideration for sustainable urban development strategies and for urban and territorial planning as they still offer the opportunity for precautionary action and targeted urban development towards sustainability [UNEP 2011].

BMBF's Funding Priority on Future Megacities

With its funding priority "Research for the Sustainable Development of Megacities of Tomorrow", the German Federal Ministry of Education and Research (BMBF) is focusing on energy-efficient and climate-responsive structures in large and fast-growing cities or megacities. The programme is a globally focused component of the Federal Government's High-Tech Strategy in the field of action on "Climate and Energy". Moreover, it is a part of the framework programme "Research for Sustainable Development" (FONA) of the BMBF.

In its main phase (2008-2013), the funding priority currently covers nine international projects in Future Megacities of Asia (Tehran-Region, Hyderabad, Urumqi, Hefei, Ho Chi Minh City), Africa (Casablanca, Addis Ababa, Johannesburg region), and Latin America (Lima). Each project focuses on a particular city working on a locally-relevant thematic issue within the broader context of energy efficiency and climate change [project descriptions, p. 201 ff.].

An outstanding characteristic of the programme is the integration of the sustainable development concept. Ecological, economic, and social facets of the development of energy-efficient and climate-responsive structures in urban growth centres are to be considered in a comprehensive and long-term manner. In this context, the programme follows an innovative methodology that includes analysing spatial, social, and technical dimensions in combination with applied research, using broad methodological approaches such as pilot projects, action research, and research by design. The research approach thus differs from other forms of fundamental research due to its practice-oriented focus that takes into account local needs as a basis for the development of applicable solutions. The transdisciplinary research is conducted through interdisciplinary consortia with partners from research institutions, civil society, politics, administration as well as the private sector. International collaboration among project partners from Germany and the partner countries is an essential aspect of the programme.

The objective of the Future Megacities Programme (FMC) is to create good practice solutions for sustainable urban development. Therefore, the bilateral teams:

1. research, plan, develop, and realise technical and non-technical innovations for the establishment of energy-efficient and climate-responsive structures in an exemplary way,
2. enable the city, along with its decision-makers and inhabitants, to bring about increased performance and efficiency gains in energy production, distribution, and use, and
3. demonstrate that resource consumption and greenhouse gas emissions by high-energy consumption sectors can be reduced in a sustainable way in the future [DLR-PT 2012].

Outcomes and Results of the Research Programme

Outcomes of the nine projects have been generated in different thematic fields of action, which also serve as a structure for this publication series. Within these thematic areas, a great variety of good practice for building energy-efficient and climate-responsive structures in urban growth centres has been generated, ranging from scientific knowledge, analytical instruments and strategic models, all the way up to realised pilot-projects, innovative technologies, applied products and locally implemented processes. In the field of action on "Energy and Sun", concepts for the urban use of renewable energies with particular focus on solar power have been elaborated for different sectors in order to decrease the use of fossil fuels and reduce carbon-dioxide emissions and air pollution. The topic "Mobility and Transport" comprises concepts for sustainable transportation through intelligent management approaches, innovative planning instruments and systems for enhancing public transit. Within the area of "Planning", solutions for increasing energy efficiency in architecture and urban design, instruments for integrated urban planning, as well as efficient management tools for climate change mitigation and adaptation have been developed. The programme's area of action on "Resources" focuses on generating new approaches for the sustainable management of waste, the careful use of scarce resources such as water, as well as efficient material cycles in the industrial sector. In the field of "Governance", models for multistakeholder systems, new approaches to inclusive decision-making processes, as well as community participation and bottom-up engagement have been developed. Outcomes within the area of action on "Capacities" include measures for vocational training in various practical fields, as well as new concepts for education and awareness raising focusing on the younger generation.

This book series presents results generated within these thematic fields of action in terms of cutting-edge research as well as practical outcomes. Whereas the other volumes emphasise one specific topic, this particular volume focuses on almost all the topics mentioned above. This is because the aim of this volume is to present and appreciate the particular contributions of rather young researchers to the research programme as a whole. Answers are given on innovative aspects, applicability, transferability, or dissemination of the solutions in the framework of future megacities in general.

Additionally, all nine participating cities and projects are presented in the appendix, where the complexity of the research priority, the different approaches, and a short overview of the most important outcomes are shown.

The Role of Young Researchers within the Future Megacities Programme

Without a doubt, senior scientists and project coordinators were responsible for the project layout and programme outcomes. But they were usually accompanied and supported by many PhD, master, and bachelor students. All of these young researchers have provided substantial input to the research on megacities and to the efforts to implement innovative ideas in the nine cities. Many of them have invested not only time, ideas, and enthusiasm, but personal financial means as well. Hence, their work was an integral part of the success that the Future Megacities Programme has impressively achieved. Therefore, and on behalf of the many institutions and universities, we would like to express our gratitude for their valuable contributions.

As a sign of our appreciation towards young researchers, this additional volume of the book series has been published, even though it presents only a small selection of the vast amount of scientific work accomplished by young researchers. Providing a just overview of all the scientific papers written in the context of this research programme would be an almost impossible undertaking; basing the selection on the winners of the Young Researchers' Award 2013 has therefore eased this challenging task (see more details below).

DAAD's Scholarship Programme on Future Megacities

The special programme on "Study and Research Scholarships of Today for the Megacities of Tomorrow" was part of the Future Megacity Programme and was thereby also financed by the BMBF. The programme offered highly qualified students, doctoral candidates, postdocs, senior scientists, and senior experts from the above-mentioned countries the opportunity to study or conduct research in project-relevant subject areas at German universities and German research institutes that were contributing to the collaborative projects. On behalf of the BMBF, the German Academic Exchange Service (DAAD) has implemented the sub-programme.

The announcement of the DAAD programme was published twice, in 2009 and 2010. Within the funding period from 2009 to 2013, DAAD received a total of 218 applications. Out of these, 116 applicants finally received a scholarship for one of the nine projects in their respective cities: twenty-eight Indians (Hyderabad), twenty-five Iranians (Karaj-Tehran), nineteen Vietnamese (Ho Chi Minh City), fourteen Chinese (Urumqi), thirteen Peruvians (Lima), four Ethiopians (Addis Ababa), five Moroccans (Casablanca), four South Africans (Gauteng), and two Chinese each for Hefei and a project in Shanghai, which had already been finished much earlier than the other nine projects.

By integrating the scholarship holders into the work of the collaborative projects, the programme aimed to create sustainable networking between the scholarship holders themselves and the German project partners. So the DAAD invited thirty-two senior experts and twenty-seven scientists visiting the German project partners for between two weeks and three months, sixteen postdoctoral fellows conducting research up to two years, thirty-three doctoral candidates accomplishing their PhD-studies up to thirty-eight months, and eight graduates working on their Master theses for three to six months. Out of the forty-one young scientists, nineteen agreed to publish their research topics and contacts in the last section of this chapter [p. 21 ↗].

A highlight of the scholarship programme was the "Young Researchers' Symposium on Future Megacities" in the German city of Essen and the first "Young Researchers' Award". It was organised by DAAD together with the University of Duisburg-Essen under the patronage of the BMBF in October 2010. DAAD published the discussions, presentations, and findings out of this fruitful meeting in a conference volume.[2]

2nd Young Researchers' Forum and Award, Hamburg 2013

In addition to the applicants for the DAAD-scholarships, many other young scientists were involved in the research on Future Megacities. Either they were studying at German universities or research institutions that were involved in the nine FMC-projects mentioned above, or they were graduates from universities in one of the nine countries. These scientists were the focus of the Young Researchers' Forum and the second call for the Young Researchers' Award in 2013. Both events were organised by the support team for the FMC-programme from Technische Universität Berlin and TÜV Rhineland in collaboration with the German Aerospace Center/ Project Agency.

Around seventy young researchers participated in the forum. They also took the opportunity to present their work on posters during the international conference "Future Megacities in Action" in May 2013 in Hamburg and during the forum itself, which was organised as a pre-event of the conference. A rather small number of applicants for the Young Researchers' Award was

also among forum participants. Finally, this number presented only the tip of the iceberg of the many scientific works done in the context of the FMC-programme. This was mainly due to the fact that only finalised and formally assessed works were admitted for the award.

In addition to the criteria for proper scientific work, the applicants were asked to comply with criteria such as the applicability of their work to practice, the transferability or importance of the research to other future megacities, the degree of technical or non-technical innovation for the energy-efficient and climate-responsive design of cities, the consideration of the concept of sustainability, or whether the work took a cross-sectoral approach or tackled only an isolated sectoral problem. The awarded winners were granted a financial bonus and the promise that their work would be published. That promise is now accomplished with this book.

The Young Researchers' "Hamburg Declaration"

During the Young Researchers' Forum, the graduates worked on a declaration and used the opportunity to present their remarks and demands during the conference held in May 2013 in Hamburg. Due to the location, they called it the "Hamburg Declaration". They recognised firstly the successful involvement of several generations of PhD, Master, and Bachelor students in various projects throughout the programme's duration. Secondly, they highlighted the importance of the emerging transdisciplinary science of megacity studies and efforts of international organisations to attain the Millennium Development Goals, the World Summit on Sustainable Development objectives, and other key international development strategies. Furthermore, they highlighted the importance of megacity research and the interdependence of basic or practice-oriented research and applied solutions for a sustainable urban development in the future.

But they also demanded the need for continuity and long-term partnerships for ensuring the success of megacity research and development. They called upon the BMBF, the DAAD, and all other contributing organisations, institutions, and individuals (1) to establish lasting networking opportunities for the alumni of this project programme; (2) to assist in the continuation of capacity building efforts; (3) to establish new or connect existing knowledge databases, including contact information and research results as an information reference for project participants and others; (4) to ensure continued study opportunities for German and foreign students and graduates, for example through the organisation and support of follow-up initiatives; and (5) to establish a fund for the development and realisation of research projects initiated by young researchers dealing with the issues of Future Megacities [Hamburg Declaration 2013].

The Book Series' Volume on the Scientific Work of Young Researchers

The volumes of the book series tackle respective topics with specific emphasis on the sustainable development of megacities: energy and resources, mobility and transportation, planning and design, capacity development, and governance (local action). Whereas the topic of energy plays an important role in some of the articles in this book (e.g., Kimmich, Ntuli), the field of capacity development is not represented at all. But this is only due to the fact that no one contributed a thesis with this topic to the Young Researchers' Award.[3] However, the four topics (I) mobility, (II) urban resources, (III) planning and design, and (IV) governance are the main chapters of this volume on young research. Each chapter starts with extended articles by winners of the Young Researchers' Award summarising their PhD, Master, or Bachelor theses. The chapters end with few abstracts of research papers by applicants to the award who were not granted a prize or special recognition.

Furthermore, almost all articles are connected to one of the nine projects. Therefore, most of the articles in this volume can be read as additional and valuable information to contributions in other volumes of this series. Respective special notices in the following section, which describes the contributions in brief, will give you an overview of these connections with other volumes.

Governance in the Energy Sector in India and South Africa

Decision-making processes in cities often go beyond formalised procedures of local authorities and result in rather informal processes of negotiation. Formal governments are no longer the only key stakeholders on urban issues; many actors are on stage competing for resources and decisions. Negotiations involve multiple players ranging from politicians and public administrators, to civil society and the private sector. Furthermore, the effectiveness of planning and governance depends upon the persuasive power that can lead to collective actions [UN-Habitat 2009]. In this wide thematic field of governance, two papers were submitted for the award.

In his dissertation, **Christian Kimmich** focuses on the situation of farmers close to Hyderabad. He argues that agriculture is a crucial sector either enabling or impeding a transition path towards the sustainable development of urban areas. Rural-urban linkages touch topics, such as migration, food security, water allocation for agricultural production versus drinking water supply in the city, or electricity allocation for agricultural production versus urban consumption. Decisions on these topics are crucial and have long-lasting consequences for both urban and rural spheres. Kimmich limits his analysis to the electricity-irrigation nexus and includes as stakeholders, farmers, the electricity provider, and local governments. He describes electricity providers as having reduced investments, monitoring capacities, and grid maintenance. The connectedness of decisions of all stakeholders contributes to high voltage fluctuations, poor power quality, pump-set burnouts in the countryside, and to increasing blackouts in Hyderabad as well. Pump-sets of poor quality in combination with unqualified repairs increase energy inefficiency and further deteriorate power quality. But this situation leads to high costs and various heavy burdens on farmers as well. To ease the situation and to assist technology adoption, Kimmich recommends the application of social learning and governance mechanisms. The results have served to design a pilot project which is described in detail in the first edited book *Energy and Sun* of the book series ↗.

Ntombifuthi Ntuli also describes governance issues in the field of energy in her master's thesis. She focuses on the Clean Development Mechanisms (CDM). This arrangement was established under the Kyoto Protocol to reduce global greenhouse gas emissions. It allows rich countries to virtually meet their emission reduction targets through investing in projects that reduce CO_2 emissions and contribute to a sustainable development in emerging and developing countries. These projects generate credits called Certified Emission Reductions (CERs) which help the buyers to meet their national reduction obligations. Once they are sold, CERs create revenues for the authorities in the developing countries. Using different qualitative research techniques, she illustrates the perspectives of European CER buyers, the CDM project developers in South Africa, and the Gauteng municipal officials responsible for CDM project development. With only twenty registered CDM projects by June 2011, South Africa lagged far behind other developing regions. Ntuli's research identifies obstacles that prevent the implementation of more CDM projects by municipalities in the Gauteng region. Furthermore, she investigates reasons why municipalities lagged behind the private sector in CDM project development (e.g., inadequate capacity in responsible administrations, high CDM transaction costs, or scepticism regarding the benefits of CDM). Because there is no significant revenue stream from the sale of CERs, the study indicates that the CDM is not an appropriate way for South Africa to substantially reduce global greenhouse gas emissions. Moreover, South Africa's contribution to climate protection must be financed through other mechanisms.

Studies on Water Issues in the Arid Cities of Urumqi and Lima

While the general issue of urban resources touches topics like material cycles, (re)use and management of waste or water, a chapter in this book deals exclusively with water due to the applications for the Young Researchers' Award. The massive and still rising consumption of water is a huge challenge in emerging megacities especially in arid and semi-arid areas. The demand for water often exceeds existing natural water resources further deteriorated by climate change, leading to more scarcity. This overexploitation becomes visible by falling groundwater tables or polluted streams and calls for urgent action—e.g., decentralised water treatment, reuse of treated wastewater, or upgrading of water and wastewater infrastructure. Moreover, often missing is basic knowledge of existing water resources.

Katharina Fricke's PhD thesis covers a wide range on questions on future ground water resources in Urumqi. Set in a semi-arid climate and close to high mountains feeding the city's water resources mainly with melting water, Urumqi will receive more water flow in the higher mountain areas and up to 12% less in the lower areas due to climate change reducing snowfall and meltwater in the coming years. Groundwater recharge thus will decrease and actual evapotranspiration will rise, especially in agricultural areas. Fricke's water forecasts are based on a combination of a hydrological water balance model simulating water supply with a socio-econometric model projecting future water demand. By doing so, she considers five different climate scenarios. Adaptation strategies focus on measures to reduce the absolute or relative water demand, especially in the agricultural sector. A shift of production and infrastructure into areas with lower evapotranspiration and higher precipitation, even outside Urumqi Region, is proposed. Fricke's essential contribution has a high value as basic research for the efforts of the Urumqi-Project in its task force on water-resource efficiency.

The interdisciplinarity of the Future Megacities research programme becomes evident in **Kara Jean McElhinney's** master's thesis. Starting in the field of water resources engineering and management, the author links her study with the subject of landscape planning: with regard to a necessary energy-efficient and climate-responsive urbanisation, a fundamental change in the way water is managed is required. Such a change must focus on sustainability and integration. The author proposes "water-sensitive urban design" as a tool. Departing from the traditional design paradigm, water-sensitive urban design takes a renewed approach to urban water management. It considers the total water cycle and infrastructure as experienced by city inhabitants via its integration into the urban landscape. Such integration supports the natural habitats of flora and fauna, creates urban green and recreational spaces, alleviates water scarcity, and integrates wastewater treatment. Based on her knowledge of engineering, McElhinney collects data regarding quantity, temperature, oxygen balance, salt content, acidity, nutrient content, microbiology, and heavy metal content in local water sources using a variety of tools including observation, estimation, and field and laboratory testing. These audit results were then very practically applied to water-sensitive urban designs developed for different kinds of water resources in specific neighbourhoods by a group of architecture students (i.e., constructed wetlands for water treatment, dikes for flood protection, et cetera).

Like Urumqi, Lima is also situated in a dry climate and surrounded by high mountains and melting glaciers. Touching these natural and topographical similarities, **Myriam Laux** describes comparable problems in her diploma thesis about Lima. Lima's water availability is completely based on resources from the Andes. Severe problems will occur if no actions are taken to adjust the high future water demand to the scarce water availability. Laux bases her scenarios and solutions for Lima on a mass-flow analysis called LiWa-tool, which has been developed in the context of the LiWa-Project in Lima. In her simulation model, she considers the construction of big reservoirs, as well as more decentralised measures producing and using more treated wastewater.

Connected to both research projects on Lima, and possibly serving as a small-scale solution, **Zarela García Trujillo** writes in her master's thesis about domestic wastewater treatment with aquatic plants. She describes a very local, decentralised and individualised solution for getting more treated waste water at the household level.

Planning, Space, and Design: Case Studies on Ho Chi Minh City and Climate-responsive Architecture in Iran

Mainly in the twentieth century, but in certain regions even today, rational comprehensive planning has been recognised as a discipline that can solve major urban problems. Often resulting in master plans, this planning paradigm has repeatedly been criticised. Today, cities and with them urban planning, are confronted with many future challenges: besides the often referred-to urban spatial growth, cities are both contributors and victims of climate change. Located in different climatic areas, each city has to address the challenges of climate change in an individual and local manner. Although ruled by different political frameworks, probably all cities will be confronted with certain demands for decentralisation, and multi-level or collaborative governance far beyond administrative boundaries. Furthermore, the growing unwillingness among citizens to passively accept top-down planning decisions will lead to the demand for more participation. Economic changes in the shape of rising inequality and poverty, or high levels of informal activities may perform the tasks that ought to be considered by urban planning in the future. While some ideas of comprehensive planning may have been maintained, a growing number of governments and municipal authorities reform their planning systems or parts of them to match these tasks and local demands. Nowadays, planning processes and results have thus become increasingly participatory, flexible, strategic, and action oriented [UN Habitat 2009].

A stunning description of such a process towards a more flexible, participatory, and environmentally oriented planning culture is **Ngoc-Anh Nguyen's** master's thesis. Her paper on the integration of environmental components in land-use planning in Ho Chi Minh City is mainly based on expert interviews done in various planning administrations. The rapid urbanisation and dense population growth in the past twenty years has significantly affected the city's land use, as well as had adverse effects on urban flooding, urban climate, and its vulnerability to climate change. Land-use planning, at the same time, is a key measure for helping the city to adapt to the environmental consequences and climate change impacts through the integration of environmental components and urban climate management. The article reveals three main obstacles to the desired adjustments: (1) land-use planning in the contradictory framework of other spatial plans; (2) challenges in the policy and legal frameworks; and (3) challenges in procedures, policy, and management frameworks. To foster the integration of environmental and climate parameters in Ho Chi Minh City's land-use plan, two tools are discussed: the Strategic Environmental Assessment (SEA) and land-use zoning. While the SEA requires nationwide policy and enforcement as well as methodological tools, land-use zoning needs more careful management adjustment for acceptance and adoption at the city and local levels.

As the former article could also be placed in the chapter on governance, the next paper deals with almost the same topic in the same city but in the field of geomatics. In his bachelor's thesis, **Jakob Kopec** detects and analyses the land-use change of Ho Chi Minh City for three periods starting in 1989. This has been achieved by remote-sensing techniques and methods on the basis of Landsat satellite imagery. Based on the derived data, he describes and evaluates urban growth by urban density gradients, the jaggedness degree, the centre-oriented entropy, and the fractal dimension. As a result of his very sophisticated research, he highlights interesting phenomena such as the fact that Ho Chi Minh City has an urban growth rate of 70% almost every two years, or that nowadays the density of buildings is much higher in areas outside the centre than in previous years. Furthermore, he shows that the combination of remote sensing techniques and geostatistical methods creates a useful tool and monitoring system for establishing effective spatial control plans. Having these enormous growth rates in mind, and remembering the administrative difficulties discussed by Ngoc Anh Nguyen, it is obvious that Günter Emberger in the volume *Mobility and Transportation* ↗ has serious doubts as to whether HCMC will reach its CO_2 targets for the transportation sector. Further issues referring to planning topics in Ho Chi Minh City can be found in the volume *Space, Planning, and Design* ↗.

The chapter closes with three abstracts. In his diploma thesis in landscape architecture, **Yassine Moustanjidi** takes Casablanca as a case study and proposes approaches, methods, and tools to integrate a green and productive infrastructure based on urban agriculture as a multifunctional component of urban planning.

Two abstracts on architecture-related topics follow. Not only urban planning with its wide range of issues, but also urban design and architecture will be confronted by some of the challenges mentioned above, specifically by climate change. As a result, architecture needs to find answers on how to approach new demands on insulation, energy saving up to energy production, or recyclable building materials. In her PhD, **Shabnam Teimourtash** investigates the impacts of climate-responsive construction on reducing the energy demand of residential buildings in Iran on the basis of vernacular architecture. **Nadia Poor Rahim**'s diploma thesis offers a feasibility study for an office building in Hashtgerd New Town, Iran. This building stands as an example of a new generation of buildings in terms of energy efficiency. The study has considered interdisciplinary scientific aspects like sociology, urban planning, construction, ecology, economy, and project management.

Mobility and Transportation: Public Transport in China

In 2005, 47% of all trips in urban areas worldwide were private and motorised. In 2009, transportation has caused 22.6% of worldwide CO_2 emissions; the highest in Latin America with 34.8%, and the lowest in China with 6.9% [UN Habitat 2013]. Generating this large proportion of greenhouse gas emissions, transportation bears a high share of responsibility for global climate change. Moreover, traffic accidents are among the main reasons for premature deaths in many cities, and noise and air pollution significantly affect public health. Due to the enormous growth of cities, distances between residential areas and places of employment become longer as well. This leads to an increasing amount of commuting time and an increasing proportion of income spent on it. Those who cannot afford transportation are among the urban poor to whom this development leads to social isolation.

The remaining trips in urban areas are either non-motorised, 37%, or made by public transport, 16% [Ibid.]. Emissions from these two traffic modes are insignificant compared to those from motorised transport. Despite these facts, many cities in developing countries come up with solutions to build even more streets and flyovers for cars. Yet, the investments in public transport and infrastructure for pedestrians or cyclists are still comparably low. Thus, the relative share of public transport has decreased or stagnated in many of these countries [Ibid.] To accelerate a more sustainable transportation development, this trend needs to be stopped.

Much of the complexity described above is illustrated in the Chinese cities of Hefei and Shenzhen. Two authors analyse the cities' public transport and thereby contribute to urgently needed answers for sustainable mobility. In her master's thesis, **Xiaoli Lin** states that Shenzhen's transport structure has changed dramatically together with its rapid population growth to more than ten million inhabitants. Situated in the industrial hub of Hong Kong and the Pearl River Delta, motorisation and traffic congestion turn out to be a huge challenge. By following the so-called Transit-Oriented Development, the city tries to increase the number of passengers in public transport by constructing a new public transport system and by developing mixed land use around the stations. But empirical studies show that the approach did not mitigate traffic congestion in the city. The author therefore recommends, among many other detailed proposals, that a holistic Transit-Oriented Development strategy should consider the public transport system as an integral system that integrates the public transport network with different mobility modes into its planning framework.

Like Xiaoli Lin, **Manuel Fiechtner** has done work in the context of the METRASYS project. In his bachelor's thesis, he provides insights into the public transportation system of Hefei, the capital of Anhui province with about 5.7 million inhabitants. Although not as dramatically as Shenzhen, Hefei is characterised by growth, reconstruction, and massive increase in traffic volume. Huge investments in transport infrastructure are necessary. Based on interviews, accessibility analyses, and GIS analyses, Fiechtner offers an extensive analysis of the current quality, major deficits, and an assessment of the effects and importance of Hefei's public transportation system. As a result of his studies, he proves on the one hand that the bus system is not only best in the centre, but also makes vast areas of the city and the administrative district of Hefei accessible. On the other hand, he states that many residential areas suffer from bad access to bus stops in an appropriate radius and thereby do not fulfil governmental standards and goals. In an extensive outlook, Fiechtner notes that Hefei will undergo dramatic changes in the upcoming years with the implementation of Bus Rapid Transit and Metro systems, and due to new intermodal train stations. Additional urban traffic planning and the adjustment of planned urban traffic projects will be necessary to keep pace with coming urban developments.

There are more articles about Hefei's traffic challenges and some solutions: The volume *Mobility and Transportation* ↗ contains an article on intelligent traffic management based on Floating Car Data (FCD).

Caused by the rising interest in traffic surveillance for simulations and decision-making, many planners are in urgent need of data. As conventional data collection systems often do not meet the demands, **Karsten Kozempel** has developed and evaluated the Airborne Traffic Detection System, which is more flexible and based on cameras. The innovation of this PhD refers to the combination of rapid preselection and more reliable verification of object hypotheses.

In his diploma thesis, **Steffen Bubeck** describes perspectives for Gauteng's transportation sector and its impact on the reduction of greenhouse gas emissions. The results show a significant potential for Bus Rapid Transit systems at relatively low costs. Investments in trains can increase passenger volumes as well, but at much higher costs. As both continue to have a low share of total transport demand until 2040, their impact on the reduction of greenhouse gas emissions is negligible.

This book collects contributions by young researchers. But this is no verdict on the papers' quality as being "junior research" in comparison to "senior research". On the contrary, the various topics are of general interest and the scientific quality of the articles are convincing according to their respective thesis level (BA, MA, PhD). Because young research lacks a clear definition, lines are fluid to senior research—especially for PhDs. Nevertheless, what counts is the authors' outstanding and fabulous passion for knowledge in the challenging field of megacity research.

DAAD's "Study and Research Scholarship of Today for the Megacities of Tomorrow":
List of Young Researchers and Research Topics

Resources	
Ana María Acevedo Interdisciplinary Research Unit on Risk Governance and Sustainable Technology Development University of Stuttgart aacevedo@fovida.org.pe	Risk Management in the City of Lima in Climate Change Scenario
Keerthi Kiran Bandru Division of Resource Economics Humboldt University Berlin bandrukk@hu-berlin.de	Enforcement in Environmental Pollution Regulation: The Case of Environmental Complaint System in Hyderabad, India.
Ruhi Gandhi Division of Resource Economics Humboldt University Berlin ruhi_123@yahoo.com	Vulnerability of Urban Poor to Changes in Food Accessibility: A Study of Opportunities and Constraints for Adaptation to Climate Change and Rapid Urbanisation in Hyderabad
Ivan M. Lucich Helmholtz Centre for Environmental Research-UFZ ivanlucich@yahoo.es	Drinking Water Regulation
Rajeshwari S Mallegowda Institute for Cooperative Studies Humboldt University Berlin ranjuhcp@gmail.com	An Institutional and Economic Analysis of Vegetable Production and Marketing in the Emerging Megacity of Hyderabad, India.
Mabel Morillo Viera Regulatory Agency of Water and Wastewater Services – Peru mmorillo@sunass.gob.pe	Methodology To Determine the Tariff for the Service of Rain Drainage
Vikram Patil Division of Resource Economics Humboldt University Berlin vickyagrico@gmail.com	IoS Framework To Analyse the APWALTA (Andhra Pradesh Water, Land and Tree Act)
Ben Solis Sosa Helmholtz Centre for Environmental Research-UFZ bensolis37@hotmail.com	Water and Sanitation Services

Space, Planning, and Design	
Vahabi Moghaddam Department of Urban and Regional Planning Berlin Institute of Technology d.vahabi@gmail.com	Achieving Sustainable Urban Form for the Young Cities of Tomorrow: A Contextual Study of the Relationship between Housing Consumption and Physical Urban Planning in Iran–Case of Tehran-Karaj Region
Nguyen Anh Tuan Ho Chi Minh City Architecture & Planning Research Centre tuankts@gmail.com	Productive Landscape System in the Fringe Area of Ho Chi Minh City
Maryam Zabihi Centre for Technology and Society Berlin Institute of Technology zabihi.maryam@gmail.com	Application of Transit-Oriented Development Criteria in Developing Hashtgerd New Town

Mobility and Transportation	
Bhuvanachithra Chidambaram Division of Resource Economics Humboldt University Berlin bhuvanavignaesh@gmail.com	Vehicle Emission Reduction–An Experimental Approach for Analysing Sustainable Traffic Strategies and Solution
Brian Mubiwa Department of Geography, Environmental Management & Energy Studies University of Johannesburg brianwangu@yahoo.com	Impact of Transport Corridors on Urban Development and Transport Energy in the Gauteng City-Region
Xue Yang Institute for City Planning and Urban Design University of Duisburg-Essen aickaf@gmail.com	A Contribution to Dynamic Methods of Calculating the Energy Demand of Mobility in Urban Areas

Governance	
Brijesh Bhatt Division of Resource Economics Humboldt University Berlin bhattbrx@cms.hu-berlin.de	Governance Structure for Enhanced Energy Efficiency in Irrigation Electricity Distribution System of Andhra Pradesh (India)
Phungmayo Horam Division of Resource Economics Humboldt University Berlin phungmayo@gmail.com	Institutions and Emergence of Credible Governance Structure: The Case of Solar Electricity Sector in India

Capacity Development	
Saikumar C. Bharamappanavara Division of cooperative Sciences Humboldt University Berlin saikumarbc@gmail.com	Collective Action in Rural versus Urban Group-based Microcredit Organisations: Lessons from the Greater Hyderabad Area (India)
Bui Thi Minh Ha Urban Planning Department Brandenburg Technical University Cottbus hambui2002@yahoo.com	Social Vulnerability And Adaptive Capacities of Communities to Urban Flooding, A Case Study in Ho Chi Minh City, Vietnam
Jun Zhang Department of Sociology Tongji University, Shanghai cheungjun@163.com	Social Behaviour and the Construction of Low Carbon City

Sources

DLR-PT – Deutsches Zentrum für Luft- und Raumfahrt e. V. – Projektträger im DLR (2012): *Research Programme Main Phase: Energy- and Climate Efficient Structures in Urban Growth Centres.* http://future-megacities.org/index.php?id=48&L=1, 15.02.2013

Hamburg Declaration (2013): *The Hamburg Declaration–15 May 2013.* http://future-megacities.org/fileadmin/documents/konferenzen/Megacities_in_Action_2013/YR_Declaration_paper.pdf, 12.08.2013

Seto, K. C./ Güneralp, B./ Hutyra, L.R. (2012): "Global forecasts of urban expansion to 2030 and direct impacts on biodiversity and carbon pools". In: *Proceedings of the National Academy of Sciences of the United States of America.* www.pnas.org/content/early/2012/09/11/1211658109.full.pdf+html?with-ds=yes, 07.03.2013

Soya, E. (2010): "Regional Urbanization and the Future of Megacities". In: Hall, P./ Buijs, S./ Tan, W./ Tunas, D.: *Megacities–Exploring A Sustainable Future*, Rotterdam, pp. 57–75

UN-DESA United Nations Department of Economic and Social Affairs/Population Division (2012): *World Urbanization Prospects: The 2011 Revision. Highlights.* http://esa.un.org/unup/pdf/WUP2011_Highlights.pdf, 15.02.2013

UNEP United Nations Environment Programme (2011): *Cities investing in energy and resource efficiency.* http://www.unep.org/greeneconomy/Portals/88/documents/ger/GER_12_Cities.pdf, 15.02.2013

UN-Habitat (2009): *Planning sustainable cities: global report on human settlements 2009.* http://www.unhabitat.org/pmss/listItemDetails.aspx?publicationID=2831, 26.11.2013

UN-Habitat (2011): *Cities and Climate Change: Policy Directions. Global Report on Human Settlements 2011,* Abridged Edition. www.unhabitat.org/downloads/docs/GRHS2011/GRHS.2011.Abridged.English.pdf, 15.02.2013

UN-Habitat (2012): *State of the World's Cities Report 2012/2013: Prosperity of Cities.* www.un.int/wcm/webdav/site/portal/shared/iseek/documents/2012/November/UNhabitat%20201213.pdf, 15.02.2013

UN-Habitat (2013), *Planning and design for sustainable urban mobility: global report on human settlements*, Nairobi.

Notes

1 The current coverage of urban land on the earth's surface is often referred to as '2%' (UNEP 2011). The predicted increase of urban land is dramatic: by 2030, urban land coverage will increase by 1.2 million km^2, thereby tripling the global urban land areas compared to the year 2000. In other words: 65% of the urban land coverage on the planet by 2030 was, or will be, under construction between 2000–2030, 55% of that expansion arising from urbanisation will occur in India and China (Seto 2012). According to Soya, cities tend to "grow well beyond their defined administrational limits, typically spawning a multitude of suburbs in expanding annular rings. The outer edges thus came to be defined as ... part of the Functional Urban Region (FUR)" (Soya 2010, 58).

2 *Dok & Mat Band 66 Future Megacities in Balance.* The volume can be ordered from DAAD: kasperek@daad.de

3 Some theses of young researchers in the field of capacity development are listed in the table: Participants of the DAAD- Scholarship Programme: "Study and Research Scholarships of Today for the Megacities of Tomorrow" [p. 21 ↗].

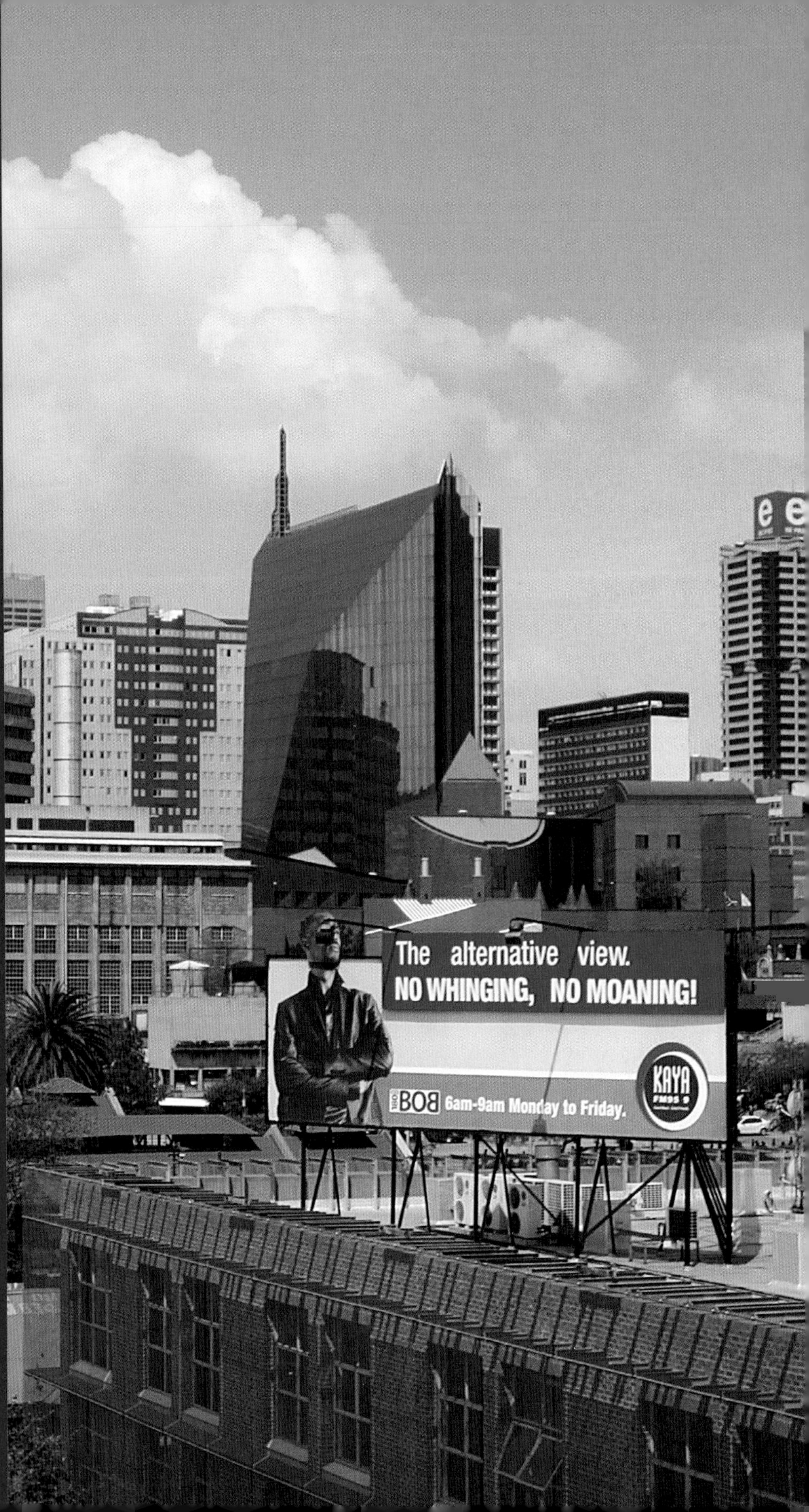

GAUTENG: Downtown Johannesburg [Carsten Zehner]

GOVERNANCE

HYDERABAD: Transformer repair- collective action [Carsten Zehner]

Christian Kimmich
Dissertation at Humboldt University Berlin, Division of Resource Economics

The Agricultural Water-Energy Nexus of Rural India under Climate Change: How Learning Coordination Becomes Key to Technology Adoption

Abstract

Surprisingly or not, agriculture can be a crucial sector that either enables or impedes the transition towards sustainable development of urban areas. This is also the case for the emerging megacity of Hyderabad. Several rural-urban linkages support this perspective: (a) migration patterns, dependent on agricultural and rural income, and development paths; (b) the food security and provisioning dimension, especially relevant in the case of perishable agricultural commodities that cannot be traded over long distances; (c) water allocation for agricultural production versus drinking water supply in the city; and (d) electricity allocation for agricultural production versus urban consumption. This research focuses especially on the latter linkage (d), as electricity provision is one of the most crucial factors of sustainable development for Hyderabad, becoming either a driver or inhibitor.

In India, electricity supply for agricultural irrigation is highly subsidised, increasing the scarcity for urban, industrial, and commercial uses. With a share of 36% of all electricity consumption in the state of Andhra Pradesh, agriculture has a very high potential for energy efficiency and mitigation measures. Based on background studies and stakeholder analyses, the thesis analyses two levels: (I) the macro level on the political economy of infrastructure regulation, and (II) the micro level of electricity distribution and utilisation in irrigation. Through this two-fold approach, the level and measures enabling a transition towards sustainable resource use can be identified. At the macro level, a model of regulation and party competition is applied. This model is tested against the empirical background generated through an analysis of the law, the discourse in newspapers and semi-structured interviews with experts and practitioners.

The micro level, which is the focus of this article, sets up an analysis of the agricultural production economy based on interviews and a farm-level survey. The analysis at the level of electricity distribution and agricultural production systems indicates that, although farmers do not have to pay per unit of electric energy utilised, the costs of poor infrastructure impose heavy burdens on agricultural enterprises. Adding the current kWh unit generation costs of electricity would by far exceed those for each of the other input factors of production. The absence of unit costs has led to highly inefficient groundwater irrigation and the high costs of pump-set burnouts to severe voltage fluctuations. These problems work as indirect incentives or striking reasons for farmers to improve the electricity quality by adopting new technologies through coordinated social learning practices or concerted, joint action. These solutions can be combined with energy efficiency measures. Effective measures and new technologies are most feasible at the level of the electricity sub-station, isolating an agricultural electricity feeder and the connected distribution transformers for the installation of capacitors.

The findings have served as the basis for designing a pilot project and capacity building measures. More on the pilot project can be found in the volume *Energy and Sun* of this book series [pp. 37–46 ↗]. In addition to the mentioned article, this article focuses on the preconditions, such as costs and incentives, and provides the theoretical background. This article summarises some of the core results of the underlying PhD research for an interdisciplinary audience. From these findings, more general implications for other infrastructures can be drawn where coordination is crucial.

Introduction: Scope of the Study

Highly Subsidised Electricity for Irrigation Has Severe Consequences

Electricity provision for irrigation is highly subsidised in most Indian states, including Andhra Pradesh, the subject of this thesis. The subsidisation regime led to the diffusion of groundwater-based irrigation, reducing dependence on irregular rainfall and decisively contributing to the success of the Green Revolution [Badiani/Jessoe/Plant 2012; Kondepati 2011; Repetto 1994; Rosegrant/Evenson 1992]. Besides a drastic increase in energy consumption and connections, with a share of 33% of all end-use electric energy utilised for irrigation, the policy also led to a steady deterioration in the quality of electric infrastructure [Shah 2009; Tongia 2007]. Although being partly compensated for subsidised agricultural electricity supply by the state, state-owned distribution companies have steadily reduced investments, maintenance, and staff budgets for rural distribution. This resulted in reduced monitoring capacities and grid maintenance, and contributed to high voltage fluctuations, poor power quality, and increasing pump-set and electricity transformer burnout rates [Dossani / Ranganathan 2004], but also challenged electricity supply in urban areas [Hanisch et al. 2010]. Non-standardised, unbranded, and often locally manufactured [Narayan 1999] pump-sets of poor quality, in combination with unqualified repairs, increase energy inefficiency and further deteriorate power quality [Tongia 2007].

Low Adoption Rate of New Technologies

The main objective of this analysis is to explain the low adoption rate of demand-side technologies and the underlying barriers to efficiency improvements in the electricity-irrigation nexus. The analysis reveals learning and governance mechanisms that can facilitate technology adoption and are transferrable to other technologies and environments. The results have served to design a pilot project, which is described in detail in *Energy and Sun*, the first book in the "Future Megacities" book series [Kimmich/Sagebiel 2013]. The core challenge for increasing energy efficiency is a coordination problem that requires the simultaneous adoption of technology by all farmers with pump-sets connected to the same grid in order to affect power quality improvements and to reduce damages to the irrigation equipment. Due to the properties of the technologies, sequential learning heuristics through experimentation by only few farmers does not yield the expected outcome of improved power quality, and adoption is thus impeded. The findings reveal the importance of taking into account the social dimensions of social-ecological and technological systems and the ecology of connected action situations.

Methods and Data: Interviews and Surveys

For the selected research questions, a mixed method approach including interviews and surveys is the most useful for gaining empirical knowledge. Many interactions and institutional arrangements can best be covered through open questions. The interviews conducted between January 2009 and October 2011 included farmers, repair workshop owners, pump-set manufacturers and local retailers, utility managers and ground staff at sub-stations, as well as village revenue officers, elected heads of the village level government, and members of the Electricity Regulatory Commission. These interviews helped in preparing the cross-section survey design. The qualitative data also informed the model building process to develop more robust formal models. Crucial basic data on agricultural cropping, irrigation and electricity patterns are best covered through standardised survey questions. Hence, the following method structure for the survey was set up:

1. Standardised farm-level survey with 305 participants (N) and 52 survey items
2. Standardised village-level survey with 18 participants (N) and 29 survey items
3. Focus Group Discussions on village-level with 18 participants (N) and 8 open questions

The four rural districts adjacent to Hyderabad were chosen for drawing a sample for the analysis. Based on the demographic Census data of 2001 and the village directory of the Census 2001 [India 2001], a stratified village sample selection was conducted. Two Mandals[1] in each district and two villages in each Mandal were chosen for analysis. The stratification selection criteria were:

- Average agricultural holding size: representativeness of average holding size with induced variance, i.e., selection of large and small holding size structures
- Population characteristics according to castes: representativeness of caste composition with induced variance, i.e., selection of differing village types
- Share of groundwater irrigation in total agricultural land use: high share of groundwater irrigation, and half of the villages with alternative irrigation source, i.e., surface irrigation reservoirs

Findings: The Costs of Failing to Coordinate

Overview

The following chapter focuses on four issues that are the main findings of this research.

- First, the text focuses on the various high costs of the necessary irrigation that impose a heavy burden on farmers.
- The second section describes the technical device of a capacitor that could on the one hand have a positive effect by stabilising the power grid, but on the other hand, could only

do so if many farmers install them on their pumps. Individual solutions alone may even have a negative effect. Regarding this phenomena and dilemma, theoretical background will be given and solutions mentioned.
·   The third section describes the increased burdens on farmers' shoulders, such as under-voltage, unauthorised connections, and shrinking groundwater tables leading to indebtedness of farmers.
·   The fourth section tries to reveal and illustrate the ambiguous role of different actors such as the energy provider in relation to the farmers. These linkages lead to a state of inter-connectedness, which needs to be considered in order to come up with real solutions and improvements for farmers and utilities. Initial ideas for such solutions will be presented in the last chapter.

High Cost of Irrigation as a Burden for Farmers

Energy consumption patterns are heavily influenced by economic incentives as well as ag-ronomic conditions. Along with the policy of electricity subsidisation, several other contin-gencies exist. To make the research questions operational, they were broken down into the following steps:

1. What are the actual costs incurred for each farmer for electricity-driven irrigation?
2. Given the rapid growth of electricity connections and electricity consumption for irrigation, what is the average consumption and costs of electricity per pump-set?
3. Which energy- and cost-efficient solutions are feasible and can be translated into capacity development measures and a pilot project?

Costs of Electricity-driven Irrigation for a Single Farm

An analysis of the actual costs generated by the irrigation system is crucial to understanding the economic incentives of a farm. For this purpose, the survey covered the following varia-bles in Figure 1 ↗.

Given the year of drilling the bore, a recovery period for the costs of twenty years is de-rived. For the pump-set, a recovery period of fifteen years is derived. The costs for connecting to the electricity grid will be set to twenty years, as the replacement of a pump-set does not require a new connection. Given the average interest rate of 19.2% [Figure 1 ↗], the annuity is calculated. This results in the following costs for groundwater irrigation in Figure 2 ↗.

With an average annual cost of 4,285 INR per acre (= 69.1 €$_{2010}$),[2] the costs of irrigation are only slightly below the costs for fertilisers and pesticides (4,518 INR = 72.9 €$_{2010}$) and the costs for seeds (5,977 INR = 96.4 €$_{2010}$). The costs for pump-set repairs contribute the highest share to the overall costs of groundwater irrigation. At 48%, a very high share of farmers uses locally manufactured (assembled) and no-name motors for their pump-sets.

Costs of Electricity

The consumption per pump-set has stabilised at around 6,000 kWh per year since the early nineteen-nineties. Based on Electricity Regulatory Commission regulations, the tariff for agricultural connections [Low Tension Tariff No. 5] is set at 1.18 INR (0.019 €$_{2010}$) per kWh [APERC 2009, 118]. This is what the government pays to the distribution companies for providing elec-

Fig. 1   Summary statistics for the costs of production [Author's calculations based on the survey]

Variable	Mean	SD	Min	Max
Acres cropped / year	4.12	6.43	0	60
Acres irrigated / year	3.99	4.53	0	42
Seed costs / year[1]	5,977	6,732	400	49,000
Fertiliser & Pesticide costs / year[1]	4,518	4,083	167	34,335
Drilling costs[1]	23,169	18,682	0	150,000
Pump-set costs[1]	22,343	8,998	2,000	72,000
Electricity connection costs[1]	7,180	8,742	0	100,000
Informal connection costs[1]	947	1,456	0	10,000
Interest rate	0.19	0.14	0.03	0.80

1: 62 INR = 1 €$_{2010}$

Fig. 2   Costs of irrigation [Author's calculations based on the survey]

Type of cost	Rupees (INR)
Annuity bore	4,531
Annuity pump-set	4,600
Annuity connection	1,608
Maintenance	414
Pump-set repair	5,412
Transformer repair	547
Total	17,112
Acres irrigated / year	3.99
Costs per acre	4,284.56

tricity for agriculture. The average cost per pump-set would then be 7,080 INR (114.2 €$_{2010}$), surpassing the costs for the bore well and pump-set itself and the costs for fertilisers, pesticides, and seeds.

The Need for Common Action: Stable Power Quality Requires Simultaneous Installation of a Sufficient Number of Capacitors

Capacitors as Grid-balancing and Money-saving Devices

Given the flat-rate power supply regime, financial incentives to implement measures on the demand side—i.e., by farmers—to improve energy efficiency are essentially absent. Inefficient pump-sets contribute to deteriorating power quality, increasing pump-set and transformer damages. Farmers and distribution utilities incur high repair costs, discouraging any investment in better equipment [Tongia 2007]. Farmers even pay part of the costs of repairing transformers, even though transformers belong to the distribution companies. Some demand-side measures—such as the use of standard-approved pump-sets with energy-efficient motors ("ISI-marked" by the Bureau of Indian Standards) and the installation of capacitors—could simultaneously reduce equipment damage and energy consumption. A capacitor or condenser is a small and cheap technical device and circuit element that can correct the power factor in an electricity grid. It balances the phase between current and voltage in three-phase supply [Dugan 2003; Meier 2006] and thus can improve power quality and energy efficiency. If implemented, farmers and utilities could save on repairs, and public expenditures on subsidies could be reduced, contributing to the viability of agriculture and benefitting distribution utilities as well as the overall economy through reduced fiscal burdens.

The survey of 305 farm households revealed that only 10% of the farmers have a capacitor installed, but at least 37% use ISI-marked pump-sets, equipment that is approved by the Bureau of Indian Standards. Only 6% use a BEE-rated pump-set, energy-efficiency labelled by the Bureau of Energy Efficiency [Kimmich/Sagebiel 2013]. At a price of 200-300 INR (3.23-4.84 €$_{2010}$), capacitors are a highly cost-effective way for farmers to reduce repair costs. The low adoption rate of capacitors seems surprising, given that capacitors are supposed to be beneficial for power quality and adoption could be in the farmers' best interest. The low adoption rate is explained in the next section through an analysis of the core action situation.

Capacitors: Only a Sufficient Number Simultaneously Installed Leads to Cost Reductions

The low numbers of installed capacitors can be explained using a game-theory model based on the characteristics of the electricity infrastructure. The electricity grid creates interdependence among the farmers' adoption strategies through the network structure and the common-pool resource properties of power quality. Because using a poor quality pump-set and not using a capacitor have a negative impact on power quality for all other farmers located at the same distribution transformer in the electricity grid, the choice of one farmer to invest in capacitors depends on the choice of every other connected farmer. When no farmer invests in the use of a capacitor or an ISI-marked pump-set, one farmer's investment does not improve conditions, for him or for others. The adoption of these capacitors may then even have a negative effect on power quality, as *"the equipment installed to increase the productivity is also often the equipment that suffers the most from common power disruptions. And the equipment is sometimes the source of additional power quality problems"* [Dugan 2003, 3]. However, if a sufficient number of farmers simultaneously invest in capacitors, the overall power quality can surpass a threshold level such that the positive effects of such a common action on pump-sets can be observed.

A common theme crystallised: Almost no farmer was aware that the simultaneous installation of capacitors was required, and the expected results had not been communicated to them. Farmers resorted to another practice with the adoption and implementation of new technologies: only individual farmers experimented with the use of a capacitor and their neighbours and peer network adapted to these experiences. Because of this, no experience with coordinated use by all farmers has been possible, impeding any beneficial experience. This situation exemplifies a social-learning strategy. From an evolutionary perspective, this is a dominant adoption strategy for many production technologies, but when faced with a coordination problem, it is unlikely to work. In fact, sequential adoption even works against simultaneous experimentation and the emergence of successful variation. Yet, when the coordination problem becomes resolved in one instance, social learning can potentially catalyse adoption by neighbouring farmers, if coordination requirements are learned and transmitted. This evolutionary stable strategy can then outperform sequential experimentation.

This finding demonstrates the necessity of not only analysing the characteristics of a core factual action situation as generated by the physical properties, but also how the action situation is actually dealt with by actors, which, in the given case, involves evolved shared routines and heuristics concerning the adoption of technologies.

The Underlying Principle: Game Theory

This constellation of interdependent decision-making and strategies can be analysed with the economic model of game theory. The underlying structure is a coordination problem, more specifically an assurance problem [Sen 1967], with one risk-dominant and one payoff-dominant equilibrium [Harsanyi/Selten 1988]. Coordination problems emerge in all fields of infrastructure, from telecommunication and mobility to water, drainage, and energy networks and agricultural technologies [Drèze/ Sharma 1998; Dutton/ Schneider/ Vedel 2012; Janssen 2007]. A simplified bi-matrix model of the coordination problem highlights the two Nash equilibria[3] in pure strategies in bold print [Figure 3 ↗]. The equal payoff for the strategy not to invest ~I, and the loss incurred by the one not coordinating, makes this model type an assurance problem.

An econometric analysis revealed that, under the given conditions, the rational strategy is not to adopt any demand-side measures [Kimmich 2011b]. This is the low Nash equilibrium of the underlying coordination problem.

Fig. 3   The focal action situation (AS1) is modelled as an assurance problem for power quality. The two farmers (F1; F2) have the choice of investing (I) or not investing (~I) in measures to improve power quality. Outcomes are ordinal ranks [Kimmich 2011a].

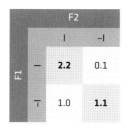

More Barriers for Technology Adoption within Interconnected Action Situations

Undervoltage Prevents the Proper Functioning of Capacitors

In addition to the problem of capacitors, the farmers are in several other situations that have an impact on their technology adoption strategy. Not only low power quality, but also low-voltage levels prevent capacitors and ISI-marked motors from working. Only locally as-sembled, non-standardised pump-sets can stand such low-voltage conditions. Undervoltage levels are partly caused by the total load connected [Dugan 2003], exceeding the transformer capacity. The simultaneous start of large loads, which require high starting currents, can cre-ate short-duration voltage variations [Ibid.]. There is, then, a conflict resulting from infrastruc-ture under-provision or, respectively, overuse of existing capacity. The conflict only emerges if the maximum capacity of the infrastructure is surpassed; in which case providing sufficient capacity for every additional connection becomes necessary. This constellation results in a social dilemma.

The relationship between energy utilisation and groundwater is crucial. Decreasing groundwater tables require deepened wells, which steadily increases energy use and respective loads on the electricity grid. The depth of wells has increased tremendously since the nineteen-eighties [Figure 4 ↗]. This makes successful coordination more difficult. While on a global scale many actors dependent on aquifers have not surmounted this dilemma, there have also been few successful cases [van Steenbergen 2006], one of them being a village located in Andhra Pradesh where the council introduced a ban on tube wells and the community voluntarily imposed limitations on crop choices to reduce water intensity. This unique case shows how the core situation of electricity utilisation can practically vanish in others cases as well. But we encountered no similar situation in our case study area, although the small hard-rock aquifers of the Deccan plateau could potentially ease cooperation to restrict groundwater exploitation [Shah 2009]. On the other side of the nexus, improvements in pump-set efficiency through successful coordination and infrastructure capacity provision could aggravate groundwater exploitation.

Several interviewees mentioned the large investments for the pump-set and tube well, financed through credits, as impeding additional payments for authorising the connection. Many farmers are already highly indebted, partly due to the risky investment into a large share of failed tube wells. Access to groundwater is decisive for the economic success of such farms. For indebted farm households, subsistence is not an option because they have payment obligations. Under these circumstances, it is conceivable that norms of solidarity have developed, and neighbouring farmers support access to the electricity grid, although the transformer may already be overloaded. Even some sub-station personnel are aware of the circumstances and tolerate open access.

Access to the Electricity Grid without Official Authorisation Leads to Insufficient Power

A distribution utility manages infrastructure provision, which requires a connection authorisation charge to be paid by every farmer utilising power. This charge regularises the connection and covers costs required for the provision of additional transformer capacity. The authorisation process is influenced by many informal arrangements at the sub-station level, including the amount of "informal payments" in addition to the official connection charge reported by the farmers. While all surveyed farmers paid connection charges, there is also an unknown share of unauthorised connections. The survey statistics indicate that, for 11% of the transformers, the calculated capacity per farmer is insufficient for the average power per pump-set, and only 37% of the surveyed farmers saw present capacity to be sufficient for an additional pump-set connection. Regulators, farmers, and electrical engineers estimated between 20 and 30% of connections to be unauthorised. Informal arrangements with sub-station personnel enable such unauthorised connections.

These cases show that farmers are involved in several other situations that exert influence on the coordination problem. An implicit conflict, secret agreements of some farmers with the energy provider's (electric utility) sub-station personnel that enable the unauthorised connections, has not been explicitly analysed here. The established relations between farmers and sub-station personnel, but also solidarity among farmers with those who cannot afford the connection charge play a role in shaping capacity provision. Although most of the

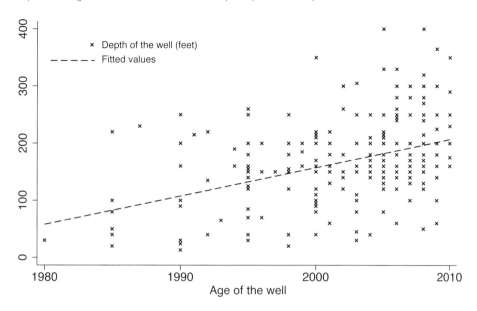

sub-station personnel do not reside in the villages, kinship links or evolved personal relations can strengthen mutual exchange. Obtaining access to the electricity grid without an
authorised connection is an "open secret" in many cases. In a discussion with an electrical
engineer from a sub-station including several villagers, a farmer openly admitted to having an
unauthorised connection.

The Ambiguous and Complicated Roles of the Energy Provider

The interaction shown above between the electric utility and farmers for capacity provision
influences the coordination problem. If the provider does not install sufficient capacity, or
delays the process even after a regular authorisation, then capacity is insufficient to install
demand-side measures. Local electricity infrastructure, covering several districts in a state,
is provided and managed by a utility that is in most cases a fully state-owned company,
controlled by a commission which regulates according to aggregate revenue requirements
[Pani/ Sreekumar/ Reddy 2007]. After some fundamental power sector reforms, including the
organisational separation (unbundling) of generation, transmission, and distribution, state
electricity regulatory commissions have been set up to develop many of the collective rules
in the sector. Thus, unlike many common-pool resource conditions, the formal institutional
setting for provision and appropriation is not developed by the farmers. Even the utility itself
is only partly involved in designing the formal institutions for its governance. The action network is larger, involving the regulatory agency and its governance [Thatcher 2002], with some
discretionary power to shape the institutional environment for the utilities, but itself being a
product of contextual factors [Dubash/ Rao 2008].

  The sub-station personnel are part of several situations within the utility itself. Effective monitoring of unauthorised connections by a vigilance unit might influence the payoff
structure of some of the sub-station personnel and farmers. Although not directly involved,

farmers' associations influence political and regulatory actions. A broader and more complex network is involved in creating an exchange of services for votes among the local constituency, which is itself embedded in the state-level political system, where party competition has led to "vote bank" policies of electricity subsidisation.

Directly linked to groundwater exploitation is the development and maintenance of tanks, the traditional South Indian water reservoirs. Surface irrigation and percolation can reduce the pressure on groundwater exploitation. Alternative income sources extend the choices available, reducing the pressure on irrigation use, and were found to have a statistically significant influence on appliance damages. Education and training play another significant role in shaping the focal action situation. Subsistence farming, as well as the presence of markets for different crops and labour markets all influence conditions for the farmers.

Conclusion and Solutions: Learning Coordinated Technology Adoption

Conclusive Reflections

The action situations analysed above influence each other and can negatively affect the coordination of technology adoption: if the infrastructure capacity provided is insufficient, the measures to improve power quality cannot work. Reduced capacity thus also reduces the payoffs of demand-side measure adoption. Similarly, a reduced groundwater level requires additional energy and thus negatively affects the capacity of the electricity grid. The adjacent network is also linked through one or more of the actors involved. While coordination for power quality and groundwater exploitation are interactions between farmers, many of the other action situations involve the electricity provider, which can itself exert a positive influence on improving power quality and thereby increase energy efficiency.

The action situations can also co-determine each other. Sufficient capacity can intensify groundwater exploitation. Only through collusion can the option of unauthorised connections actually emerge. Successful coordination requires sufficient capacity as a precondition. This makes electric load crucial in those instances in which capacity is insufficient. Infrastructure capacity is only a problem in some of the empirical cases, which makes a focus on coordination and social learning a practical guidance in the other cases.

This network of adjacent action situations has several practical implications for the implementation of a pilot project, as the concluding section points out. The coordination problem shows that a local governance mechanism is necessary to prevent sequential social learning and to enable concerted action for coordination. The problem of capacity appropriation and provision reveals that either a project has to take into account the internal governance of the electric utility and requires reducing corruption, or the project is conducted together with a utility that is not as susceptible to unauthorised connections, such as a cooperatively governed utility. The dilemma of excessive groundwater exploitation and resulting insufficient electric infrastructure capacity indicates that either rules for sustainable groundwater governance are necessary or a region with low levels of groundwater exploitation has to be selected.

The analysis revealed why existing policies to improve energy efficiency through demand-side measures has remained ineffective, neglecting the concerted investments necessary to overcome coordination failure and improve power quality. A top-down implementation policy would require bottom-up coordination strategies that cannot easily be prescribed. Not only do many strategies of sequential social learning and experimentation by farmer peer-groups counteract concerted action, but even the knowledge and hence ability to operate an electrically engineered power system is only modest and often absent in the field. Due to budget constraints within the utilities, the operational ground level at transformer sub-stations is often understaffed with few assistant electrical engineers and linemen. Tensions and mistrust between the distribution utilities and the farmer communities, but also illegal payments and corruption further complicate the situation. This happens despite the fact that utilities could profit from improved power quality through reduced transformer damages.

Given these challenges, a carefully designed pilot project can reveal best practices to the utilities and the farmers, when improvements can be observed, and thus enable social learning and best practice technology adoption by others.

In Search for Solutions: A Pilot Project as an Example of Application-Oriented Research

A pilot project has been built upon the findings and earlier experiments [Mohan/ Sreekumar 2010] to develop a best practice model of social learning for technology adoption. The project partner composition and phase descriptions indicate how such an intervention can be translated into practice. Measures of transferability and up-scaling enable a sustainable transition after the pilot project is phased out. The project thereby aims to contribute to agricultural viability. For the pilot project, a group of local partners was selected according to the project needs to facilitate collaboration, ownership and commitment. As an implementing partner, a local electric utility that is cooperatively governed has been selected to reduce problems of insufficient infrastructure capacity due to unauthorised connections. Only with sufficient capacity can the coordinated adoption of demand-side technology be successful. The project also involves a local scientific partner, specifically a power system research centre that can select the appropriate technology with the specifications necessary for the electricity system. A technology-transfer company has been included to support collaboration with technology providers and the selection of the best technology available in the local market. A committee of local NGOs has been appointed to enable local mobilisation of farming communities and increase ownership after the project intervention phases.

There is more about the practical issues of this pilot project in the volume *Energy and Sun* of this book series [pp. 37–46 ↗]. Both, the pilot project and this analysis can be seen as an example of an application-oriented research approach as promoted by BMBF's research programme.

References

Andhra Pradesh Electricity Regulatory Commission. (2001): *"Tariff Order: Review of Tariff Filings FY2001–02"* APERC, ed. 4/2001

APERC. (2009): *Wheeling Tariffs FY2009-10 to FY2013-14 and Retail Supply Tariffs FY2009–10* A. P. E. R. Commission, ed. Hyderabad

Badiani, R./ Jessoe, K.K./ Plant, S. (2012): "Development and the Environment: The implications of agricultural electricity subsidies in India". In: *The Journal of Environment & Development* 21(2), pp. 244–62

Dossani, R./ Ranganathan, V. (2004): "Farmers' willingness to pay for power in India: conceptual issues, survey results and implications for pricing". In: *Energy Economics* 26(3), pp. 359–69

Drèze, J./ Sharma, N. (1998): "Palanpur: population, society, economy". In: P. Lanjouw and N. H. Stern, eds. *Economic development in Palanpur over five decades*. Oxford, New York: p. xxviii, 640 p

Dubash, N.K./ Rao, D.N. (2008): "Regulatory practice and politics: Lessons from independent regulation in Indian electricity". In: *Utilities Policy* 16(4), pp. 321–31

Dugan, R.C. (2003): *Electrical power systems quality* 2nd ed. New York

Dutton, W.H./ Schneider, V./ Vedel, T. (2012): "Ecologies of Games shaping Large Technical Systems: Cases from Telecommunications to the Internet". In: J. Bauer, A. Lang, and V. Schneider, eds. *Innovation Policy and Governance in High-Tech Industries The Complexity of Coordination*. Berlin, Heidelberg: Springer, p. 1 online resource

Hanisch, M./ Kimmich C./ Sagebiel, J./ Rommel, J. (2010): "Coping with power scarcity in an emerging megacity: a consumers' perspective from Hyderabad". In: *International Journal of Global Energy Issues* 33(3–4), pp. 189–204

Harsanyi, J.C./ Selten, R. (1988): *A general theory of equilibrium selection in games*. Cambridge, Mass.

India, C. of. (2001): *Census of India, 2001. Series 1, India. Paper*. New Delhi: Office of Registrar General & Census Commissioner

Janssen, M.A. (2007): "Coordination in irrigation systems: An analysis of the Lansing-Kremer model of Bali". In: *Agricultural Systems* 93(1–3), pp. 170–90

Kimmich, C. (2011a): "Concerted action and the transformer dilemma: overcoming uncertainty in electricity provision for irrigation in Andhra Pradesh, India". In: *13th International Conference of the International Association for the Study of the Commons*. Hyderabad

Kimmich, C. (2011b): "Incentives for energy efficient irrigation through appliance quality: Empirical evidence from Andhra Pradesh, India". In: *1st International Conclave on Climate Change*. Centre for Climate Change, Engineering Staff College of India, Hyderabad

Kimmich, C. (2013): "Linking action situations: Coordination, conflicts, and evolution in electricity provision for irrigation in Andhra Pradesh, India". In: *Ecological Economics*, 90(0), pp. 150–58

Kimmich, C./ Sagebiel, J. (2013): "Peri-Urban Linkages: Improving Energy Efficiency in Irrigation to Enable Sustainable Urban Transition". In: L. Eltrop, T. Telsnig, and U. Fahl, eds. *Energy and Sun: Sustainable Energy Solutions for Future Megacities*. Berlin

Kondepati, R. (2011): "Agricultural Groundwater Management in Andhra Pradesh, India: A Focus on Free Electricity Policy and its Reform". In: *International Journal of Water Resources Development* 27(2), pp. 375–86

Mohan, R./ Sreekumar, N. (2010): "Improving efficiency of groundwater pumping for agriculture: thinking through together". Discussion Paper

Narayan, J. (1999): "Energy sector reform and governance". In: *India in the new millenium: energy, environment and development*

Pani, B.S./ Sreekumar, N./ Reddy, M.T. (2007): "Power sector reforms in Andhra Pradesh: Their impact and policy gaps". In: Centre for Economic and Social Studies, ed. *Governance and Policy Spaces* 11:62

Reidhead, W. (2001): "Achieving agricultural pumpset efficiency in rural India". In: *Journal of International Development* 13(2), pp. 135–51

Repetto, R.C. (1994): *The "Second India" revisited: population, poverty, and environmental stress over two decades*. Washington, DC

Rosegrant, M.W./ Evenson, R.E. (1992): "Agricultural Productivity and Sources of Growth in South Asia". In: *American Journal of Agricultural Economics* 74(3), pp. 757–61

Sant, G./ Dixit, S. (1996): "Agricultural pumping efficiency in India: the role of standards". In: *Energy for Sustainable Development* 3(1), pp. 29–37

Sen, A.K. (1967): "Isolation, Assurance and the Social Rate of Discount". In: *The Quarterly Journal of Economics* 81(1), pp. 112–24

Shah, T. (2009): *Taming the anarchy: groundwater governance in South Asia*. Washington, D.C., Colombo, Sri Lanka: Resources for the Future; International Water Management Institute

Suri, K.C. (2002): *Democratic process and electoral politics in Andhra Pradesh*, India. London: Overseas Development Institute.

Thatcher, M. (2002): "Delegation to independent regulatory agencies: Pressures, functions and contextual mediation". In: *West European Politics* 25(1), pp. 125–47

Tongia, R. (2007): "The political economy of Indian power sector reforms". In: D. G. Victor and T. C. Heller, eds. *The political economy of power sector reform: the experiences of five major developing countries*. Cambridge; New York, p. xviii

Van Steenbergen, F. (2006): "Promoting local management in groundwater". In: *Hydrogeology Journal* 14(3), pp. 380–91

von Meier, A. (2006): *Electric power systems: a conceptual introduction*. Hoboken, NJ

Notes

1 "As part of the decentralisation of the administrative system set up in 1986, each district is divided into a number of Mandals (intermediate territorial and administrative unit, with a population of about 50,000 to 70,000 between the village and district levels) and Gram Panchayats (village councils or the area that falls under a village council)" (Suri 2002, 5).

2 62 INR (Indian Rupees) = 1 €$_{2010}$

3 A Nash equilibrium results when each player in a game responds to the given strategy of the other players with his best strategy. For the assurance problem of capacitor installation, this means: install a capacitor if the other farmers have done so and do not install a capacitor if nobody else has done so. The two Nash equilibria are where either all or nobody has installed a capacitor.

GAUTENG: Landfill gas collection in Gauteng [Carsten Zehner]

Ntombifuthi Ntuli

Master's Thesis at University of Johannesburg, Department of Geography, Environmental Management and Energy Studies

(Co-Authors: Harold J. Annegarn, Ludger Eltrop, Ralf Kober)

Implementation of the Clean Development Mechanism (CDM) in Gauteng Municipalities: Barriers, Opportunities, and Post-2012 Outlook

Abstract

The Clean Development Mechanism (CDM) can be defined as a project-based mechanism established under the Kyoto Protocol to help Annex 1 parties meet their emission reduction targets through investing in project activities that reduce greenhouse gas (GHG) emissions and contribute to sustainable development in Non-Annex 1 countries [Curnow/ Hodes 2009]. Even though South Africa is leading in terms of the number of registered CDM projects in Africa, it is still lagging far behind other developing regions in this regard, having registered only twenty CDM projects by June 2011.

This research is aimed at identifying the constraints that inhibit large-scale implementation of CDM projects by Gauteng municipalities, investigating the reasons why South African municipalities are lagging behind the private sector in CDM project development, and identifying opportunities for further development of CDM projects.

The study was conducted using qualitative research techniques, using methods such as in-depth interviews and/or focus groups. Three different groups of respondents were identified: (i) European Certified Emission Reduction (CER) buyers; (ii) project developers/ CDM consultants in South Africa; and (iii) Gauteng municipal officials responsible for CDM project development. A separate questionnaire was compiled for each of the three target groups with the purpose of drawing conclusions about the prevailing status of the South African CDM market from the perspectives of each of these three groups. The objective of examining the perspectives of international CER purchasers was to gain an outsiders' perspective of the barriers to South African CDM implementation and to assess their appetite for South African CERs.

The main barriers to CDM implementation that were identified include: inadequate project development capacity, insufficient financing opportunities, low electricity tariffs, post-2012 uncertainties, additionality, price volatility of CERs, high CDM transaction costs, and scepticism regarding the benefits of CDM. That some of the barriers (applicable in the earlier years of CDM) have since been addressed—either through direct action or by means of policy measures—was established. The opportunities identified included energy efficiency, landfill gas, renewable energy and increased focus on Programme of Activities (POAs).

The findings revealed that several of these barriers remained applicable to conditions in South Africa. Most importantly, the European Union made a decision that its Emission trading Scheme (EUETS) would only trade CERs with the least developed countries, which excludes South Africa. The study concluded that these factors would make it improbable that South Africa would continue to generate a significant revenue stream from the sale of CERs beyond 2012. It was therefore recommended that South Africa's contribution to climate protection and greenhouse gas emission reductions be financed through other mechanisms.

Introduction: Framework of Research

This Research in the Framework of Other Scientific Studies

Article 12 of the Kyoto Protocol [United Nations 1998] defines the Clean Development Mechanism (CDM) as a mechanism allowing Annex 1 Parties[1] to invest in project activities that reduce greenhouse gas (GHG) emissions and contribute to sustainable development in Non-Annex 1 countries [Curnow/ Hodes 2009]. In reducing GHG emissions, these projects generate credits called Certified Emission Reductions (CERs), which the Annex 1 Parties can use to meet their emission reduction obligations under the Kyoto Protocol [Curnow/ Hodes 2009].

Three previous studies investigated CDM barriers and opportunities in South Africa. Little et al. [2007] conducted a study that focused on inhibiting and facilitating factors affecting implementation of the CDM by South African industries. Wilson [2007] focused on the barriers and drivers to implementation of the CDM within a single municipality—the Nelson Mandela Bay Municipality. Winkler and van Es [2007] dealt with opportunities and constraints of the implementation of the CDM in energy efficiency projects throughout South Africa. Their paper focused on dispelling the misconception that energy efficiency projects might not qualify under the "additionality" criterion of the CDM.

This study built on these previous studies by investigating CDM implementation by metropolitan and municipal administrations of Gauteng Province, the industrial and commercial heartland of South Africa. In addition, this study examined the perspectives of international CER purchasers, giving an outsiders' perspective of the barriers to the CDM from both the demand and the supply side of CERs. Differences between CDM projects developed by the private and municipal sectors were analysed.

This research forms part of the EnerKey Sustainable Megacities Gauteng project. EnerKey is a collaborative project between Gauteng and German institutions, which focuses on energy as a key element in addressing climate protection [www.enerkey.info]. Module 6 of the EnerKey project focuses on the Climate Policy and the Clean Development Mechanism (especially the problems that Gauteng municipalities encounter when implementing the CDM) and contributes towards formulating solutions for use by municipalities to fast track CDM implementation.

In the earlier years of the CDM, South Africa was amongst a group of five countries identified by Jung as "CDM Stars" [2005]. These are countries with a high potential for generating carbon credits under the CDM. But evidently, the CDM has generated marginal benefits for South Africa. By June 2011, two hundred CDM projects had been submitted to the South African Designated National Authority, comprising 163 Project Idea Notes (PINs) and thirty-seven Project Design Documents (PDDs). Of the thirty-seven PDDs, twenty have been registered by the CDM Executive Board (a CDM approval committee of the UNFCCC in Bonn) as CDM projects, six of which have been issued CERs. The thirty-seven PDDs are at different stages of the project cycle [DOE 2011].

Goldblatt expressed dismay at the slow growth of CDM project in South Africa [2009]. In South Africa, emission intensity is extremely high compared to similar middle-income developing countries. The highly energy-intensive South African economy makes the country one of the highest emitters of greenhouse gasses in Africa [DEAT 2007]. In 2000, South Africa was the nineteenth most carbon-intensive economy, accounting for 9.2 mt of CO_2 per capita by 2004 [Ibid.]. These figures highlight South Africa's potential for CDM project development [Goldblatt 2009]. This large potential is affirmed by Pegels, who views South Africa's coal energy history as providing potential for major emission reductions, considering the high levels of technological and economic development in the country [2010]. She further describes South Africa's abundant renewable energy resources as providing a favourable climate for project development and investment.

Analysis of the South African CDM pipeline revealed that only three municipal projects had been registered by the CDM Executive Board by June 2011. The aim of the research was to identify the constraints that inhibit and opportunities that facilitate large scale implementation of CDM projects by Gauteng Municipalities and to investigate the reasons why South African municipalities are lagging behind the private sector in CDM project development.

Methods: Qualitative Research Techniques

Although the purpose of the study was to draw conclusions about the South African CDM market specifically for the municipal sector, the study was designed to examine the entire sequence of supplier, broker, and buyer. Suppliers were selected as the municipalities of the Gauteng Province, South Africa, represented by Gauteng municipal officials responsible for CDM project development. Gauteng was selected because of its high level of industrial and economic activity and thus a considerable potential for CDM project development. A new category of professional intermediary agents has evolved–CDM consultants, who are usually lawyers by training–due to the complexities of CDM trading. The researcher canvassed the views of this category to obtain a comprehensive assessment of the CDM implementation chain. The client group selected were CER buyers and investors (companies and agencies) in Germany and Denmark. These countries strongly support the UNFCC CDM programme on a political level and have purchased large volumes of CERs.

Qualitative research techniques were used as the study methodology as the topic deals with a subjective assessment of attitudes, opinions, and behaviour [Kothari 2004]. The study sought to clarify reasons for the opinions, interpretations, and perspectives of the selected respondents on the issue of CDM project development in South Africa. Qualitative research enables the researcher to produce detailed snapshots of the participants under study [Ramchander 2004].

The data used was sourced by administering a questionnaire as well as interviews with the identified respondents, and from the South African Designated National Authority, the UNEP Risoe website [http://www.cdmpipeline.org] and the UNFCCC website. In 2009, the first author (PNN) organised a CDM workshop for Gauteng municipalities in cooperation with the German partners of the EnerKey sustainable megacities programme [www.enerkey.info]. The papers presented at this workshop and the breakout discussions gave a preliminary overview of the CDM implementation scenario in Gauteng municipalities.

The researcher (PNN) conducted interviews in person where possible, otherwise by telephone, avoiding bias by maintaining objectivity on the topic and excluding leading questions [Valentine 2005]. The data requested from the respondents concerned finding out factual details and seeking responses to firm pre-identified categories. The numbers of respondents and response rates in the three categories of client, intermediary, and supplier are indicated in Figure 1 ↗. The interviews with European CER purchasers took place from March 2010 to June 2010. Interviews with the intermediaries and the municipal officials took place between October 2010 and February 2011.

Findings: Barriers and Opportunities for CDM in South Africa

CDM in Municipalities

CER Buyers' Perspective (Client)

The perspectives of the carbon credit buyers (clients) on the performance of municipalities in generating Certified Emission Reductions (CERs) were considered relevant. This would assist in establishing whether the lack of development of CDM projects in municipalities is due to a lack of interest in the municipal sector from carbon credit buyers, or a lack of initiative from municipalities themselves to create a supply of CERs. The purchasers were asked whether they are contemplating purchasing CERs or investing in municipal CER projects (globally), which project type they prefer, and where these projects are located.

The majority (88%) of the buyers indicated past dealings with municipal projects. Of these, 88% had purchased CERs from renewable energy projects, 63% from energy efficiency projects, and 63% from landfill gas projects (multiple choice questions allowed for selection of more than one answer). Most purchases of municipal CERs were from projects in China. Only 12% of the buyers responded that they had no concerns about the specific types or technologies of potential CDM projects.

The next question asked buyers to assess municipal versus private sector CDM projects in terms of quality. This question was intended to find out the influence of municipal administrative procedures on the success of CDM projects. 63% of the buyers regarded municipalities as lacking project management acumen. Only 38% considered municipalities poor in CDM project management. The private sector project management performance was positively (good) evaluated by 63%, while 25% rated the level as average, and 12% as very poor. In terms of knowledge and understanding, 25% of the respondents rated municipalities as good, 50%

Fig. 1   Number of respondents, suppliers and consultants, and rates of response [Author]

Group of Respondents	Original Sample	Number of Respondents	Response Rate
CER buyers in Europe	20	12	60%
Municipal officials (suppliers of CERs)	15	10	67%
CDM consultants (proponents)	20	10	50%

rated municipalities as average, and a further 25% rated them as having poor knowledge of the CDM. The private sector was rated good by 12% of the respondents; the remainder rated them as poor.

Municipalities are said to be doing well with "Stakeholder engagement", with 38% of CER respondents agreeing to this statement. 25% of the respondents thought that private sector performance in this aspect was poor; 63% thought it was average. In terms of "Punctual CER delivery", 75% of buyers were of the opinion that municipalities do not perform very well. 63% thought that the private sector delivers CERs punctually.

The final aspect that the respondents were asked to rate was "Top management support" in the development of CDM projects. 35% thought municipal senior management is not supportive of CDM projects, while all respondents thought top managers in the private sector often demonstrate support for CDM projects. This indicates the critical importance of senior management support to the success of CDM projects. The top-down vs. bottom-up approach in project development may play a major role in influencing management decisions. Management is more likely to support project ideas that come from their level (more often the case in the private sector), whereas in municipalities project ideas usually come from project staff (bottom-up) and it may take time to convince management of the benefits of proposed projects.

CDM Consultants' Perspectives

CDM consultants in South Africa were asked the same questions about their assessment of municipal performance in CDM projects relative to the private sector [Figure 2 ↗]. The private sector was perceived as performing well in "Project management" (50% good or very good). By contrast, 50% of the project developers rated the municipalities as poor performers in this regard. Only 20% of these respondents rated them as performing well. All the CDM consultants rated the private sector as very good (100%) with regards to "Knowledge and understanding" of the CDM, with the municipalities scoring less well, with 60% rated as good and 40% as poor. Both the municipalities and the private sector were said to be doing well with "Stakeholder engagement".

"Punctual delivery" of CERs seems to be an obstacle for both the private sector and municipalities. Overall, both CDM consultants and CER buyers perceived the private sector as a better performer in project development. These findings indicate that municipalities are lagging behind the private sector in CDM project development. The CDM consultants expressed disappointment with the slow development of CDM projects by municipalities. Most consultants and project developers had been active in encouraging municipalities to use carbon financing for greenhouse gas emission reduction projects. However, one project developer expressed disappointment: "the biggest barrier in municipal projects is procurement rules.

Fig. 2 Consultants' perspective of CDM in municipalities [Author]

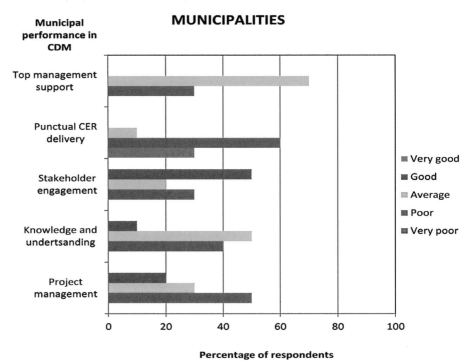

We have spent a lot of time selling ideas to municipalities and even dedicated free consulting time in pre-feasibility stage of the projects ... with all the time spent... we do not get awarded (contracts) for one reason or another".

Similarities and Differences

From the CER buyers' perspective, buying carbon credits from projects developed by the private sector is preferred because of better performance in project delivery. When the opinions of the CDM consultants and CER buyers are compared, the difference is that although both groups preferred projects developed by the private sector, CER buyers still have some misgivings, while CDM consultants favoured private sector projects (100%). Both groups' evaluation of municipality developed projects bordered on the negative.

The Perspective of Municipal Officials

Knowledge and Experience in the Field of CDM: For municipal officials with responsibility for CDM matters, the questionnaire elicited information about their relevant experience—30% have expert knowledge, while a further 50% have an intermediate understanding of CDM. This indicates that there is a lack of internal expertise in municipalities for dealing with the complexities of CDM project development and negotiation.

Future Projects for Municipalities: The municipal officials were asked to rate the probability of projects being developed within four project categories. All interviewed officials ranked energy efficiency and landfill gas projects as the most likely to be developed in the near future (100% for both), followed closely by renewable energy projects (90%). Least likely to be developed were transportation projects. These four types of projects were identified because they are prioritised in the energy and climate change strategies of various municipalities.

Factors that Motivate CDM Development in Municipalities

The municipal officials were asked, "What are driving factors that lead to the development of a CDM project?" This question intended to establish whether the slow development of CDM projects is because of a lack of motivation or due to other reasons. A high percentage (80%) of municipal respondents thought that CDM projects were initiated as a result of a consultant or a project developer approaching a municipality with a project idea. 80% indicated that they also look at what other municipalities have done and whether such projects succeeded, i.e., they rely on the success or failure of other municipal projects as a basis for generating project ideas. Approximately 55% stated that municipal integrated development plan (IDP) strategies were the main driving force in formulating project ideas, while 45% disagreed that the projects were initiated because they were part of the IDP or other strategies.

For most municipalities that have successfully implemented CDM projects, it had been a trial-and-error process. The need for landfill-gas disposal had triggered their involvement, rather than a desire to generate CER revenue, thus supporting the 45% who disagreed with the statement that CER revenue had been the primary motivating factor. Municipal officials did not agree that political motivation is a driver for CDM project development. They commented that politicians tend to focus on short-term projects with completion during their limited five-year terms of office rather than on long-term payoff issues (e.g., climate protection)

Barriers to Implementation of the CDM in South Africa

Globally, the barriers that hinder local governments from engaging in CDM include: the complexity of the CDM process, upfront investments required, institutional problems, inadequate capacity, uncertainties regarding the post-2012 continuation of the Kyoto Protocol, political obstacles and the lack of ownership of CDM projects [Sippel/ Michaelowa 2009].

The Perspective of CER Buyers and CDM Consultants

CDM project development is a protracted process. Project developers encounter a number of obstacles, some of which are project related while others are of a more general nature. On the other hand, CDM consultants and project developers in South Africa have been very active in growing the CDM market. These developers, including local companies and foreign companies with established presence in South Africa, intended to participate in the business opportunities presented by the nascent CDM market. Six years after the approval of the first CDM project in South Africa, it appears that the market is still struggling to grow and has yet to reach its potential. CDM consultants and project developers were interviewed to gain insight into their experiences regarding the slow growth of the CDM market.

In terms of project-specific obstacles, 90% of the buyers agreed that lack of "CDM knowledge" is an obstacle [Figure 3 ↗]. Knowledge of the CDM process, in any country, often resides

Fig. 3   Barriers to CDM implementation in SA: CER buyers' perspective [Author]

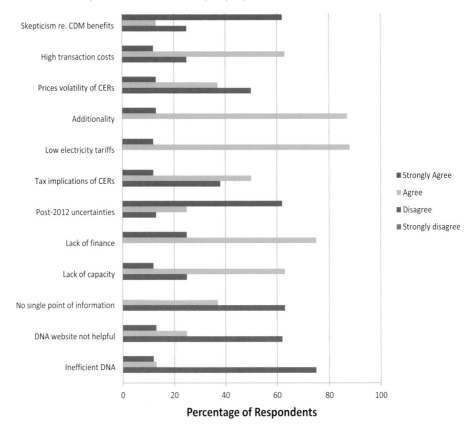

Percentage of Respondents

within a limited group of project developers and consultants, making it difficult for someone who does not already understand CDM to become involved. Despite the majority of CDM consultants believing that capacity building is still a barrier, 30% indicated that there has been an increase in CDM capacity building activities (including conferences, workshops, and seminars) and that these have increased general awareness of carbon trading.

A large number of CER buyers (60%) disagreed with the statement that there is "no single point of information" regarding CDM in South Africa, and 80% of the project developers disagreed. This indicated that both groups of respondents were of the opinion that the South African market is mature and that CDM information is readily available. However, there is still a lack of capacity, as indicated by 75% of the buyers. A majority of buyers (88%) agreed that the implementation of sustainable development criteria in South Africa is transparent. The South African "Designated National Authority" (DNA) has published "Sustainable Development Assessment Guidelines" on its website, which demonstrates transparency. This feature thus is not considered an obstacle for a CDM project. Charikleia et al. agree that "CDM technologies should be linked to developing countries' national strategies instead of acting as a source of demonstration projects, which therefore leads to the enhancement of local economic activity, capacities and infrastructure" [2009, 83].

The South African CDM consultants agreed with their European counterparts that the DNA is not the main constraint responsible for the small number of approved projects in

South Africa. 70% of the respondents ruled out the statement that "CDM information is not readily available". Several CER buyers praised the South African DNA as the most effective in Africa. 75% of the respondents disagreed with the statement "DNA inefficiency" is a barrier in CDM development in South Africa. A majority (60%) of the CER buyers agreed that "misunderstanding of technology" is an obstacle to project development. "Poor communication" among stakeholders can also be an obstacle in any project, as conceded by 50% of CER buyers. The biggest obstacle in terms of developing large-scale projects is the lack of finance and risk coverage. Financial institutions remain cautious in financing carbon projects as such investments they are still considered risky. Furthermore, uncertainty regarding the future of CDM after the first commitment period ends in 2012 remains a challenge, as concurred by 80% of the CER buyers. The majority of the CDM project developers share the same sentiments.

Most CER buyers regarded the uncertain tax implications of CER revenue as a barrier. However, 80% of the consultants held a contrary view, based on a recent South African government decision to exempt carbon revenue from taxation—an indication that the government is committed to supporting growth of the CDM market. "This measure is also aimed at improving South Africa's attractiveness for CDM projects" [Pegels 2010, 4950].

Both CER buyers and CDM consultants believed that South African electricity prices are inexpensive by international standards—thereby confirming that renewable energy projects to provide expensive forms of electricity are not financially viable. Therefore, the low electricity price in South Africa acts as a barrier to CDM development. However, electricity prices in South Africa have sharply increased over the period 2008–2011, with far above inflation increases scheduled for 2012 and 2013. Because of these anticipated increases, electricity prices may no longer persist as a barrier in CDM implementation, hence 30% of the interviewed consultants disagreed on this point.

Project developers need to ensure that their projects are "additional", which means that a project could not be developed without carbon funding. This is a high risk factor as projects may be rejected for inadequate proof of additionality at the validation stage by the Designated Operational Entity, far into the project cycle. All buyers agreed that proving additionality is an impediment to CDM project development. "Price volatility of CER": 50% of the buyers did not agree that this is a barrier because, as with all other financial markets, the CER price is dependent on several factors and is bound to fluctuate. Project developers saw volatility of CER prices as a serious barrier because, if there is a price crash, this could a negative impact on their cash flow projections. All the project developer respondents agreed that both "additionality" and "price volatility of CERs" are substantial barriers beyond the control of CDM project developers.

"High transaction costs" have been a major hurdle in the carbon markets, not just in South Africa but globally. It is not surprising, therefore, that 75% agreed with this statement. Finally, 75% of the CER buyers regarded the "scepticism" surrounding the benefits of CDM as a barrier to implementation. Almost 90% of the consultants felt that post-2012 uncertainty is an additional barrier to CDM development, especially since, at the time of the interviews, the deadline for the first commitment period of the Kyoto Protocol was approaching, with little prospect of a second commitment period. Michaelowa & Jotzo argued that the transaction costs and institutional rigidities would reduce the attractiveness of the Kyoto Protocol flexibility mechanisms compared to domestic greenhouse gas abatement options [2005].

Municipal officials were provided questions on a range of potential barriers for CDM project development in their respective municipalities. The main intention was to determine what municipalities regarded as barriers, both in their own CDM project development activities, and across the country in general. Regarding the efficiency of the "Designated National Authority" (DNA), the municipalities believed the South African DNA was reasonably effective and was actively involved in building capacity on CDM issues throughout the country. Some municipal officials (40% of the respondents) were unaware of sources of CDM information. As observed in the interviews with the CDM consultants and CER buyers, the following factors were listed as accepted barriers to CDM implementation:

· lack of capacity
· lack of financing
· uncertainty around post–2012
· price volatility of CERs
· high transaction costs
· scepticism regarding CDM benefits
· legal restrictions
· lack of municipal knowledge of CDM
· lack of understanding of relevant technology

Municipalities that have developed CDM projects agreed with the consultants that the procurement provisions of the Municipal Financial Management Act (MFMA) had caused delays in project development. 60 % disagreed that "lack of municipal ownership of projects" is a barrier. Municipalities thus may be implying that, even though the projects may be managed by external agents, they are still extensively involved because external agents cannot make decisions on the municipality's behalf. Although 60% agree that the lack of good examples (in South Africa) is a barrier to project development, 40% oppose this view on the basis that the project developer should be learning from projects in other countries as well as South Africa.

In listing the main hurdles municipalities encounter when implementing CDM projects, the respondents cited two notable barriers: lack of capacity and lack of insight on how long the CDM process would take. CDM projects are not a municipal priority. Politicians pay more attention to delivery of essential services for which they can derive electoral support. Many (67%) regarded political obstacles as a barrier, especially in those municipalities where project implementation may require political support.

Opportunities for CDM Project Development in Gauteng Municipalities

CDM provides new opportunities for municipal and local authorities to channel additional investment from developed countries into their own sustainable development projects, while contributing to the reduction of greenhouse gas emissions. This simultaneously allows municipalities to move closer towards the targets set in their energy and climate change strategies. UN ESCAP identified several potential areas for such projects including the improvement of urban planning, transportation development, and energy efficiency, as well as improved strategies for solid waste management and conversion to energy [2009].

To date, most of the municipal CDM projects in South Africa have been landfill gas projects, of which several involve only methane flaring, without secondary use of the gas energy. According to Couth and Trois, landfill methane emissions are increasing in developing countries partly due to increased quantities of waste, urban populations, economic development and, to some extent, the replacement of open burning and dumping by engineered landfills [2012]. Many landfill sites in Gauteng have not been evaluated for potential CDM or renewable energy landfill gas projects. One serious challenge of such projects in South Africa is the difficulty in estimating the potential gas production.

There are several lessons to be learned from the eThekwini Landfill gas project, as one of the first projects to navigate the CDM approval process amidst municipal procurement and legislative barriers. An article analysing the eThekwini landfill gas CDM project implementation by Couth et al. highlights time and cost, complexity of the CDM process, as well as conservative and inflexible methodologies as the main issues stalling implementation. They further associate these issues with "the lack of security of the CDM process to guarantee CERs and ensure that GHG emissions have been reduced by such projects" [Couth et al. 2011]. Methane recovery, whether flaring or electricity generation, however, remains the most viable option for municipal CDM projects in Gauteng.

Energy efficiency is one of the main areas where municipalities can develop CDM projects. South Africa has significant potential, across all sectors, for the development of energy efficiency projects [Winkler/ van Es 2007]. "However, analysis of the emerging CDM portfolio shows that energy-efficiency projects are much better represented at the concept stage than in fully designed CDM projects" [Ibid.]. Although conditions have become more favourable for energy efficiency projects, further actions are required to increase the number of these project types under the CDM.

The generation of electricity from renewable energy technologies within Gauteng has a large, but limited potential [Eltrop/ Annegarn 2011]. Concentrated solar has the best potential for large-scale, relatively low greenhouse gas mitigation technologies. Solar photovoltaic generation is more expensive with a low overall capacity, but prices have been falling dramatically in recent months, exhibiting a growing potential. Electricity from biomass is expensive with a small capacity factor, due to climate, water, and land limitations. Gauteng is in a geographic location of low wind speeds, eliminating this as a viable energy source. Renewable energy generation from waste remains the most accessible, low-risk entry point for renewable electricity and fuel generation in Gauteng.

If the opportunities contemplated above are too small to consider as stand-alone CDM projects, they can be clustered into "Programme of Activities" (POAs). The Programme of Activities mechanism allows project developers to include an unlimited number of small-scale CDM project activities (CPAs) throughout the life of a project, without going through the registration process for each additional activity. This is especially beneficial for municipalities, because it eliminates the procurement process barrier (previously experienced by municipalities each time they registered a new CDM project). Some of the municipal officials interviewed advised that they had not registered some of the emission reduction projects for CDM because of the relatively small size of rewards to be gained in relation to high transaction costs, and the potential delays in project initiation while awaiting CDM approval. Although a POA registration process has high initial costs in comparison to a normal CDM project, in the long run, the financial benefit makes up for the initial financial burden.

Conclusion: CDM Won't Finance South Africa's Contribution to Climate Protection

The majority of barriers to CDM implementation in South Africa identified in earlier studies were found to be still relevant. One crucial barrier that has been removed is the tax implication of carbon credits. South Africa announced that from 2009 the revenue from the primary generation of CERs would be tax exempt, a decisive step taken to support the CDM market.

Landfill gas was identified as a key opportunity that Gauteng municipalities could utilise to participate in the CDM market. While municipalities can earn CERs already by simply flaring landfill gas, an opportunity exists to generate even more carbon credits by using the gas for the generation of electricity or compressed natural gas for vehicle propulsion. So far only one project in South Africa has achieved such approval.

Most of the barriers pertaining to these project types related to internal municipal procedures, including the stringent procurement rules set by the Municipal Financial Management Act. A remaining challenge is that such projects generate insufficient volumes of CERs for South Africa to take up a significant share of CDM investment funds. CER buyers expressed the view that electricity prices in South Africa are low relative to international rates, making it difficult for renewable energy electricity projects to compete. However, since the country's 2008 power crisis, electricity prices have increased drastically (25% per annum for three successive years). This, together with the new bidding process for renewable energy power purchase agreements, will strengthen the case for renewable energy CDM projects.

It has been established that there is a substantial pool of expertise available that could assist municipalities to increase the number of CDM projects. However, bureaucracy in decision-making and complicated rules in engaging external consultants were identified as hindrances. The inherent conservative nature of South African municipalities when venturing into new initiatives and technologies, reinforced by the constraints of the Municipal Finance Management Act, remain challenges—these have been limitations to South Africa's development of CDM projects.

Several European buyers actively seek CERs from African projects. These CER buyers, CDM project developers, and consultants have extensive knowledge about the South African CDM market. Nevertheless, because of the uncertainties regarding the CDM status after 2012, South African project developers have been increasingly reluctant to initiate new projects, especially in the period leading up to 17th Conference of the Parties (COP17) to the United Nations Framework Convention on Climate Change (UNFCCC). The discounted price of post-2012 CERs (a drop of >50% in the spot price) has further contributed to scepticism.

While a decision was taken at COP 17 to extend the Kyoto Protocol for a second commitment period up to 2017, several key players in the CDM market (including Russia, Japan, and Canada) have withdrawn from the Kyoto Protocol. These countries join the USA, which has never ratified the Kyoto Protocol, effectively leaving the EU as the only significant player in CER trading under CDM. It should be noted that most CER buyers in Europe are also signatories to the European Union Emission Trading Scheme (EU–ETS). Under this scheme, the EU–ETS signatories will trade CERs only with the Least Developed Countries (LDCs) after 2012. This excludes Advanced Developing Countries (a group including South Africa, China, India, and Brazil). It is, therefore, apparent that the CDM market in South Africa is indefensible. South Africa will have to seek buyers from outside the EU to sustain its carbon market.

CER purchasers who actively sought projects during 2011 were particular about project eligibility. Projects in the early stages of the CDM registration process were the least likely to be considered, since the risk of non-delivery would be high compared with already validated projects. Market uncertainty and high upfront transaction costs inhibit project developers from initiating registration of CDM projects. This is especially the case with municipalities, as, in addition to the CDM barriers, there are internal barriers within municipal administrations that may further delay the registration process.

To the extent CDM continues post-2012, the level of benefit for South Africa is unclear considering the reduction in the pool of CER buyers. Unfortunately, South Africa did not take full advantage of the opportunity when CDM was at its peak. South Africa stood a reasonable chance of capitalising on carbon financing, but the conservative nature of the country in implementing large-scale projects restricted the growth of the CDM market.

Overall, besides the large pool of expertise and multiple players, there remain a formidable number of barriers for the implementation of municipal CDM projects in South Africa, which makes it improbable that the country will generate a significant revenue stream from the sale of CERs beyond 2012. South Africa's contribution to climate protection and greenhouse gas emission reductions will have to be financed through other mechanisms.

Acknowledgements

We acknowledge contributions by Dr. Maike Sippel (IER), Dr. Axel Michaelowa, Yuriy Lozensky, Elisabeth Frewin, and all of the individuals who responded to our questionnaires. Financial contributions are acknowledged from the German Academic Exchange Programme (DAAD), TÜV Rheinland (Cologne, Germany), the IER (University of Stuttgart), the University of Johannesburg, the National Research Foundation (NRF), the EnerKey Sustainable Megacities Programme, the German Federal Ministry of Education and Research (BMBF) (EnerKey Project support), the South African National Energy Research Institute (SANERI) (EnerKey Project Support). Parts of this work have been presented at two conferences: "Carbon Markets and Climate Finance Africa", January 2011, Sandton; and the "South African Energy Efficiency Convention", November 2011, Johannesburg.

References

Couth R./ Trois C. (2012): "Sustainable waste management in Africa through CDM projects". In: *Waste Management*, 32, pp. 2115–25

Couth R./ Trois C./ Parkin J./ Strachan L.J./ Gilder A./ Wright M. (2011): "Delivery and viability of landfill gas CDM projects in Africa: A South African experience". In: *Renewable and Sustainable Energy Reviews*, 15, pp. 392–403

Curnow, P./ Hodes, G. (2009): *Implementing CDM Projects: Guidebook to Host Country Legal Issues*. Risoe, Denmark

Department of Environmental Affairs and Tourism (2007): *Environmental Sustainability Indicator Report–Global Stewardship*. Pretoria

Department of Energy (2009): *Department of Energy official website*, Pretoria. (http://www.energy.gov.za/files/esources/kyoto/kyoto_frame.html), 14.10.2009

Department of Energy (2011): *South African CDM Project Portfolio* (Up to June 2011), South African Designated National Authority, Pretoria. (http://www.energy.gov.za/files/esources/kyoto/kyoto_frame.html), 25.06.2011

Eltrop, L./ Annegarn, H.J. (2011): "Energy as a Key Element of an Integrated Climate Protection Concept for the City Region of Gauteng, South Africa". *Energy & Climate Protection Conference*, 5–6 October 2011, Johannesburg (www.enerkey.info)

Gilder, A. (2006): *Support for the Development and Uptake of CDM projects in the Industrial Sector: Country Report South Africa. UNIDO Pilot Project in Cooperation with Austrian Industry*. Johannesburg

Goldblatt, M. (2009): *City of Johannesburg Carbon Finance Guidelines*. City of Johannesburg

Hong J./ Guo G.X./ Marinova, D./ Jia R./ Yuang F (2011): "Distribution characteristics and prospects for CDM projects in China". Paper presented at 19th International Congress on Modelling and Simulation. Perth. 12–16 December 2011

Jarman, M. (2007): *Small Guide to Big Issues: Climate Change*. Johannesburg

Jung, M. (2005): "Host country attractiveness for CDM non-sink projects". In: *Energy Policy*, 34, pp. 2173–84

Karakosta, C./ Doukas H./ Psarras J. (2009): "Directing Clean Development Mechanism towards developing countries' sustainable development priorities". In: *Energy for Sustainable Development*, 13, pp. 77–84

Kothari, C.R. (2004): *Research Methodology Methods and Techniques*. Second ed. New Delhi

Little G./ Maxwell, T./ Sutherland, M. (2007): "Accelerating implementation of Clean Development Mechanism in South Africa". In: *South African Journal of Economic and Management Sciences*, 4, pp. 395–411

Michaelowa A./ Jotzo F. (2005): "Transaction costs, institutional rigidities and the size of the Clean Development Mechanism". In: *Energy Policy*, 33, pp. 511–23

Pegels, A. (2010): Renewable energy in South Africa: Potentials, barriers and options for support". In: *Energy Policy*, 38, pp. 4945–54

Ramchander, P. (2004): *Towards the responsible management of socio-cultural impact of township tourism*, Unpublished PhD thesis, University of Pretoria, South Africa

Sippel, M./ Michaelowa, A. (2010): *Does global climate policy promote low carbon cities? Lessons learned from the CDM.* Paper presented at UNFCCC Climate Talks. June 2010, Bonn

UN ESCAP (2007): *Climate Change Action in Asia and the Pacific. United Nations Economic and Social Commission for Asia and Pacific (UN ESCAP)*. Bangkok, Thailand

United Nations (1998): *Kyoto Protocol to the United Nations Convention Framework Convention on Climate Change*, Bonn

Valentine, G. (2005): "Tell me about …: using interviews as a research methodology". In: Flowerdew R.A./ Martin D. (Eds.), *Methods in Human Geography—A Guide for Students Doing a Research Project*, second ed. Upper Saddle River NJ

Wilson, C.M. (2007): *Barriers and drivers to the implementation of the Clean Development Mechanism within Nelson Mandela Bay Municipality: A case study*, Unpublished MBA thesis. Rhodes University. Grahamstown, South Africa

Winkler, H./ Van Es, D. (2007): "Energy efficiency and CDM in South Africa: Constraints and opportunities". In: *Journal of Energy in Southern Africa*, 18, pp. 18–38.

Notes

1 Annex I countries of the United Nations Framework Convention on Climate Change (UNFCCC), adopted 1992 in Rio, include all OECD countries and economies in transition. They committed themselves to the aim of returning to their 1990 levels of greenhouse gas emissions by the year 2000. Non-Annex I countries have ratified to the UNFCCC but are not included in Annex I. Annex II countries are all OECD countries. They are expected to provide financial resources to assist developing countries to comply with their obligations (e.g.:. transfer of environmentally sound technologies to developing countries). (http://unfccc.int/2860.php; http://www.ipcc.ch/pdf/glossary/ar4-wg3.pdf; both 2013-11-07)

URBAN RESOURCES: WATER

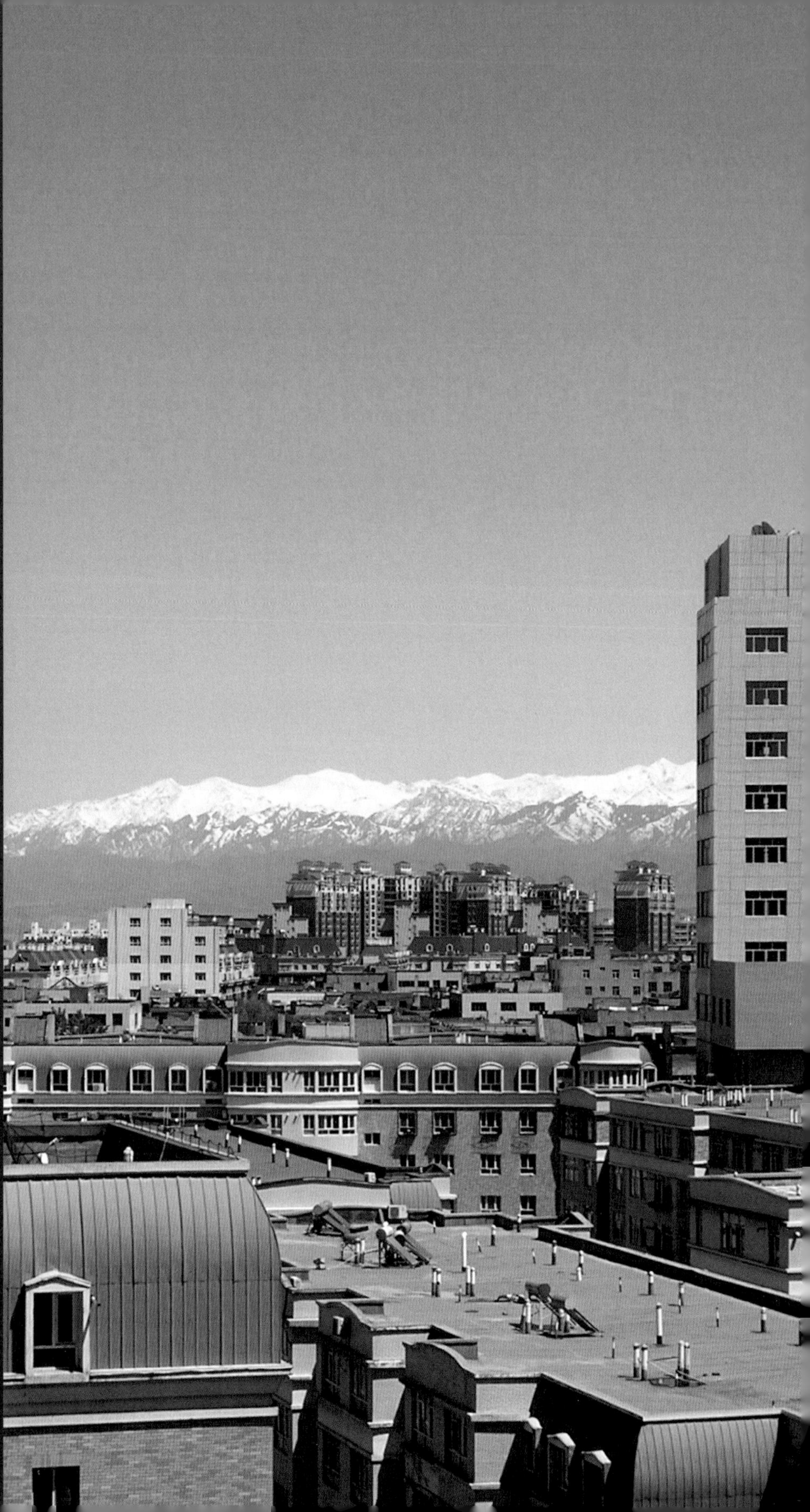

URUMQI: Panorama with snowy mountains [Katharina Fricke]

Katharina Fricke

Dissertation at Heidelberg University, Institute of Geography

Strategies for a Sustainable Megacity Development under the Water Resource Challenge in Urumqi Region, Northwest China

Abstract

Located between the semi-desert Junggar Basin and the Tianshan Mountains in Northwest China, the research area Urumqi Region is—despite its semi-arid climate—in a relatively favourable hydrological situation. The nearby mountains provide water, making human development possible in the first place. Due to socio-economic development during the last sixty years and increasing water consumption, a demand- and population-driven water scarcity exists today. Quantitative effects of climate and land-use change on the hydrological system in the future are uncertain. This study aims to evaluate the projected changes by combining a hydrological water-balance model simulating water supply with a socio-econometric model projecting future water demand. With model input mainly acquired from global datasets, references or remote sensing data, this approach is transferable to other areas.

The water balance model is used to calculate the annual water balance and the hydrological processes for five different climate scenarios and one scenario for land use transformation. The simulation results show that, on average, in the last decade more water has been available than during the last thirty-six years. Within the next forty years, total water flow will increase in the mountain areas, but decrease up to 12% in lower areas due to reduced snowfall and meltwater. Groundwater recharge will decrease and actual evapotranspiration will rise, especially in agricultural areas. Only a climate scenario with the maximum projected precipitation provides a total water flow equivalent to the last decade.

The socio-econometric model is used to simulate water demand for six development scenarios. The most probable scenarios lead to an annual water demand equal to available water resources. Thus, water scarcity will increase and adaptation strategies be developed for local geographical and hydrological conditions based on the modelling results. They focus on measures to reduce absolute or relative water demand, especially in the agricultural sector. A shift of production and infrastructure into areas with lower evapotranspiration and higher precipitation, even outside Urumqi Region, is proposed. In urban areas, households and industries should optimise usage efficiency and water treatment. But the natural advantage of the hydrological system, the water supply from the mountains, and the extensive groundwater bodies, should also be cautiously further exploited where suitable.

Introduction: Challenges of Urumqi's Future Waterhousehold

Focus of the Research: Analysis of Water Demand and Supply

Water is an essential resource and a factor in human development and well-being, as well as for ecological processes [Martin/ Sauerborn 2006]. The concentration of human activities in and around megacities aggravates the pressure on the city's natural environment and local water resources, especially where water availability is limited, such as in the future megacity Urumqi. Within the BMBF-funded research project "RECAST Urumqi—Meeting the Resource Efficiency Challenge in a Climate Sensitive Dryland Megacity Environment", the sub-project on water aimed at the facilitation of a sustainable megacity development through improvement of water resource efficiency in Urumqi. One aim was to analyse the actual situation of water resources and simulate future water supply and demand. The simulations should provide quantitative estimations of the possible changes and emphasise the necessity of adaptation measures, but also provide information about the spatial distribution of hydrological processes, taking into account the special geographic location of Urumqi City. The results support the development of a water management and conservation strategy adapted to the local characteristics and options.

Water Scarcity in Central Asia's Biggest City

A Growing Megacity on the Slopes of the Tianshan Mountains

The research area Urumqi Region is located in north-western China between the Junggar Basin and Gurbantünggüt Desert in the north and the Tianshan Mountains in the south [Fricke et al. 2009]. Originally an oasis with a semi-arid climate on the Silk Road, the capital of Xinjiang Uygur Autonomous Region is now part of an agglomeration of more than 3.8 million inhabitants [2009], experiencing an enormous growth in population and economy [Statistics Bureau of Xinjiang Uygur Autonomous Region 2010]. The settlement area has expanded from under 10 km^2 in 1949, to over 260 km^2 in 2010 [Dong et al. 2007; Reinl 2012] and also led to the development of new urban districts, the latest in Midong New District. The urban area is located on the alluvial fan and plains adjacent to the foothills of the Tianshan Mountains, and has relatively good water availability due to surface runoff from precipitation and meltwater in the mountains, and several groundwater layers below the city [Roberts 1987; Zhou et al. 2007]. The mountain areas serve as storage of winter precipitation such as snow and ice [Berkner 1993; Zhu et al. 2004], which causes 70% of the runoff to occur from June to August in the Urumqi River [Zhou et al. 2007]. The large sediment bodies allow the infiltrating surface runoff and percolation into the groundwater, thus preventing transpiration losses.

Growing Water Consumption

In 2007, agriculture still accounted for 65% of total water consumption, followed by households with 23% and industry with only 12%. The consumption ratio of total water resources is 74%, while surface water consumption rate is 89% due to its accessibility. Groundwater is more important for domestic usage, providing 69% of the water supply [Fricke et al. 2009]. The

Fig. 1 The research area Urumqi Region with the administrative area of Urumqi City, elevation, rivers and water bodies [Reprinted from Fricke 2014, Chap. 2, p. 16 with kind permission of Springer Science + Business Media]

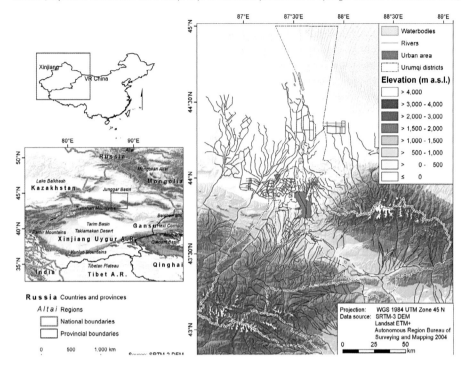

spatial patterns of water consumption are not homogeneous, agricultural water consumption is high in peri-urban areas, while city districts are characterised by higher water consumption by households and industry [cf. Fricke/ Bubenzer 2011]. Most agricultural areas were originally located next to the foothills above the city and at a spring zone below the city [Roberts 1987]. With the reclamation and expansion of the settlement area, the agricultural areas shifted towards the basin and groundwater extraction increased. Due to the growth of the population and economy, urban and sealed areas aumented and more land use transformations are planned in the future.

Limited Water Resources and Deteriorating Water Quality

Several problems related to limited water resources emerge [Figure 2 ↗]: on the one hand, there is natural water scarcity due to the semi-arid climate. On the other hand, there is demand- and population-driven water scarcity due to an unsustainable level of water consumption [cf. Falkenmark et al. 2007]. The decrease of river flows to downstream basins leads to a deterioration of natural vegetation, salinisation, and large-scale land desertification as well as reduced water quality [cf. Chen/ Cai 2000, Hao 1997; Wang/ Cheng 1999; Zhou et al. 2007]. Another indicator is the falling groundwater tables below the city [Water Affairs Bureau Urumqi 2004, 2005 and 2007], for which the irrigation water demand, sealed reservoirs, canals and diverted river flows are responsible [Zhou et al. 2007]. Treatment capacities have been expanded, but are not yet fully used due to an incomplete sewage system and fees for water and waste water treatment [Fricke 2008; Yao 2011]. A poor information system for the public and for decision-makers

Fig. 2 Hydrologic system, future changes and consequences for Urumqi Region.
(E: evaporation, ET: evapotranspiration, + increase in the future, - decrease in the future) [Fricke et al. 2009]

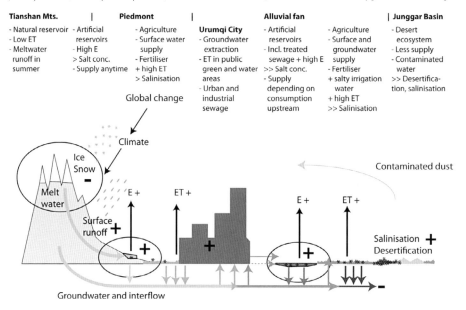

discourages an improvement of this situation [Zhou et al. 2007]. Du et al. summarise that new requirements for water supply and discharge of pollutants and waste water will become one of the largest challenges for urban infrastructure and municipal governments [2006].

Ambiguous Water Supply Forecasts due to Climate Change

In addition to this problem, Urumqi Region will experience changes due to climate change and human development. An analysis of weather data from Urumqi [Barth 2011] shows that in the past thirty-five years, air temperature has increased by more than the average global warming trend published by the IPCC [2007]. This was also confirmed by the modelled regional temperature change [Trenberth et al. 2007] and several publications about the notable changes in Xinjiang and the Tianshan Mountains [Aizen et al. 1997; Piao et al. 2010; Shi et al. 2007]. The expected effects of climate change on the runoff were not necessarily clear since both temperature and precipitation increased, which might increase evapotranspiration losses, but also net precipitation. The precipitation also increased, but with a higher variability [Aizen et al. 1997; Barth 2011]. The consequences for snowfall and snow cover so far are ambiguous [Qin et al. 2006]. However, the glaciers in the headwaters of Urumqi River have notably decreased in mass and length due to rising temperatures [Aizen et al. 1997; Fuchs 2011; Han et al. 2006; Piao et al. 2010; WGMS 1991-2009], resulting in a temporary increase in glacier meltwater runoff [Li et al. 2003 in Shi et al. 2007; Ye/ Chen 1997]. Recently, glacier meltwater contributed to up to 10% of the total river runoff in Urumqi Region and the increase of ablation could lead to an additional 2 to 4% in the future, but break off after ice melts or a new equilibrium state has been reached [Fricke 2013].

Besides aggravating a supply-driven water scarcity, population growth, rising living standards, and economic and industrial development can lead to an additional demand- and population-driven water scarcity [Du et al. 2006]. Qualitative problems and probable changes have been assessed [Fricke et al. 2009], but a quantitative projection and estimation of water supply and demand in the future is still missing, although these projections are necessary to develop a strategy for adaptation to the expected changes.

Methods: Simulations and Scenarios on Water Supply and Demand

Future supply and demand of water resources in Urumqi were projected by separate models. A hydrological model was used to simulate water supply under different climate and land-use scenarios and a socio-econometric model was applied to project the demand of water resources.

Water Balance Model: Simulation of Water Supply

Several requirements and limitations influenced the hydrological model; because the watersheds of the research area extend over an area of more than 7,000 km², modelling at the macro-scale was chosen [Uhlenbrook 1999]. In order to also enable the investigation of spatial differences at a smaller scale and make practical predictions for the effects of climate and land-use change, the resolution of the input data and results should be raster-based and model the responsible hydrological processes. Models that require an extensive calibration of parameters and coefficients could not be applied as in situ measurements, input, and calibration as well as validation data were limited. The dominant processes were simplified and a combination of physical and index models with indices related to soil and land cover characteristics simulated the water balance of the region's catchment area.

The design of the hydrological model is based on the water balance model ABIMO [Glugla/ Fürtig 1997 in Haase 2009], which was further developed by Messer [1997] for calculating long-term groundwater recharge rates, including a runoff model by Schroeder/ Wyrich [1990 in Haase 2009]. The available net runoff Q_n is derived from the water balance equation and then divided into surface runoff Q_{sf} and groundwater recharge Q_{gw}, which was calculated for monthly calculation steps [Schmidt et al. 2003]:

$$Q_n = P - ET_a = Q_{sf} + Q_{gw}$$

with precipitation P and actual evapotranspiration ET_a [Figure 3 ↗]. In contrast to ABIMO, the potential evapotranspiration ET_p was calculated with the Penman-Monteith equation according to Allen et al. [1998], based on average climate data. ET_a was then calculated based on ET_p and P [Fricke 2013].

Storage in snow and ice is important for the timing of the water supply, as about one-third of the precipitation in Urumqi Region falls as snow. Thus, a module based on temperature and snowmelt indices to account for the accumulation and melting of snow was included [Rango/ Martinec 1995]. The water available for surface runoff and groundwater recharge was also simulated with an index-based module. Lacking the necessary field measurements or calibration data, the processes were simplified to an infiltration coefficient based on soil, land cover type and slope [cf. Haase 2009; Messer 1997]. Groundwater flow, interflow or glacier

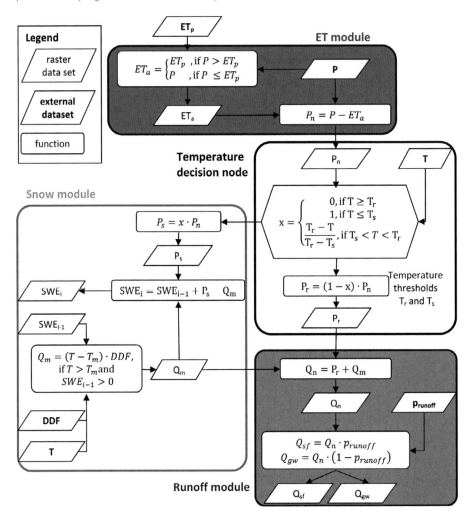

melt were not specifically modelled. The input parameters and land surface characteristics necessary for the calculation of ET_p, melting factor and runoff coefficient were derived from remote sensing data (land surface temperature, monthly precipitation, elevation, radiation and sunshine hours, land use and cover classification) in combination with climatological station data.

Scenarios

Several scenarios of climate data have been developed as input data to simulate and evaluate the effects of climate change on the water balance. These include two scenarios representing past climate by the average monthly values for the period 1975–2010 and for the last decade 2001–2010. Changes in the hydrological system due to climate change are mainly attributed to changes in precipitation and evaporation [Arnell 1996]. For a climate change scenario,

Fig. 4   Overview over climate change scenarios [Reprinted from Fricke 2014, Chap. 4, p. 130 with kind permission of Springer Science + Business Media]

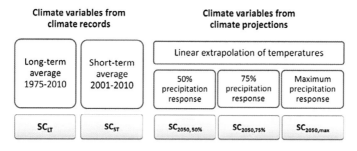

Fig. 5 a/b Temperature (red, left) and precipitation values (blue, right) for 1975–2010 and 2001–2010 for Urumqi station from NCDC climate data and projected values for 2050 with the three different projections for precipitation values (dotted) [Reprinted from Fricke 2014, Chap. 4, p. 130 with kind permission of Springer Science + Business Media, data from NOAA NCDC]

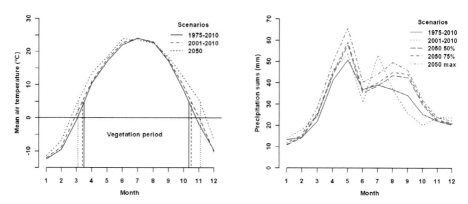

the hypothetical changes of monthly mean temperatures and precipitation sums should be modelled as this approach is more consistent with observed trends [Stadler et al. 1998] than just increasing mean air temperature. This hypothetical trend for temperature was assessed until 2050, using a linear regression analysis after smoothing and padding the time series [Mann 2008]. Unfortunately, the precipitation data was not suitable for linear extrapolation and did not exhibit a significant trend during the last thirty-six years. Therefore, the precipitation values were extrapolated based on regional climate projections for A1B emission scenarios and their 50%, 75% and maximum precipitation response published by the IPCC [2007]. Feedback mechanisms between climate variables or effects on land cover and soil characteristics were not taken into account. As a scenario of future land use transformation, the land use plan until 2050 for the new district Midong Northeast of Urumqi City was used [Fricke 2008].

Evaluation of the Water Balance Model

Before applying the water balance model, model sensitivity and uncertainty were assessed to be able to evaluate the quality of the model results. The most important input parameters for the model were consequently improved, but the results of a global sensitivity analysis showed that the model uncertainty of a single calculation for a selected location is larger than the average resulting value because of the unavoidable parameter uncertainty. Subsequently, the simulation results were compared to other models and data sources to evaluate the model's overall performance. The comparison showed that model performance is comparable to other models such as the semi-distributed SWAT model [Grassmann et al. 2007]. In addition, it can simulate the annual water balance on the catchment level [Fricke 2013]. However, the input data apparently was also insufficient to simulate monthly runoff dynamics as the storage function of interflow and groundwater flow was not well represented.

Socio-Econometric Model: Projection of Water Demand

Along with the growth of population and economic output in industrialising regions, water demand usually also increases, driven by quantity and patterns of production and consumption in the spatial unit. The relationship between development and water demand is not necessarily linear, but influenced by technological improvements and changing production and living standards. Previous publications have modelled the relationship between the socio-econometric development of Urumqi City and water consumption in the past, but could not offer a projection of future water consumption [cf. Du et al. 2006]. Here, a socio-econometric model developed by Trieb/ Müller-Steinhagen [2008] is used to project future water demand and the relative consumption of the user groups for agriculture, industry and population. Water demand is used synonymously with water consumption which is a combination of the theoretical water demand and adaptation to actual water availability through technical improvements or competition for resources. The water demand ω of each, population, agriculture and industry, is calculated separately as a function of the time t:

$$\omega\left(t\right) = \omega\left(t-1\right) * \left(1 + \gamma\left(t\right)\right) * \frac{\eta\left(t-1\right)}{\eta\left(t\right)} * \left(1 - \mu\right)$$

The driving factors are the growth rate of population or GDP $\gamma(t)$, the efficiency of the water distribution system $\eta(t)$, the end-use efficiency enhancement $\mu(t)$. The water demand of agriculture, industry and population was calculated based on the drivers, population growth, GDP growth and a combination of both growth rates, respectively. In the distribution efficiency η, the progress factor α and best practice factor β accounted for improvements of technical applications and water management.

To project population development in Urumqi Region until 2050, extrapolation based on a linear regression analysis and on the high growth prediction of the UN World Population Prospects for overall China were compared [UN 2009]. Similarly, three studies predicting the probable economic development of China have been evaluated [Hawksworth 2006; Keidel 2008; Wilson/ Stupnytska 2007], as projections for Urumqi or Xinjiang were not available.

Water distribution efficiency, best practice and progress factors in the three sectors were adapted from several publications and references dealing with the non-revenue water and irrigation water use efficiency [Andrews/ Yñiguez 2004; AWWA Leak Detection and Water Accountability Committee 1996; Cornish 2005, Deng et al. 2004; McIntosh et al. 1997; Khan et al. 2004; Tian 1986; Xinhuanet 2006]. The socio-econometric model and the general end-use efficiency enhancement were then calibrated with available data about sectoral water demand from 2003–2008, taken from Water Reports and Statistical Yearbooks.

Sector	Agriculture	Municipal	Industrial
Driving force	γ_{pop}	γ_{GDP}	γ_{ind}
Efficiency of distribution	$\eta_{irr} = 45\,\%$	$\eta_{mun} = 80\,\%$	$\eta_{ind} = 80\,\%$
Best practice	$\beta_{irr} = 90\,\%$	$\beta_{mun} = 95\,\%$	$\beta_{ind} = 95\,\%$
Progress factor	$\alpha_{irr} = 50\,\%$	$\alpha_{mun} = 65\,\%$	$\alpha_{ind} = 65\,\%$
General end use eff. enhancement	$\mu_{irr} = 1\,\%\,y^{-1}$	$\mu_{mun} = 2\,\%\,y^{-1}$	$\mu_{ind} = 2\,\%\,y^{-1}$

Fig. 7 Water demand 2003–2008 and estimated water demand 2003–2050 for the minimum and maximum scenarios (black lines) and the medium projection (dark grey) [Reprinted from Fricke 2014, Chap. 6, p. 168 with kind permission of Springer Science + Business Media]

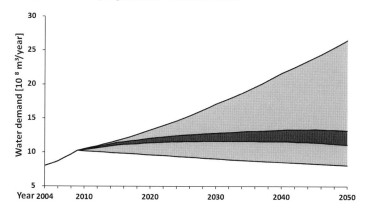

Findings: Urgent Need to Increase Water Usage Efficiency

Simulation Results: Growing Water Demand vs. Decreasing Resources

Water demand was calculated with six different scenarios for population and GDP development from 2009 until 2050. A restricted economic development and a self-regulating process in the region were assumed. Furthermore, the GDP scenario by Wilson/ Stupnytska [2007], which is also consistent with the recent development, combined with the linear regression model for population growth, was chosen. Accordingly, water demand would increase from 2008 to 2050 from $1,000 \cdot 10^6\,m^3$ to about $1,100–1,300 \cdot 10^6\,m^3$. This projected rise of 10 to 30% could just be met by the available water resources.

The absolute amount and the proportion of agricultural water demand is projected to decrease while industrial water demand will continuously increase and the amount of municipal water demand will remain quite stable. Since the agricultural sector offers the highest potential for improvement and Urumqi experiences the transition to a more industry oriented economy, these changes are realistic.

By comparing the long-term and short-term climate scenarios, the availability of water resources in the past was analysed. The modelled increase in precipitation of 4.3% exceeded the ET_a and led to more available water resources, as meltwater, surface runoff and groundwater recharge increased on average over 30% [Fricke 2013]. The proportion of water percolating into the groundwater also increased slightly, as Aizen et al. suggest [1997].

From the three climate scenarios for the future, the average net precipitation for Urumqi Region simulated with the short-term climate scenario was only reached by the scenario with the highest precipitation. This scenario could compensate the rising temperature and ET_p, but for the other two scenarios, total water flow was reduced by 9 to 12%. In all three future scenarios, meltwater flow in Urumqi Region would decrease by 28 to 34% and groundwater recharge by 4 to 15%, respectively. Surface runoff is the dominating process in the larger part of the catchments, but it is also prone to evaporation and contamination. Due to the increased ET, recession of river flows in the downstream basins will worsen—e.g., -5 to -19% surface runoff in the Urumqi City catchment area or -2 to -14% in the Midong catchment. With rising air temperatures, the vegetation period in Urumqi based on thermal criteria will be further prolonged while lacking the necessary water supply [Fuchs 2011]. The effects of climate change on the water balance components are not equally distributed in space as for example ET_a rises mainly in areas with denser vegetation. In most agricultural areas, the net precipitation available for vegetation will decrease in all three scenarios.

According to the simulation results, the planned land-use change in Midong District will increase the ET_a and sublimation of snow in winter, but reduce transpiration in summer as predicted by Messer [1997]. Unfortunately, groundwater recharge will decline under the urbanisation process and further reduce the amount of water stored in groundwater bodies.

Sectoral Evaluation and Strategies for Improvement

Urban and economic development would have to stagnate to cope with the limited local water resources and create a bottleneck situation for further development with real and severe water scarcity [Falkenmark et al. 2007]. To support further development and an optimised usage of water resources, a water management strategy and possible measures based on the simulation results were developed. The focus is on adaptation measures with regard to water resources management and a sustainable usage of available water resources.

Water, like other ubiquitous resources, suffers from the "tragedy of the commons" [Hardin 1968] as over-using this resource has more advantages for the user than negative consequences, thus a "negative externality" [Gao 2009]. Although economic theory indicates that reduced availability of resources will lead to increased prices and support more efficient usage, substitution, and technical improvements [Turner et al. 2001], this assumption might not apply to Urumqi Region. The continuous attraction, growth, and production in Urumqi Region can be attributed to other factors, such as existing infrastructure and production, transportation, centrality, and policies. The limited carrying capacity of the regional ecosystem and water resources will not prevent further development, but the comparative advantage is increasingly influenced by the environmental standards implemented and environmental production costs [Guan/ Hubacek 2007].

Measures for an improved water supply, usage efficiency and conservation have been presented in Fricke [2009] for Midong New District with recommendations for the different water user groups and economic sectors. Similarly, the water management strategy and measures had to be adapted to the different sectors, but also take into account the spatial distribution of water availability and the hydrological processes that have been modelled.

Fig. 8 Simulated total water flow for the short-term climate scenario and how it differs from the three climate scenarios for 2050 with agricultural areas [Reprinted from Fricke 2014, Chap. 7, p. 184 with kind permission of Springer Science + Business Media]

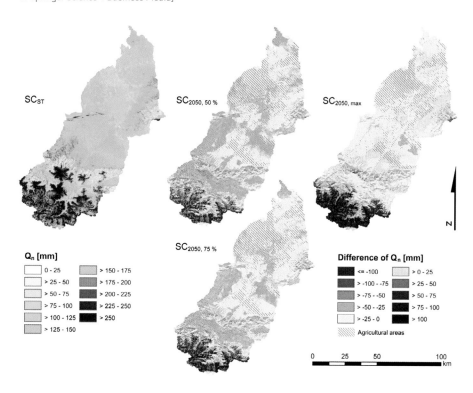

Agricultural Water Consumption

Agriculture is the largest water consumer and therefore the focus of the water conservation strategy. Due to the recent water supply, the total sown area increased by 20% from 1998 to 2008 [Statistics Bureau of Urumqi 2009]. The larger part of agriculture depends on irrigation (85% of cultivated land), but surface runoff and available water resources are expected to decrease in the lower catchment areas. The difference between the recent and simulated water availability can serve as a "risk map" of increased water scarcity in the future [Figure 8 ↗]: most agricultural areas will experience reduced local water availability. Thus, the strategic assumption is that agricultural water demand will have to decrease. The ascending trend for food, oil and cereal prices suggest rising revenues from agricultural products in the future [FAO 2012]. However, revenue per water consumed from industry was recently still ten times higher (28.36 RMB m^{-3} vs. 2.76 RMB m^{-3}, based on data from the Statistics Bureau of Urumqi 2009 and Water Affairs Bureau Urumqi 2007).

Measures to increase water usage efficiency should first of all aim at improving the supply infrastructure as this would reduce "white water" losses to transpiration and could lead to an estimated 30 to 40% water savings [Blanke et al. 2007]. The reuse of treated waste water is suggested, but its extent is limited—e.g., to 20% in Tunisia [Neubert 2005]—as the advantage of lower water prices and substitution of fertilisers are offset by opportunity costs. Additionally, better irrigation management with a reduction in irrigation of up to 40% "would not adversely affect crop production under the appropriate timing and irrigation dose" (less than 10% drop in yield) for example in wheat production [Hu et al. 2010, 229].

A change in crop management to less water-intensive crops would contribute, as well as an improved soil management increasing the amount of precipitation and irrigation directly used or infiltrated into the soil as "green water". But the downside of advanced crop and soil management is often the accompanying use of fertilisers, which further pollute infiltration and drainage water. Incentives, promotion, and regulation of the desired practices are needed from political and regulatory bodies, because the main reason that farmers do not adopt water-saving measures is the lack of incentives [Blanke et al. 2007]. The most effective way to reduce agricultural water consumption would actually require a shift in existing agricultural areas within the region, according to predicted water availability or "virtual water trade" through the import of agricultural goods from other regions that have better climatic conditions for agricultural production.

Urban Areas with Non-Agricultural Production and Population

Expanding urban areas will decrease the accumulation of snow, total water flow, and especially groundwater recharge. Urban supply, which is covered to almost 70% by groundwater resources, will be strongly affected by the predicted reduced groundwater recharge. The groundwater consumption rate (consumption divided by available water resources) was "only" at about 62% in 2007; therefore, further exploitation can be expected. Hence, water users in urban areas could profit from measures improving infiltration and groundwater recharge by reducing their degree of impermeability.

Guan/ Hubacek [2007] observed that North China has not exhausted the possibilities for importing "virtual water". Apparently, the export-oriented economic strategy is not compatible with water-saving policies. Water-saving in urban areas can instead be achieved by the redevelopment and improved maintenance of the distribution network to reduce leakage, as well as the installation of more efficient devices and technologies for water usage. These investments in infrastructure have to be balanced by the revenue earned from saved water, which is difficult with the very low recent water fees. Expanding the connection of households and industry to the sewer system and a consequently higher rate of wastewater treatment should be combined with the advanced treatment of wastewater, water recycling, and the usage of treated wastewater. Directly through these measures or indirectly through the control of regulations, combined with economic benefits and incentives, water authorities could influence water cycle networks in industrial production [Lehn et al. 1996].

Ecosystem and Environment

The environment in Urumqi Region provides an ecosystem function with regard to water such as decomposition of pollutants, and filtering of percolating water. Water scarcity and environmental water stress raise the question: when will the carrying capacity and the border to reversibility be overstepped? Reasonable measures to prevent the collapse of the ecosystem would include an increase in the environmental flow in rivers and green water of natural landscapes or a reduction in the contamination of water resources. Besides the environmental water flow, groundwater recharge, and underground storage of water resources to avoid evaporation losses could be increased when the natural process of runoff infiltration in and outflow out of the alluvial plain at the transition to the accumulation basin would be amplified [cf. Zhou et al. 2007]. Also in terms of urban and industrial water supply, the focus of a water management strategy should be on protecting soil and water quality and recharging groundwater resources, which is actually a major hydro-geologic advantage of Urumqi Region in the first place.

Outlook

In the end, the applicability and transferability of the models and methods used is briefly evaluated and a methodological outlook is given. The socio-econometric model proved to be practicable for the projection of water demand even with a small data base when efficiency parameters are available. The hydrological model can be transferred to another catchment area at a fixed scale, based on the assumption that a similar relationship between most of the model parameters and physical and climatic characteristics exist in another basin. Most of the data used for modelling in Urumqi Region was derived without extensive field research and with freely available data from international datasets or remote sensing data. For a more detailed investigation, additional local references might be necessary for other climates, soils and land cover types. Not all processes of the hydrological system could be accounted for by the simulation, but the water balance model proved to be sufficient for calculating an annual water balance, still offering possibilities for expansion.

References

Aizen, V.B./ Aizen, E.M./ Melack, J.M./ Dozier, J. (1997): "Climatic and Hydrologic Changes in the Tien Shan, Central Asia". In: *Journal of Climate*, 10, pp. 1393–403

Allen, R.G. (1998): *Crop evapotranspiration: Guidelines for computing crop water requirements*. Rome

Andrews, C.T./ Yñgiuez, C.E. (2004): *Water in Asian cities: Utilities' performance and civil society views*. Manila

Arnell, N. (1996): *Global Warming, River Flows and Water Resources*. Chichester

AWWA Leak Detection and Water Accountability Committee (1996): "Committee Report –Water Accountability". In: *Journal AWWA*, 88 (7), pp. 108–11

Barth, N.C. (2011): *Auswertung der Temperatur- und Niederschlagsdaten von 15 Klimastationen im Umkreis von Urumqi (AR Xinjiang, China)*. Unpublished bachelor's thesis, Heidelberg University

Berkner, A. (1993): "Wasserressourcen und ihre Bewirtschaftung in der Volksrepublik China". In: *Petermanns Geographische Mitteilungen*, 137 (2), pp. 103–26

Blanke, A./ Rozelle, S./ Lohmar, B./ Wang, J./ Huang, J. (2007): "Water saving technology and saving water in China". In: *Agricultural Water Management*, 87 (2)

Chen, M./ Cai, Z. (2000): "Groundwater Resources and Hydro-environmental Problems in China". In: Chen, M./ Cai, Z. (eds.): *Groundwater Resources and the Related Environ-Hydrogeologic Problems in China*. Beijing

Cornish, G.A. (2005): *Performance Benchmarking in the Irrigation and Drainage Sector: Experience to date and conclusions*. http://www.dfid.gov.uk/r4d/pdf/outputs/R8164.pdf, 18.10.2011

Deng, X.P./ Shan, L./ Zhang, H./ Turner, N.C. (2004): "Improving Agricultural Water Use Efficiency in Arid and Semi-arid Areas of China". In: Fischer, T. (ed.): *4th International Crop Science Congress*, 26.09.–1.10.2004. Brisbane

Dong, W./ Zhang, X./ Wang, B./ Duan, Z. (2007): "Expansion of Urumqi urban area and its spatial differentiation". In: *Science China Series D: Earth Sciences*, 50 (Supp. I), pp. 159–168

Du, H./ Zhang, X./ Wang, B. (2006): "Co-adaptation between modern oasis urbanisation and water resources exploitation: A case of Urumqi". In: *Chinese Science Bulletin*, 51 (Supp. I), pp. 189–95

Falkenmark, M./ Berntell, A./ Jägerskog, A./ Lundqvits, J./ Matz, M./ Tropp, H. (2007): *On the Verge of a New Water Scarcity: A Call for Good Governance and Human Ingenuity*. Stockholm (SIWI Policy Brief)

Food Agricultural Organisation (FAO) (2012): *Annual real food price indices (2002–2004=100 %)*. http:\\www.fao.org/worldfoodsituation/wfs-home/foodpricesindex/en/, 25.03.2012

Fricke, K. (2008): *The development of Midong New District, Urumqi, PR China: Ecological and historical context and environmental consequences*. Unpublished diploma thesis, Heidelberg University

Fricke, K. (2009): "Integriertes Wassermanagement – Strategien für das Industriegebiet Midong in Urumqi, NW-China". In: *UmweltWirtschaftsForum*, 17 (3), pp. 291–98

Fricke, K. (2014): *Analysis and modelling of water supply and demand under climate change, land use transformation and socio-economic development–The water resource challenge and adaptation measures for Urumqi Region, Northwest China*. Springer Thesis, Heidelberg

Fricke, K./ Bubenzer, O. (2011): "Available Water Resources and Water Use Efficiency in Urumqi, PR China". In: German Academic Exchange Service (ed.): *Future Megacities in Balance, Young Researchers' Symposium in Essen 9.-10. October 2010*. DAAD Dok&Mat, 66, pp. 134–40

Fricke, K./ Sterr, T./ Bubenzer, O./ Eitel, B. (2009): "The oasis as a mega city: Urumqi's fast urbanisation in a semi-arid environment". In: *Die Erde*, 140 (4), pp. 449–63

Fuchs, J. (2011): *Multitemporale Detektion der Gletscherveränderung im östlichen Tian Shan (AR Xinjiang, China) im Kontext des Klimawandels: Untersuchungen am Beispiel der Flusseinzugsgebiete von Toutun, Shuixi und Urumqi*. Unpublished bachelor thesis, Heidelberg University

Gao, C. (2009): "An Analysis of Externality Economy of Xinjiang Water Resource Development". In: *Journal of Sustainable Development*, 2 (2), pp. 143–47

Grassmann, P.W./ Reyes, M.R./ Green, C.H./ Arnold, J.G. (2007): "The Soil and Water Assessment Tool: Historical Development, Applications and Future Research Directions". In: *Transactions of the American Society of Agricultural and Biological Engineers*, 50 (4), pp. 1211–50

Guan, D./ Hubacek, K. (2007): "Assessment of Regional Trade and Virtual Water Flows in China" In: *Ecological Economics*, 61, pp. 159–70.

Haase, D. (2009): "Effects of urbanisation on the water balance: A long-term trajectory". In: *Environmental Impact Assessment Review*, 29, pp. 211–19

Hao, Y. (1997): "Water environment and sustainable development along the belt of Xinjiang section of the new Eurasian Continental Bridge". In: *Chinese Geographical Science*, 7 (3), pp. 251–58

Hardin, G. (1968): "The Tragedy of the Commons: The population problem has no technical solution; it requires a fundamental extension in morality". In: *Science*, 162, pp. 1243–48

Hawksworth, J. (2006): *The World in 2050: Implications of global growth for carbon emissions and climate change policy*. http://www.pwc.com/gx/en/world-2050/pdf/world2050carbon.pdf, 2.10.2010

Hu, Y./ Moiwo, J.P./ Yang, Y./ Han, S./ Yang, Y. (2010): "Agricultural water-saving and sustainable groundwater management in Shijiazhuang Irrigation District, North China Plain". In: *Journal of Hydrology*. 393 (3–4), pp. 219–32

Intergovernmental Panel on Climate Change (IPCC) (2007): *Climate Change 2007: Synthesis Report*. http://www.ipcc.ch/pdf/assessment-report/ar4/syr/ar4_syr.pdf, 16.11.2011

Keidel, A. (2008): *China's Economic Rise: Fact and Fiction (Policy Brief, 61)*. http://carnegieendowment.org/files/pb61_keidel_final.pdf, 1.10.2010

Khan, S./ Tariq, R./ Cui, Y./ Blackwell, J. (2004): "Can Irrigation Be Sustainable?" In: Fischer, T. (ed.): *4th International Crop Science Congress*. 26.09.-1.10.2004, Brisbane

Lehn, H./ Steiner, M./ Mohr, H. (1996): *Wasser–die elementare Ressource: Leitlinien einer nachhaltigen Nutzung*. Berlin

Mann, M.E. (2008): "Smoothing of climate time series revisited". In: *Geophys. Res. Lett.* 35 (16), pp. L07214.

Martin, K./ Sauerborn, J. (2006*): Agrarökologie*. Stuttgart

McIntosh, A.C./ Yñiguez, C.E./ Asian Development Bank. (eds.) (1997): *Second water utilities data book: Asian and Pacific region*. Manila

Meinrath, G./ Schneider, P. (2007): *Quality assurance for chemistry and environmental science: Metrology from pH measurement to nuclear waste disposal*. Berlin, Heidelberg

Messer, J. (1997): "Auswirkungen der Urbanisierung auf die Grundwasserneubildung im Ruhrgebiet unter besonderer Berücksichtigung der Castroper Hochfläche und des Stadtgebietes Herne, Essen". In: *DMT-Berichte aus Forschung und Entwicklung*, 58

Neubert, S. (2005): "Abwassernutzung in der Landwirtschaft: ein 'integriertes' und ökologisch nachhaltiges Verfahren?" In: Neubert, S. (ed.): *Integriertes Wasserressourcen-Management (IWRM). Ein Konzept in die Praxis überführen*. Baden-Baden

Piao, S./ Ciais, P./ Huang, Y./ Shen, Z./ Peng, S./ Li, J.Z./ Liu, H./ Ma, Y./ Ding, Y./ Friedlingstein, P./ Liu, C./ Tan, K./ Yu, Y./ Zhang, T./ Fang, J. (2010): "The impacts of climate change on water resources and agriculture in China". In: *Nature*. 467, pp. 43–51

Rango, A./ Martinec, J. (1995): "Revisiting the degree-day method for snowmelt computations". In: *Water Resources Bulletin*, 31 (4), pp. 657–69

Reinl, C. (2012): "Entwicklung und Ausbreitung des urbanen Bereichs von Urumqi, Hauptstadt der Autonomen Region Xinjiang". Unpublished diploma thesis, Heidelberg University

Roberts, B. (1987): "Die ökologischen Risiken der Stadtentwicklung und Landnutzung in Urumqi, Xinjiang/China". In: *Bremer Beiträge zur Geographie und Raumplanung*, 12

Schmidt, G./ Gretzschel, O./ Volk, M./ Uhl, M. (2003): "A concept for the scale-specific simulation of water-bound material fluxes in the project FLUMAGIS". In: Hennrich, K./ Rode, M./ Bronstert, A. (eds.): *6. Workshop zur großskaligen Modellierung in der Hydrologie - Flussgebietsmanagement*. Kassel

Shen, Y./ Lein, H. (2005): "Land and water resource management problems in Xinjiang Uygur Autonomous Region, China". In: Norwegian Journal of Geography, 59 (3), pp. 237–45

Shi, Y./ Shen, Y./ Kang, E./ Li, D./ Ding, Y./ Zhang, G./ Hu, R. (2007): "Recent and future climate change in north-west china". In: Climatic Change, 80, pp. 379–93

Stadler, D./ Bründl, M./ Schneebeli, M./ Meyer-Grass, M./ Flühler, H. (1998): *Hydrologische Prozesse im subalpinen Wald im Winter*. Zürich

Statistics Bureau of Urumqi (2009): *Urumqi Statistical Yearbook 2009*. Beijing

Statistics Bureau of Xinjiang Uygur Autonomous Region (2010): *Xinjiang Statistical Yearbook 2010*. Beijing

Tian, Y. (1986): "Tugayi in the delta and lower reaches of the Kerya River—A natural complex reflecting ecological degradation". In: *Journal of Desert Research*, 6 (2), pp. 1–24

Trenberth, K.E./ Jones, P.D./ Ambenje, P./ Bojariu, R./ Easterling, D./ Klein Tank, A./ Parker, D./ Rahimzadeh, F./ Renwick, J.A./ Rusticucci, M. (2007): "Surface and Atmospheric Climate Change". In: Solomon, S./ Qin, D./ Manning, M./ Chen, Z./ Marquis, M./ Averyt, K.B./ Miller, H.L. (eds.): *Climate Change 2007: The Physical Science Basis. Contribution of Working Group I to the Fourth Assessment Report of the IPCC*. Cambridge, New York, pp. 235–336

Trieb, F. (2007): *AQUA-CSP: Concentrating Solar Power for Seawater Desalination*. http://www.dlr.de/tt/Portal-data/41/Resources/dokumente/institut/system/projects/aqua-csp/AQUA-CSP-Full-Report-Final.pdf, 9.08.2011

Trieb, F./ Müller-Steinhagen, H. (2008): "Concentrating solar power for seawater desalination in the Middle East and North Africa". In: *Desalination*, 220, pp. 165–83

Turner, R.K./ Bateman, I.J./ Adger, W.N. (2001): "Ecological Economics and Coastal Zone Ecosystems' Values: An Overview". In: Turner, R.K./ Bateman, I.J./ Adger, W.N. (eds.): *Economics of Coastal and Water Resources. Valuing Environmental Functions*. Dordrecht, pp. 1–44

Uhlenbrook, S. (1999): "Untersuchung und Modellierung der Abflussbildung in einem mesoskaligen Einzugs-gebiet". In: *Freiburger Schriften zur Hydrologie*, p. 10

UN Population Division of the Department of Economic and Social Affairs (2009): *World Population Prospects: The 2008 Revision*. New York

Wang, G./ Cheng, G. (1999): "The ecological features and significance of hydrology within arid inland river basins of China". In: *Environmental Geology*, 37 (3), pp. 218–22

Water Affairs Bureau Urumqi (2003): *Water Report 2003*. Urumqi

Water Affairs Bureau Urumqi (2004): *Water Report 2004*. Urumqi

Water Affairs Bureau Urumqi (2005): *Water Report 2005*. Urumqi

Water Affairs Bureau Urumqi (2007): *Water Report 2007*. Urumqi

Wilson, D./ Stupnytska, A. (2007): "The N-11: More Than an Acronym". In: *Global Economics Paper*, p. 153

Xinhuanet (2006): *China's 11th Five-Year (2006-2010) Social and Economic Development Plan*. http://www.sandp-consulting.com/admin/upload/ChinaParliamentendorses11thFive-YearPlan.pdf, 24.10.2011

Yao, Y. (2011): "Water reuse: a case study of Urumqi, China". In: IWA (ed.): *1st Central Asian Regional Young and Senior Water Professionals Conference*, 22.–23.09.2011, Almaty

Ye, B./ Chen, K. (1997): "A Model Simulating the Processes Response of Glacier and Runoff to Climatic Change: A Case Study of Glacier No 1. in the Urumqi River China". In: *Chinese Geographical Science*, 7 (3), pp. 243–50

Zhou, Y./ Nonner, J.C./ Li, W. (2007): *Strategies and Techniques for Groundwater Resources Development in North-west China*. Beijing

Zhu, Y./ Wu, Y./ Drake, S. (2004): "A survey: obstacles and strategies for the development of ground-water resources in arid inland river basins of Western China". In: *Journal of Arid Environments*, 59, pp. 351–67

LIMA: The irrigated banks of the Chillón river in Chuquitanta [Emma Hillard]

Kara Jean McElhinney
Master's Thesis at University of Stuttgart, Institute for Sanitary Engineering, Water Quality and Solid Waste Management & Institute of Landscape Planning and Ecology

Auditing Water Resources for Application to Water-sensitive Urban Design—A Case Study in the Lima Metropolitan Area, Peru

Abstract

The development of lasting and effective solutions for the complex problems that Lima faces with regard to energy- and climate-efficient urbanisation requires a change in the fundamental way water is managed within the urban environment, with a renewed focus on sustainability and integration. One tool that can be implemented to support a new approach to urban water management is water-sensitive urban design (WSUD). A water audit can be carried out to support the preliminary stages in WSUD by providing information about specific water quality and quantity parameters. Data collected in an audit can be used to constrain and guide early design development, with the overall goal of quickly identifying and developing ideas that are truly feasible for the area under consideration, not only from a technical standpoint, but also economically, environmentally, and socially.

At the core of this study was the development and implementation of a water audit to collect information about the state of water resources in Chuquitanta, a neighbourhood in the District of San Martín de Porres in Lima. Several key questions about current and projected water usage in the area, typical social practices, and economic restraints were considered before deciding what information would be collected during the audit and which methods would be used to gather it. A customised set of parameters related to water quantity, temperature, oxygen balance, salt content, acidity, nutrient content, microbiology, and heavy metal content were evaluated in local water sources using a variety of tools including observation, estimation, and field and laboratory testing. Collected parameter values were then compared to quality standards for surface- and wastewater treated for reuse in irrigation.

Audit results were then applied to water-sensitive urban designs developed for four of six water resources in Chuquitanta by a group of architecture students. Conclusions were drawn about the technical feasibility of hydraulic components included (i.e., constructed wetlands for water treatment, dikes for flood protection, et cetera), and in some cases recommendations were made for adjustments which would ensure technical functionality while striving to stay true to the vision proposed in preliminary designs. Final outcomes included a recycled vertical-flow constructed wetland for treatment of domestic greywater, a surface-flow constructed wetland for treatment of river water channelled into a system of irrigation canals, and a subsurface-flow constructed wetland as green space as well as secondary wastewater treatment.

Introduction: Lima's Water Challenges and the Concept of Water-sensitive Urban Design

Challenges to Water Management in a Desert City

Potable Water from Rivers and Wells

The metropolitan area made up of the provinces of Lima and Callao is considered the world's second-largest desert city. The aridity of coastal Peru results from a combination of climatological and geographical factors which combine to minimise precipitation in Lima; on average, the city and surrounding area receive less than eight millimetres of rain per year [INEI 2011; Unger 2010]. The average flow rates of Lima's three rivers, the Rímac, the Chillón, and the Lurín, are 31.5 m³/s, 8.8 m³/s, and 4.1 m³/s, respectively [Fernández-Maldonado 2008]. The Rímac and Chillón Rivers are Lima's major sources of drinking water. Throughout the year, more than half of the Rímac river's flow is diverted to the La Atarjea water production plant operated by the Servicio de Agua Potable y Alcantarillado de Lima (SEDAPAL, English: Potable Water and Sewerage Service of Lima) [Encinas Carranza 2010]. The Chillón water production plant, operated for SEDAPAL by the Consorcio Agua Azul S.A., diverts roughly 2 m³/s of the Chillón river's flow for water production during the rainy season in the Andes from December to April; between May and November when the Chillón's flow can slow to a trickle, the Consorcio Agua Azul extracts up to 1 m³/s for water production from a system of groundwater wells in the Chillón watershed [CAA 2009]. In addition to the wells operated for SEDAPAL by Agua Azul, SEDAPAL owns and operates a network of 471 groundwater wells which are used to supplement surface waters utilised for potable water production [Encinas Carranza 2010].

Rapid, Informal Urban Growth

In recent years, the consequences of rapid, generally undirected population growth have put astrain on local water resources and their distribution in Lima Metropolitana. The population in the metropolitan area increased about fourteen times between 1940 and 2010 [Zolezzi Chocano 2005]. Large peripheral areas stretching into the hills north, south, and east of central Lima were informally settled via rural-urban migration at the beginning of this period. Unable to provide housing alternatives, authorities first tolerated and then gave support to the improvement and extension of these peri-urban neighbourhoods, setting a precedent for low-density growth. The political strife and economical insecurities that Peru faced in the eighties and early nineties led to an increase in the influx of immigrants to Lima who were forced to settle in undeveloped areas further and further from the historical urban centre [Fernández-Maldonado 2008]. Lima's most recent metropolitan development plan was developed for the period from 1990–2010, and though it has been temporarily renewed each year since then, as of early 2012, the city had no legal instrument to discourage low-density growth [CML 1990; Zolezzi Chocano 2005].

Inadequate Water-delivery Infrastructure

Understandably, water-delivery infrastructure in the metropolitan area has not been able to keep up with rapid, low-density population growth and currently serves only 80% of inhabit-

Fig. 1   Wastewater treatment technologies used in Lima [Moscoso Cavallini 2011]

Treatment Technology	Number of Facilities	Percentage of Total Collected Wastewater Treated
Facultative lagoons	10	4.6
Aerated lagoons	5	2.2
Aerated lagoons w/sedimentation & polishing	3	44.2
Anaerobic lagoons w/aeration & polishing	3	29.1
Anaerobic reactors & facultative lagoons	2	2.5
Activated sludge	14	16.9
Trickling filters	2	0.3
Constructed wetlands	2	0.1

ants, despite almost continuous efforts by SEDAPAL since 1980 to provide complete coverage [Fernández-Maldonado 2008; Unger 2010]. Furthermore, the distribution network exhibits losses estimated at 35 to 40% [Silva Nole 2011], half of which can be attributed to illegal connections [El Comercio 2012]. With network losses, average daily per capita water usage in Lima is estimated at 250 litres. The roughly 20% of Lima Metropolitana's inhabitants who lack access to the piped distribution network depend on potable water delivered by truck. Less than half of the water delivery trucks supplying these areas are operated by SEDAPAL; the balance are privately owned and operated. Water deliveries made by truck are often infrequent and no mechanism exists for controlling the source or quality of delivered water or the proper maintenance of truck water tanks. Moreover, potable water delivered by truck can cost up to nine times more than water delivered via the city's piped distribution network [Unger 2010]. The deficiencies in Lima's municipal water-supply service and the high cost of water in peripheral communities have led to a profusion of illegal groundwater wells; 1,733 unlicensed wells were counted in 2009. Without more investigation no one can be sure of the consequences that unregulated illegal groundwater wells will have on the long-term sustainability of Lima's subsurface water resources [Encinas Carranza 2010].

Insufficient Wastewater Treatment

Wastewater management presents another challenge in Lima. As with its piped water distribution network, SEDAPAL has had difficulty expanding its sewerage network rapidly enough to accommodate urban growth and only roughly 85% of the metropolitan area's households are connected to the sewage collection network [INEI 2007]. Wastewater treatment facilities have also not kept pace; currently only 16 to 17% of the 18,850 litres per second of wastewater collected by SEDAPAL receives any form of treatment at all, while the balance is discharged untreated into the Pacific Ocean [Moscoso Cavallini 2011]. Lima Metropolitana currently has forty-one facilities for treatment of the 16 to 17% of domestic wastewater collected, as summarised in Figure 1 ↗. Lima's wastewater treatment plants (WWTP) generally produce low-quality effluents because many do not function as designed or are under-designed for influent pollutant loads and types; furthermore, none of Lima's plants are designed to remove nutrients or chemical contaminants from wastewater. Though twenty-seven of Lima's plants were designed to include a disinfection step at the end of the treatment process, in the majority of cases this step is not in operation. For these reasons, treatment efficiencies achieved in Lima's WWTPs are frequently inadequate for the safe discharge of effluent into surface waters or for its use in irrigation [Moscoso Cavallini 2011].

Limited, Water-needy Urban Green Spaces

Another related difficulty faced by Lima Metropolitana is the provision of an amount of urban green space sufficient for its population. It is estimated that Lima Metropolitana has just over 2,000 ha of green space and on average only about 2.4 m² of green space per capita, far less than the 9 m² of green space per person recommended by the World Health Organization (WHO) [Moscoso Cavallini 2011]. Unbuilt spaces in Lima are in peril. Especially in the absence of a valid and current urban plan, there is pressure on authorities to allocate undeveloped and agricultural areas for residential and industrial development [Dongo-Soria S. 2011]. In areas that are already used as recreational space or for which parks are planned, green-space development is generally seen as needing to be just that—green—and expensive, limited potable water supplies are widely used for the irrigation of grass and other water-needy park plantings [PUCP 2012; Rodríguez 2012]. In order to discourage the use of potable water for irrigation, the Peruvian government passed a ministerial resolution in 2010, which effectively legalised the use of treated wastewater for irrigation and proposed the development of quality standards for domestic and municipal wastewater reused for this purpose [VIVIENDA 2010]. In 2011, Peru's Superintendencia Nacional de Servicios de Saneamiento (SUNASS, English: National Superintendence of Sanitation Services) proposed that municipalities begin to pay market rates for potable water used in green space irrigation instead of government-subsidised tariffs, and encouraged Peruvian mayors to seek financing for the construction of treatment facilities for municipal wastewater that could be reused in irrigation [La Republica 2011]. Despite this, the construction and proper maintenance of decentralised treatment plants for irrigation of urban green spaces remains financially cumbersome for municipalities, and irrigation of these areas with potable water continues [El Comercio 2010].

Conflicts with Hydropower Production

Climate change and associated conflicts with energy production ensure that Lima's challenges related to water resources will not be easily overcome. The metropolitan area's three rivers are fed by glacial meltwater, which is stored and managed in a network of upstream reservoirs. Global warming has caused the mass of all Andean glaciers to shrink by 20% since 1970, and is also responsible for reduced precipitation in Peru's mountainous regions. Both these factors have contributed to a reduction in upstream reservoir volumes, which has led not only to concerns about downstream water availability, but also to conflict with electricity providers who utilise upstream waters for hydropower production: 80% of Peru's electricity is currently generated using hydropower, and as populations in Lima and other urban centres continue to increase while mountain reservoir volumes decrease, arguments about whether to optimise water resources management for hydropower production or for drinking and irrigation water provision will surely intensify [Unger 2010].

Research Focus: Water-sensitive Urban Design (WSUD)

Improving Water Management in Lima with WSUD

It has been argued that it is the mismanagement of water, and not a lack of water resources, that is the real culprit behind water scarcity problems in the Lima metropolitan area [El Comercio 2011]. The development of lasting and effective solutions to the complex problems that Lima faces requires a change in the fundamental way water is managed within the urban environment, with a renewed focus on sustainability and integration. One tool that can be implemented to support a new approach to urban water management is water-sensitive urban design (WSUD). WSUD takes a renewed approach to urban water management, which considers the total water cycle and supports the idea that water infrastructure can and should be seen and experienced by city inhabitants via its integration into the urban landscape. Better incorporating water infrastructure into city spaces also opens up its potential to serve an additional purpose by supporting the natural habitats of flora and fauna or as an urban recreational area [Engineers Australia 2006]. The potential for more effectively and efficiently managing water resources in Lima by applying the principles of WSUD is high, and would not only alleviate issues related to water supply and distribution (i.e., water scarcity), but could also address some of the challenges related to wastewater management and the provision and maintenance of green space in the city.

Auditing Water Resources to Support WSUD

A water audit is an accounting procedure aimed at assessing the quantity and/or quality of water resources available in an area or to a project. An audit of local water resources can be implemented during the preliminary stages of WSUD to provide information about specific water quality and quantity parameters which can be used to constrain and guide early design development, leading to savings in money and time at future stages of the project. When considered alongside project goals for water usage or treatment, "boundary conditions" based on information about water flow rates or contaminant levels, which is collected via an early-stage audit, can help ensure that initial design prototypes function as envisioned. This information can also serve as a starting point for the selection of a specific water-treatment method or other technologies to complement the proposed designs. Moreover, information collected during an audit can help steer project resources away from ideas that simply work, before much time or money is wasted on investigating them more thoroughly.

At the core of this study was the development and implementation of a water audit to collect information about the state of water resources in Chuquitanta, a neighbourhood located within Lima's District of San Martín de Porres. As a next step, final audit results were then used to generate suggestions for technically feasible and design-appropriate constructed wetland configurations that could be incorporated into WSUD prototypes developed for various water sources in Chuquitanta by a group of Peruvian and German engineering and architecture students during the LiWa "Lima: Beyond the Park" Summer School, held in February/March 2012. Suggestions included an estimation of the land area the wetland configurations would require.

Methods: Developing and Implementing a Water Audit and Applying its Results

Questions Asked During Audit Development

There are six major water sources in or near the north-eastern part of Chuquitanta: the Chillón river, effluent from the SEDAPAL Puente Piedra WWTP, domestic wastewater from the Santa Cruz Hill (SCH) residential area, a network of irrigation canals channelling redirected river water through the neighbourhood, groundwater from a local pumping station, and a spring or *puquio* forming a small groundwater pond [Figure 2 ↗]. Audit development focused on the first four of these sources, and began with exploration, conversations with residents and local officials, and a literature review to gain a basic sense of the state of affairs surrounding them. Five considerations were then made in order to decide which set of parameters would give the best overview of the quantities and qualities of the four water sources:

- Which directly measurable water-quality parameters are generally considered in assessments of surface waters and wastewaters?
- Which of these are typically considered in assessments of surface waters and wastewaters in Germany and Peru?
- Which parameter levels might be affected by "upstream" activities or day-to-day use of local water sources?
- Which parameter levels are important to the intended or "downstream" uses of local water sources?
- Which parameters offer the easiest and cheapest information to obtain?

Selection of Audit Parameters and Auditing Methods

It was decided early on that information on the quantity of water contained in or flowing through each source should be collected. With regard to quality parameters, first thought was given to which parameters are generally considered in assessments of surface waters and wastewaters, and these were grouped into several broad categories [EPA 2012]:

- Temperature
- Oxygen Balance: dissolved oxygen (DO); biochemical oxygen demand (BOD_5); chemical oxygen demand (COD); total organic carbon (TOC)
- Salt Content: electric conductivity (EC); anions and cations such as chloride (Cl^-), nitrate (NO_3^-), sulphate (SO_4^{2-}), phosphate (PO_3^{4-}), bicarbonate (HCO_3^-), carbonate (CO_3^{2-}), sodium (Na^+), magnesium (Mg^{2+}), calcium (Ca^{2+}), iron (Fe^{2+} and Fe^{3+}), and aluminium (Al^{3+})
- Acidity/Alkalinity: pH; total alkalinity
- Nutrient Content: nitrogen (N), especially as ammonium (NH_4-N), nitrate (NO_3-N), ammonia (NH_3), nitrite (NO_2^-), total Kjeldahl nitrogen (TKN), and N_{tot}; phosphorous (P), especially as orthophosphate (PO_4-P), dissolved phosphorus, and total phosphorus (P_{tot})
- Microbiology: faecal bacteria indicators, especially total coliforms, faecal coliforms, and thermotolerant coliforms; bacteria, especially Salmonella, Escherichia coli, faecal streptococci, and enterococci; parasitic worm (helminth) eggs and cysts
- Other: taste, odour, and colour; total solids, total suspended solids (TSS), and turbidity; fats & oils; total hardness and carbonate hardness; heavy metals and metalloids, especially cadmium (Cd), copper (Cu), chromium (Cr), iron (Fe), manganese (Mn), lead (Pb), and

Fig. 2 Chuquitanta's six major water resources [Author, based on aerial photo from Stuttgart University]

zinc (Zn); absorbable organo-halogens (AOX); industrial, mining, agricultural, pharmaceutical, and radioactive pollutants

The questions listed above were then used to help generate a list of parameters on which to focus the investigation. Germany typically monitors a very wide variety of parameters in surface waters and wastewaters discharged into surface water bodies, which fall into all of the categories listed. On the other hand, the three most important parameters for assessing wastewater and surface water qualities in Peru are BOD_5, total coliforms, and parasitic worm (helminth) eggs/cysts. Nutrient content seems to be only very rarely measured in water bodies and effluent streams. While a consideration of the impact of the large variety of "upstream" activities on water quality was not very helpful in narrowing down the selection of auditing parameters, the intention to use constructed wetlands "downstream" to treat water from the various sources in Chuquitanta for reuse in irrigation provided some helpful constraints. Constructed wetlands are dimensioned using, among other data, the flow rate and level of BOD_5 in the incoming water. Furthermore, especially because wetlands have been shown effective in reducing levels of nutrients and microbiological parameters, having information about these parameters would help in determining projected wetland efficiencies [DEEC 2004]. The methods available for collecting information about water qualities in Chuquitanta included collecting data directly via observation, interviews, available literature, and other print sources; making estimations based on information collected via observation, interviews, and print sources; carrying out field testing or collecting samples

Fig. 3   Prioritisation of auditing methods in Chuquitanta [Author]

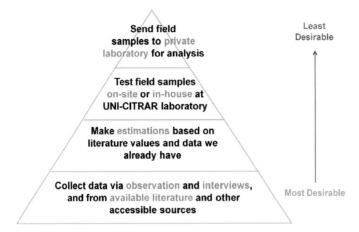

in the field for testing "in-house" at the laboratories of the Centro de Investigación en Tratamiento de Aguas Residuales y Residuos Peligrosos at the Universidad Nacional de Ingeniería (CITRAR-UNI, English: Center for Research on Wastewater Treatment and Hazardous Waste); and collecting samples to send to a private laboratory for testing. Logistics challenges and money and time constraints led to the prioritisation of auditing methods shown in Figure 3 ↗.

In the end, almost all parameters that could be directly determined for each source by observation, interviews, print sources, or reasonably determined by estimation were included in the audit. With regard to the choice of parameters selected for determination by testing, DO, temperature, EC, and pH were all chosen because of the relative ease with which they can be measured in the field using probes and meters. Because of their importance to constructed wetland dimensioning and efficiency determinations for all sources, the decision was made to measure several nutrient parameters at the in-house laboratory, along with COD, which in comparison to BOD_5 is a much easier indicator of organic content to measure accurately in the laboratory. Cl^- was also selected for measurement as a representative indicator of salt content (along with EC). Finally, the decision was made to send samples to a private laboratory for evaluation of BOD_5, total coliforms, and parasitic worm (helminth) eggs/cysts since these parameters are key indicators of water quality in Peru. Since there are so many metals and because recent information was available about heavy metal content in the Chillón River (the source most likely to exhibit high levels of these pollutants), they were not measured.

Audit Implementation

Once a decision was made about which parameters to include in the audit, various methods and sources including direct observation, interviews, and questionnaires; laws and legal norms; reports and presentations by government ministries, private enterprises, non-governmental organisations, and international organisations; statistics made publicly available by governments; published scientific research; and newspaper articles were considered in the collection of available "pre-existing" information. The flow rate of the Chillón River, the quantity of grey- and blackwater produced in SCH each day, and the concentration of various SCH greywater parameters including BOD_5, NO_3-N, TKN, P_{tot}, faecal coliforms, Salmonella, parasitic worm (helminth) eggs/cysts, and TSS were then estimated using established norms. Finally, field sampling and testing were carried out to collect information about the remaining parameters. First, a set of probes and meters were used to measure temperature, DO, pH, and EC in the field, and preliminary field testing was carried out using an Aquamerck® Compact Laboratory for Water Testing in order to determine anticipated parameter ranges for nitrite, nitrate, ammonium, and phosphate. Then, samples were collected from all sources for: a) in-house testing at CITRAR-UNI for COD, NO_3-N, NH_4-N, PO_4-P, P_{tot}, and Cl⁻ using Merck Spectroquant® Cell Tests; and b) for delivery to a private laboratory for analysis of BOD_5, total coliforms, and parasitic worm (helminth) eggs/cysts.

Using Audit Results to Estimate Required Wetland Size

A wetland's capacity to treat polluted water is directly related to its size. Consequently, a successful design would require input about the minimum wetland size required to sufficiently improve the quality of the contaminated water under consideration. An Excel-based tool was created to roughly estimate areas required for various constructed wetland types that might be included in a WSUD. The tool is based on a modified tanks-in-series model developed by R.H. Kadlec called the "P-k-C* Model." Tanks-in-series models are often used in the field of chemical engineering to represent flow through a non-ideal reactor (such as a wetland) as flow through a series of ideal continuous stirred-tank reactors. The P-k-C* Model estimates wetland area based on the target outflow concentration of a dimensioning parameter (often BOD_5, sometimes NO_3-N, P_{tot}, or faecal coliforms if the wetland is designed for specific removal of one of these pollutants, et cetera), the inflow concentration of this parameter, the background concentration of this parameter, the modified first-order areal constant for this parameter, and the number of tanks-in-series [Kadlec 2009]. Since this method requires a desired or "target" concentration of the dimensioning parameter, it was necessary to choose a standard for comparison for each of the audit parameters considered.

Findings: Constructed Wetlands as a Central Component of WSUD for Chuquitanta

Graphical representations of all audit results are shown in the figures below. In these graphics, the standard of comparison for each parameter is indicated with a "+" symbol. Where the measured value exceeded the standard, the bar is red; where it remained below the limit, the bar is green. Blue bars indicate that no appropriate standard of comparison was available, while the notation "N.V." means that no value was measured for the particular parameter. The numerical data collected during the audit, a summary of all audited parameters with audit results, an indication of the method used to collect each result, and the standard of comparison applied to each result are shown in the Figures 16, 17, and 18 at the end of this article ↗.

Fig. 4   The Chillón river during periods of high (left) and low (right) flow [left: Emma Hillard, right: Author]

Fig. 4   The Chillón river during periods of high (left) and low (right) flow [left: Emma Hillard, right: Author]

Renaturation of the Chillón River

For much of the year, the Chillón river is a major water element in the study area, though there are annual periods when it runs dry [Figure 4 ↗]. Local flooding often occurs when the volume of the Chillón river increases and results can be severe [Salazar Vega 2011].

Student design ideas focused on river renaturation via the development of a natural morphology and native bank plantings to encourage the return of local flora and fauna to the river and to provide a space for public recreation [Figure 5 ↗]. It was also suggested that the flow of the river be supplemented during dry periods using water that now flows into the *puquio* (groundwater pond) or with treated WWTP effluent, and that river banks be reinforced to provide flood protection. Final audit results indicate elevated NO_3-N levels and high levels of microbiological parameters and most heavy metals [Figure 6 ↗].

The recommended technical solution generally agrees with the student design ideas in that overall, re-establishing a more natural river morphology and installing native plantings would improve the amount of green space in the area and could have some positive effect on riverwater qualities. However, routing waters from the puquio and/or wastewater treatment plants into the river channel to supplement river plantings during periods of low flow may pose technical problems related to water qualities and raise concerns about the ethics of repurposing scarce water resources to green the banks of an otherwise neglected river. It could also lead to political unrest since the puquio is located on the border between the City of Lima and the City of Callao and both municipalities claim ownership of the puquio and the rights to its use. Particularly because of its highly variable flow rate, a free water surface constructed wetland (FWSW) might be the best wetland treatment choice for the river, though in order to accommodate the river's maximum average flow of 6,250 L/s between December and April, the area of the FWSW as given by the wetland area estimation tool would be truly huge at roughly 39 ha. Though steps could be taken to reduce this large footprint, the development of a truly effective and realistic constructed wetland treatment system for implementation with waters from the Chillón river is a major undertaking and beyond the scope of this study.

Fig. 5   Student design idea for the Chillón river during low flow periods [University of Stuttgart ILPÖ]

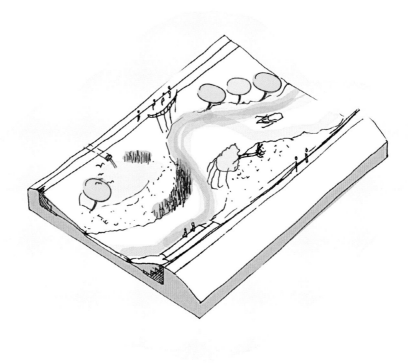

Fig. 6   Chillón river audit results [Author]

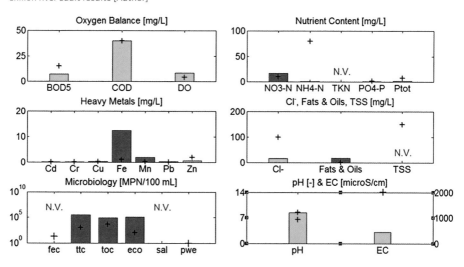

Sub-surface Constructed Wetland for Additional Treatment of Puente Piedra Wastewater Treatment Plant Effluent

The Puente Piedra WWTP was built in 2002 on six hectares of land in Chuquitanta for the treatment of 422 L/s of domestic wastewater from 150,000 inhabitants of northern Lima. However, influent volumes and organic loads higher than those that the plant was designed to handle have caused major operational problems and the effluent released into open channels in Chuquitanta is generally malodorous and of visibly poor quality [Figure 7 ↗]. Despite this, it is still used for irrigation of agriculture in the surrounding area [Moscoso Cavallini 2011].

Students envisioned SEDAPAL's new treatment system as a pair or series of lagoons, which achieve low-cost, biological (secondary) treatment of the plant's current effluent [Figure 8 ↗]. They also recommended that a recreational space be designated within the treatment area. Final audit results indicate high BOD_5 and COD levels, high levels of PO_4-P and P_{tot}, high Cl^-, and high levels of microbiological parameters [Figure 9 ↗].

The recommended technical solution is partial treatment of WWTP effluent in a horizontal sub-surface flow constructed wetland (HSSFW) which could serve primarily as a stop-gap treatment method while SEDAPAL carries out a planned upgrade/expansion of the Puente Piedra WWTP. After additional treatment in the wetland, the effluent could then be used to irrigate local agriculture. This recommendation deviates from the students' suggestions in that HSSFW do not look like or function as lagoons. However, this type is preferred to a free water-surface constructed wetland (FWSW) (the wetland type most similar to that envisioned in the student design) in this case because the quality of the WWTP effluent is too poor for it to be channelled into an open water-treatment lagoon which could successfully be incorporated into a recreational space. Treatment in a HSSFW would still provide vegetation that would contribute to an overall greening of the area, and would require considerably less land area to achieve the same treatment efficiencies. When applied to the wetland area estimation tool, collected data generate an estimated HSSFW area of roughly 8.5 ha necessary for the treatment of the full volume of WWTP effluent. This area is of course quite large. However, the recommendation made here is envisioned as an intermediary solution while SEDAPAL upgrades its plant. With every improvement in the quality of the water flowing into the wetland, the required wetland area gets smaller.

Fig. 8   Student design ideas for the Puente Piedra WWTP [University of Stuttgart ILPÖ]

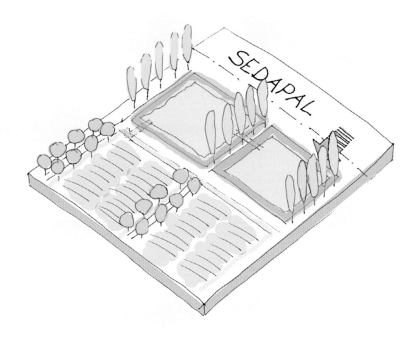

Fig. 9   Audit results for the Puente Piedra WWTP [Author]

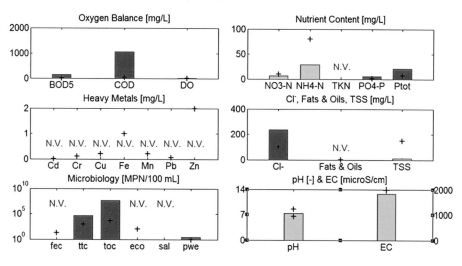

Domestic Grey- and Blackwater Treatment at Santa Cruz Hill

The residential area on Santa Cruz Hill is one of several in Chuquitanta with no connection to the public water supply or sewerage networks, though the community hopes to achieve this in the next few years [Figure 10 ↗]. For now, potable water is delivered by truck and stored in plastic or metal cisterns outside homes. Domestic greywater is generally discarded in the street, often as a means for controlling dust and no formal latrine or other hygienic facilities are available [ILPÖ 2012].

Student design ideas focused on the collection of grey- or blackwater from the settlement for transport by gravity to the base of the hill for treatment in a constructed wetland [Figure 11 ↗]. Final audit results for combined grey and black domestic wastewater indicate high BOD_5, high nutrient levels, high levels of microbiological parameters, and elevated TSS, as might be expected for untreated wastewater [Figure 12 ↗].

The recommended technical solution generally supports the design idea. In the absence of a sewerage system, grey and black wastewater streams in Santa Cruz Hill are not combined, which is an advantage in that treatment methods can be optimised for each stream. Domestic greywater (i.e., water used for bathing, washing, and in the kitchen) could be collected either at each household or at multihousehold collection points on the hill where solids and grease could be removed on-site using a filter and grease trap or a settling tank. Greywater could then be channelled by gravity through a basic pipe network to the base of the hill for treatment in a vertical flow constructed wetland (VFW) with recirculating flow—i.e., a VFW in which water that has vertically passed through a series of soil layers is collected and returned to the top of the system for reapplication to the VFW. A recirculating VFW is recommended in this case because this technology maintains high pollutant removal efficiencies while minimising the land area required to achieve these efficiencies [Gross 2007]. To some extent, blackwater generated in Santa Cruz Hill could be handled by installing ecological sanitation (ecosan) latrines equipped with urine diverting dry toilets (UDDT) to separate urine and faeces. Data collected in the audit and applied to the wetland area estimation tool under this assumption generate an estimated VFW area of roughly 50 m² necessary for the treatment of greywater generated by the 295 people living in the settlement [Residents 2012].

Fig. 11 Student design ideas for the Santa Cruz Hill residential area [University of Stuttgart ILPÖ]

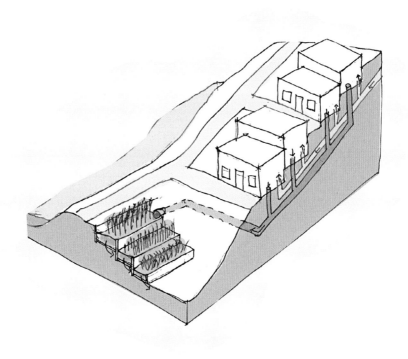

Fig. 12 Audit results for Santa Cruz Hill domestic wastewater [Author]

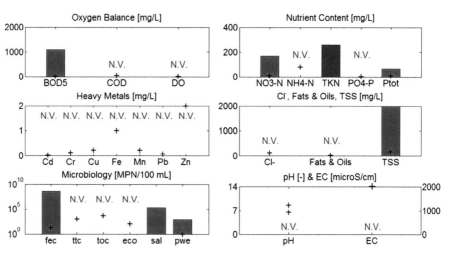

Fig. 13   Chuquitanta's network of irrigation canals [Author]

Multifunctional Free Water Surface Wetlands at the Chuquitanta Irrigation Canals

The final water source in or near Lhuquitanta considered within the context of this study is the network of irrigation canals which snakes through the neighbourhood, fed by water diverted from the Chillón river at a point upstream of the study area and used for irrigation of agriculture in Chuquitanta and farther downstream [Figure 13 ↗] [Representative 2012]. Much former agricultural land in Chuquitanta is now built up and sections of the irrigation network that serviced these areas have consequently been closed off while other parts of the network now pass through residential developments on their way to the fields. Domestic grey- and blackwater, as well as solid waste, are often dumped into these sections of the network.

Student design ideas focused on the installation of canal channels made from natural materials (i.e., not concrete) covering canals where water quality remains poor as it moves through settlements in Chuquitanta, and utilising the canals as "river-like" dual-purpose recreational/constructed wetland areas [Figure 14 ↗]. Final audit results indicate high levels of COD, NO_3-N, and total coliforms [Figure 15 ↗].

The recommended technical solution is a FWSW that doubles as a green park. FWSW have been shown to effectively reduce COD, NO_3-N, and coliform levels in polluted waters [Beutel 2009; Greenway 2005; Mandi 1996; Reilly 2000]. Canals could be covered throughout the settlement area, and then outlet into a planted basin forming the FWSW. Incorporating basins for collecting and holding canal water in the planted area lengthens contact times and makes it much more likely that adequate pollutant removal efficiencies will be reached. After treatment, the wetland effluent could be directed back into a "semi-renaturalised" (i.e., lined earthen) canal system outside the settlement area for subsequent use in agricultural irrigation; lining the canals is likely necessary to prevent water losses to seepage or irrigation. When collected data including a maximum flow rate between December and April of 900 L/s are applied to the wetland area estimation tool [Representative 2012], they generate an estimated FWSW area of roughly one hectare necessary for the treatment of the irrigation canal water. This is a large area, but not an unrealistic amount of space in Chuquitanta. However, the advantages of a multi-functional FWSW/recreational green space which incorporates irrigation canal water would have to be weighed against the loss of agricultural land to the installation.

Fig. 14 Student design ideas for Chuquitanta's system of irrigation canals [University of Stuttgart ILPÖ]

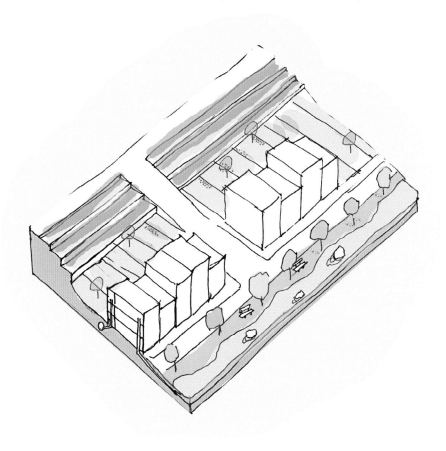

Fig. 15 Audit results for Chuquitanta irrigation canals [Author]

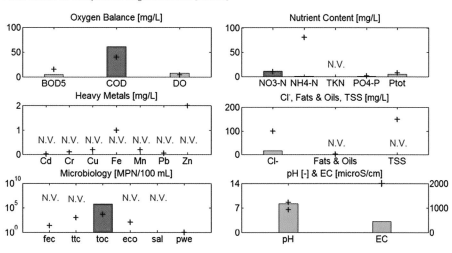

Conclusion and Outlook

Wetlands for the treatment of waste and surface waters intended for reuse in the irrigation of agricultural and other green spaces are a viable option for Lima and for inclusion in WSUD prototypes developed for Chuquitanta, in particular considering the additional objective of increasing the amount of green space in the metropolitan area. In fact, Lima Metropolitana has two natural coastal wetland areas, and several pilot-scale constructed wetlands have already been set up by city municipalities or their private partners in recent years to treat domestic wastewater for various purposes. However, in general, these initiatives did not succeed because of their very small scales and a lack of expertise in planning and maintaining the implemented wetlands. It is clear that the success of wetlands initiatives in Lima will likely depend on their implementation on larger scales and with the full support of SEDAPAL and the city government. Fortunately, there is hope that political will is moving in this direction, not only in light of recent laws passed to support the irrigation of urban green spaces with treated domestic wastewater, but also as seen in the enthusiasm for constructed wetlands demonstrated by the community in Chuquitanta and the municipal government of San Martín de Porres.

Annex: Numerical Data from the Audit

Fig. 16 Chuquitanta Audit Results & Comparison to Standards Part I: Quantity, Temperature, Oxygen Balance, Salt Content, Acidity

Parameter	SCH Domestic Waste-water	Puente Piedra WWTP Effluent	Chillón River	Chuquitanta Irrigation Canals	Standard for Comparison
Water quantity	47 L/person/day (estimated)	498 L/s (as of 2010) (INEI 2011)	6250 L/s (Dec.–Apr.); 2400 L/s (May–Nov.) (estimated)	900 L/s (Dec.–Apr.); 45 L/s (May–Nov.) (as of 2012) (Representative 2012)	–
Temperature (°C)	–	26.9	24.4	24.0	<35[1]
Oxygen balance					
Biochemical oxygen demand (BOD_5) (mg/L)	1100 (estimated)	135	7	5	15[2]
Chemical oxygen demand (COD) (mg/L)	–	1053	40	61	40[2]
Dissolved oxygen (DO) (mg/L)	–	4.78	8.24	7.63	≥4[2]
Salt Content					
Electric conductivity (EC) (μs/cm)	–	1820	440	439	2000[2]
Chloride (Cl^-) (mg/L)	–	235	17	15	100[2]
Acidity					
pH	–	7.3	8.4	8.1	6.5–8.5[2]

Fig. 17 Chuquitanta Audit Results & Comparison to Standards Part II: Nutrient Content & Microbiology

Parameter	SCH Domestic Wastewater	Puente Piedra WWTP Effluent	Chillón River	Chuquitanta Irrigation Canals	Standard for Comparison
Nutrient Content					
Nitrate (NO_3-N) (mg/L)	170 (estimated)	6	16	11	10[2]
Ammonium (NH_4-N) (mg/L)	–	28.8	< 0.2	< 0.2	80[3]
Total kjeldahl nitrogen (TKN) (mg/L)	260 (estimated)	–	–	–	–
Orthophosphate (PO_4-P)	–	5.86	0.11	0.73	1[2]
Total phosphorus (P_{tot}) (mg/L)	65 (estimated)	21	1.0	5.2	7[3]
Microbiology					
Faecal coliforms (MPN/100 mL)	440,000,000 (estimated)	–	–	–	20[4]
Thermo-tolerant coliforms (MPN/100 mL)	–	51,000[5]	340,000[6]	–	1000[2]
Total coliforms (MPN/100 mL)	–	46,000,000	79,000	490,000	5000[2]
Escherichia coli (MPN/100 mL)	–	–	130,000[6]	–	100[2]
Salmonella (MPN/1000 mL)	2,200,000 (estimated)	–		–	0[2]
Parasitic worm (Helminth) Eggs/Cysts (MPN/1000 mL)	8,700 (estimated)	30	< 1	< 1	< 1[2]

Fig. 18 Chuquitanta Audit Results & Comparison to Standards Part III: Other Parameters

Parameter	SCH Domestic Waste-water	Puente Piedra WWTP Effluent	Chillón River	Chuqui-tanta Irrigation Canals	Standard for Com-parison
Other					
Cadmium (Cd) (mg/L)	–		0.021[6]	–	0.005[2]
Chromium (Cr) (mg/L)	–		0.028[6]	–	0.1[2]
Copper (Cu) (mg/L)	–		0.226[6]	–	0.2[2]
Iron (Fe) (mg/L)	–		12.46[6]	–	1[2]
Manganese (Mn) (mg/L)	–		1.99[6]	–	0.2[2]
Lead (Pb) (mg/L)	–		0.222[6]	–	0.05[2]
Zinc (Zn) (mg/L)	–		0.518[6]	–	2[2]
Fats & oils (mg/L)	–		19.0[6]	–	1[2]
Total suspended solids (TSS) (mg/L)	2000 (est.)	11[5]	–	–	150[1]

References

Beutel, M. W./ Newton, C. D./ Brouillard, E. S./ Watts, R. J. (2009): "Nitrate removal in surface-flow constructed wetlands treating dilute agricultural runoff in the lower Yakima Basin". In: *Ecological Engineering* 35, pp. 1538–46, Washington

[CML] Concejo Metropolitano de Lima (1990): *Plan de Desarrollo Metropolitano de Lima-Callao 1990-2010 (PlanMet).* http://www.urbanistasperu.org/inicio/PlanMet/planmet.htm, 25.05.2012

[CAA] Consorcio Agua Azul S.A. (2009): *Perfil de la Empresa. Objeto Social y Plazo de Duración.* http://www.caa.com.pe/Perfil.html, 18.06.2012

[DECC] Department of Environment and Conservation of New South Wales (2004): *Environmental guidelines. Use of effluent by irrigation.* http://www.environment.nsw.gov.au/resources/water/effguide.pdf, 07.06.2012

Dongo-Soria S., D. (2011): "Desarrollo industrial mira a Lurigancho y Ventanilla. Urge celeridad en cambios de zonificación." In: *El Comercio* (Aug. 2011), p. 10

El Comercio Staff (2010): "En Miraflores postergan concesión de nueva planta de tratamiento de parque María Reiche." In: *El Comercio* (Dec. 2010)

El Comercio Staff (2011): "Afirman que hay agua suficiente pero no se usa con eficiencia. Voz de especialistas desde el congreso mundial en Brasil." In: *El Comercio* (Sep. 2011), p. 19

El Comercio Staff (2012): "Sedapal pierde S/.300 millones por año debido a robo de agua." In: *El Comercio* (Mar. 2012)

Encinas Carranza, P., Ed (2010): *Reporte ambiental de Lima y Callao, 2010. Evaluación de avances a 5 años del informe GEO.* http://www.actualidadambiental.pe/ciudadano/documentos/reporte_ambiental_2010.pdf, 10.06.2012

Engineers Australia (2006): *An Overview of Australian Runoff Quality. A Guide to Water Sensitive Urban Design.* http://www.ncwe.org.au/arq/pdfs/introduction.pdf, 19.06.2012

[EPA] United States Environmental Protection Agency (2012): *Water: Monitoring & Assessment. Chapter 5: Water Quality Conditions.* http://water.epa.gov/type/rsl/monitoring/vms50.cfm, 24.06.2012

Fernández-Maldonado, A. M. (2008): "Expanding networks for the urban poor: Water and telecommunications services in Lima, Peru." In: *Geoforum* 39, pp. 1884–96

Greenway, M. (2005): "The role of constructed wetlands in secondary effluent treatment and water reuse in subtropical and arid Australia." In: *Ecological Engineering* 25, pp. 501–09

Gross, A./ Shmueli, O./ Ronen, Z./ Raveh, E. (2007): "Recycled vertical flow constructed wetland (RVFCW). A novel method of recycling greywater for irrigation in small communities and households." In: *Chemosphere* 66, pp. 916–23

[ILPÖ] Institut für Landschaftsplanung und Ökologie, Universität Stuttgart, (2012): *Lima: Beyond the Park. Summer School 2012 Booklet.* Unpublished work, Stuttgart.

[INEI] Instituto Nacional de Estadistica e Informatica del Perú (2007): *Perfil Sociodemográfico de la Provincia de Lima.* http://www.inei.gob.pe/biblioineipub/bancopub/Est/Lib0838/libro15/index.htm, 27.06.2012

[INEI] Instituto Nacional de Estadistica e Informatica del Perú (2011): *Peru: Anuario de Estadísticas Ambientales.* http://www.inei.gob.pe/, 31.01.2012

Kadlec, R. H/ Wallace, S. D. (2009): *Treatment wetlands.* CRC Press, Boca Raton, FL

La Republica Staff (2011): "Quieren evitar seguir regando jardines con agua potable." In: *La Republica* (Oct. 2011)

Mandi, L./ Houhoum, B./ Asmama, S./ Schwartzbrod, J. (1996): "Wastewater Treatment by Reed Beds. An Experimental Approach." In: *Water Resources* 30, pp. 2009–2016

[MINSAL] Ministerio de Salud del Peru, Dirección General de Salud Ambiental (2011): *Río Chillón 2010.* http://www.digesa.minsa.gob.pe/depa/rios/2010/rio_chillon_2010.pdf, 24.06.2011

Moscoso Cavallini, J. C. (2011): *Estudio de Opciones de Tratamiento y Reuso de Aguas Residuales en Lima Metropolitana.* http://www.lima-water.de/documents/jmoscoso_informe.pdf, 28.01.2012

[PUCP] Pontificia Universidad Católica del Perú (2012): *La gente piensa que el gras verde y las lindas flores son ecología, pero no lo son.* http://puntoedu.pucp.edu.pe/entrevistas/entrevista-arquitectura/, 18.06.2012

Residents of Cerro Santa Cruz, Chuquitanta. Personal Interview, 04.04.2012

Reilly, J. F./Horne, A. J./Miller, C. D. (2000): "Nitrate removal from a drinking water supply with large free-surface constructed wetlands prior to groundwater recharge." In: *Ecological Engineering* 14, pp. 33–47.

Representative from the Chuquitanta Irrigation Board. Personal Interview, 07.03.2012

Rodríguez, S. (2012): "¿Qué parques necesitamos?" In: *Publimetro* (Mar. 2012), p. 6

Salazar Vega, E. (2011): "Crece riesgo en ribera del Chillón. Acumulación de basura estrecha cauce del río." In: *El Comercio* (Feb. 2011), p. 8

Silva Nole, L. (2011): "Agua llega de a pocos en Lima norte. SEDAPAL reparará redes en el distrito de Comas y otras zonas." In: *El Comercio* (Apr. 2011), a2

Unger, M./ Vollherbst, T./ Vera, J./ Grimm, F. (2010): *Lima: eine Stadt trocknet aus.* Reportage. http://videos.arte.tv/en/videos/lima_quand_l_eau_est_un_luxe_-3346706.html, 28.01.2011

[VIVIENDA] Ministerio de Vivienda Construcción y Saneamiento del Perú (2010): *Lineamientos de Política para la promoción del tratamiento para el reuso de las aguas residuales domésticas y municipales en el riego de areas verdes urbanas y periurbanas. 176-2010-VIVIENDA.* http://spij.minjus.gob.pe, 24.05.2012

Zolezzi Chocano, M./Tokeshi Gusukuda - Shirota, J./Noriega Jugo, C. (2005): *Densificación Habitacional. Una Propuesta de Crecimiento para la Cuidad Popular.* http://www.desco.org.pe/sites/default/files/publicaciones/files/densificacion_habitacional.pdf, 0.06.201

Notes (Tables)

1 As per Peruvian decree 003-2010-MINAM: *"Aprueba Límites Máximos Permisibles para los efluentes de Plantas de Tratamiento de Aguas Residuales Domésticas o Municipales"* (English: "Approved Maximum Allowable Limits for Effluent of Domestic or Municipal Wastewater Treatment Plants")

2 As per Peruvian decree 002-2008-MINAM: *"Aprueban los Estánderes Nacionales de Calidad Ambiental para Agua, Categoria 3: Parámetros para Riego de Vegetales de Tallo Bajo"* (English: "Approved National Standards for Water Quality, Category 3: Parameters for Irrigation of Short-stemmed Plants")

3 Maximum allowable level for treated wastewater used in irrigation as established by the Standards Institution of Israel

4 Maximum allowable level for unrestricted use of treated wastewater in agricultural irrigation as established by the Standards Institution of Israel

5 (As of 2008) [INEI 2011]

6 (Maximum monthly 2010) [MINSAL 2011]

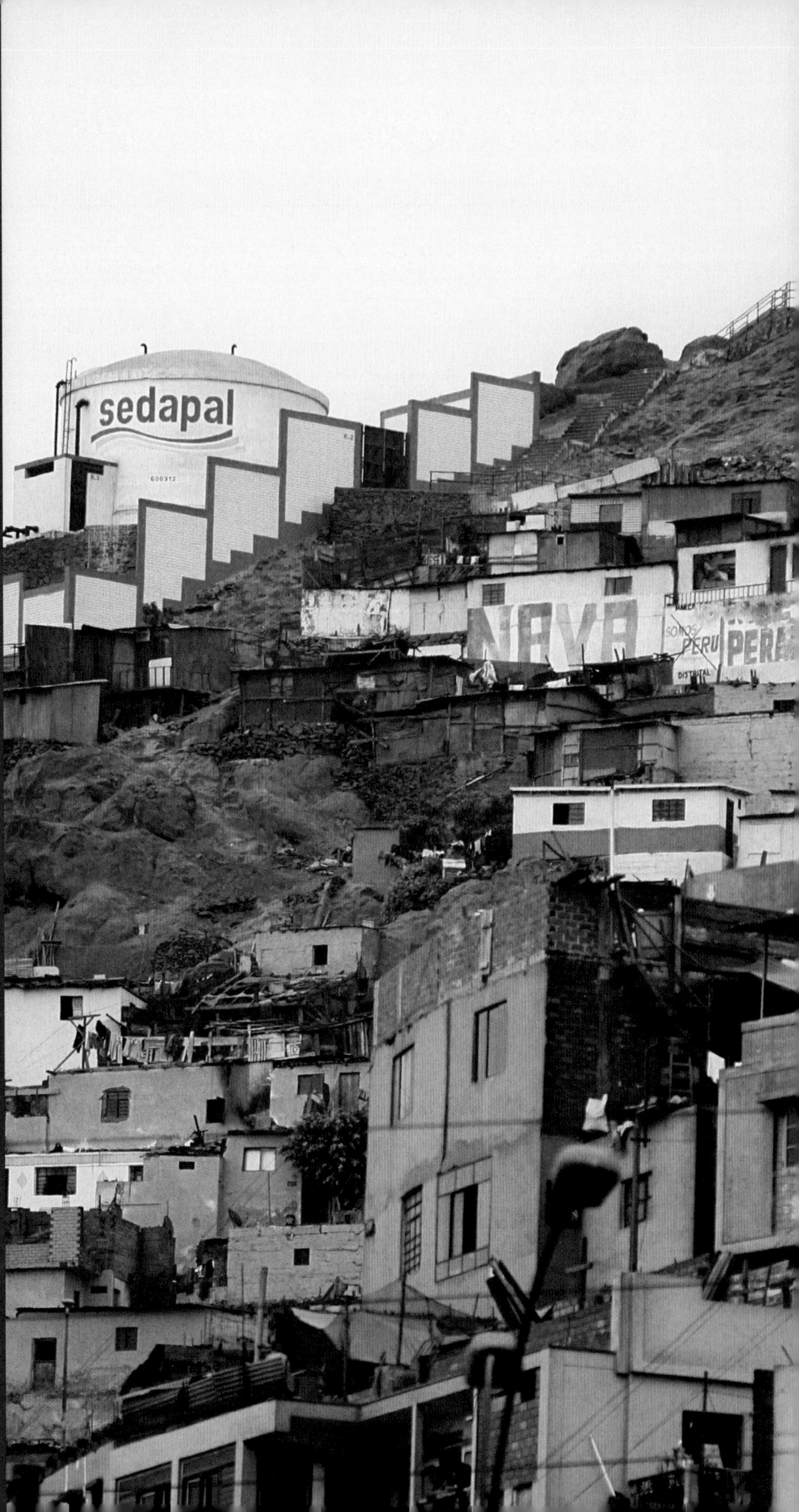

LIMA: Water tank [Marcus Mangeot]

Myriam Laux

Diploma Thesis at University of Stuttgart, Institute for Sanitary Engineering,
Water Quality and Solid Waste Management

Adaptation of the Urban Water System to Future Developments— Modelling of Different Options for Lima, Peru

Abstract

The development of megacities is a great challenge for many involved institutions, but particularly for city planners. Special difficulties have to be solved for the development of infrastructure projects such as water and wastewater systems. In the framework of the LiWa project, such a development is examined for the metropolitan region of Lima. In this work, the region's water system has been analysed, with a focus on the demand and supply of fresh water on the one hand and wastewater treatment and wastewater reuse on the other. To achieve this, many data had to be collected and Lima's water and wastewater system had to be analysed in detail. With the help of different scenarios and a macro-modelling tool called LiWatool, it was possible to develop a simulation for a sustainable water system for the region considering the welfare of further generations. The LiWatool was especially developed by ifak-Institute in the framework of its Future Megacities research project. It is based on the principle of mass-flow analysis.

An analysis of the city's water system showed that the already scarce water resources due to climate change and the rapidly growing population are increasingly at risk. Only 82.8% of Lima, which has a population of nine million, is currently connected to the public drinking water system. About 1.5 million people have to be supplied through tankers. Around 2.2 million people are not connected to the sewage system. Surface waters are highly contaminated from the direct discharge of domestic wastewater, fresh industrial effluents, untreated process water from the mines, and the intensive use of fertilisers. Below-cost water pricing prevents infrastructure expansion. Moreover, there are network losses of nearly 40% due to lagging infrastructure maintenance. A simulation of the "current state" using the LiWatool clearly indicates that the megacity of Lima will no longer get its water without implementing specific measures under certain assumptions after 2021 [Figure 2 ↗].

To counteract this trend, ways to increase the reuse of treated wastewater and improve drinking water availability were examined in this study. The simulation of a scenario with an increased amount of reuse by the conversion of a primary plant to a secondary plant, and through the construction of an additional treatment plant shows that the water demand can be covered until 2039. The increase in water availability due to major projects, such as the construction of reservoirs in the Andean region, will meet the demand until

2040. But the simulation also shows an enormous rise in demand due to the insufficient increase of water reuse. With the combination of the expansion of a primary to a secondary wastewater treatment plant, water conservation campaigns, and only one major project to increase availability, the corresponding water demand will be met by 2040. The situation should not only be improved in Lima, but also in other cities and rural areas of Peru. All stakeholders should work together on an integrated solution so that all Limeños can live with water in the future.

Introduction: Multifaceted Challenges to Establishing a Stable Water System in an Arid Megacity

Dangerously Rapid Urban Growth on Steep Slopes

With more than nine million inhabitants [INEI 2011b] and only 9 mm of rainfall per year, Lima is the second-driest megacity in the world [Kehl et al. 2007]. Due to strong rural depopulation, especially in the 1970s, Lima experienced extreme urbanisation. Nearly 30% of Peru's population now lives in Lima. The metropolitan region thus forms the cultural, political, administrative, and economic centre of the country [Brussel et al. 2008]. But with a rapid growth rate of up to 5.5%, urban development was very heterogeneous. Approximately 43% of the population lives in temporary accommodation (*Asentamiento Humano*), often on steep slopes that are almost uninhabitable [Oswald 2007].

Unequal Water Supply

However, due to the rapid population growth it is not only the city's development that is very heterogeneous, but also the development of the water and sanitation system. Currently only 82.8% [INEI 2011b] of the population is connected to the water supply system and about 1.5 million people live in Lima without drinking water. The situation is especially difficult for residents of border settlements, those areas that are "officially" regarded as uninhabited. Due to the steep slopes, it is extremely difficult to install a functioning water supply infrastructure. The residents of these areas therefore are usually served by public standpipes (*pilones*) or tanker trucks with water mainly from private suppliers. For this service, the residents of the slums often have to pay around ten times the official tap water price [Kehl et al. 2007]. The 671.6 million m^3 of drinking water is generated annually by the rivers Rímac, Chillón and groundwater sources [SEDAPAL 2009]. To regulate the strong groundwater extraction, major projects were implemented in the Andes to increase river runoff. These major projects include the nineteen reservoirs, which are intended to offset annual fluctuations, and the mega project Marca I, which supplies water to river Rímac through a tunnel and canal system from another catchment area [Kehl et al. 2007]. Although the municipal water company SEDAPAL (Servicio de Agua Potable y Alcantarillado de Lima) assures that the drinking water produced meets the World Health Organization (WHO) criteria for drinking water, NGOs dispute this. The water quality of the tanker trucks is usually worse because the trucks are not subject to state inspections, and thus the tankers containing the drinking water often are contaminated [Drehkopf 2012].

Poor Sanitation Standards

Aside from water, sanitation is not fully accessible to the entire population. Only 75% of Lima's population is connected to the sewage system [INEI 2007]. Nearly 2.2 million people need to dispose of their accumulated wastewater into latrines, into neighbourhoods' toilets, or untreated into the rivers. The discharge of untreated sewage leads to severe river contamination by sewage and organic matter. This pollution is exacerbated by the introduction of untreated, severely contaminated industrial wastewater and illegal discharges of untreated process water of the mining industry (upstream in the Andes). Furthermore, agriculture—which has settled in the upper river valleys—discharges large quantities of pesticides, fertilisers, and pesticides into the rivers as well.

Lack of Proper Wastewater Treatment

The whole City of Lima collects an average of 18 m^3/ s wastewater [SEDAPAL 2010]. However, only about 17% of sewage collected is cleaned, and the remaining 83% is released untreated into the rivers and finally into the Pacific Ocean. So far, the collected wastewater is treated in seventeen treatment plants [SEDAPAL 2009]. Wastewater lagoons form the majority of the cleaning equipment. Other cleaning methods, such as activated sludge processes, can rarely be found in the metropolitan area [Brussel et al. 2008]. However, most of these systems are overloaded with highly contaminated wastewater and cannot be used to their full cleaning power. In 2014, two new wastewater treatment plants with a total capacity of 20 m^3/s will be opened to clean 100% of the collected wastewater [Moscoso 2011]. However, unlike existing systems, the two new water treatment plants are only equipped with a primary cleaning stage.

Non-covering Tariff System and Impact of Climate Change

These problems are exacerbated by the non-covering tariff system in the water sector. The deduced price of water does not cover the resulting investment and maintenance costs for the water and wastewater system. Mechanical and apparent losses result in total network losses of almost 40% caused by the lack of maintenance of the distribution system and many illegal withdrawals [Alcázar et al. 2000].

Climate change is another factor that could exacerbate the already critical situation in Lima in the future. Different climate models have shown that the flow rate of the rivers in Lima will probably decrease in the future, especially from December to March [Loschko 2011]. Regarding the occurrence and effects of El Niño-Southern Oscillation (ENSO), no reliable statement can be made.

Methods: LiWatool as a Simulator for Lima's Entire Water and Wastewater System

To simulate Lima's entire water system on a macro level, an important tool has been newly developed by the ifak Institute Magdeburg. It is called LiWatool and is based on material flow analysis. The LiWatool can also be described as a macro-modelling simulator for the entire water system without detailed consideration. For a simulation of the water system, the tool has to be supplied with input parameters and data.

Fig. 1 (above) Temporary accommodation (Asentamiento Humano) [Lukas Born]

(middle) Treatment stages in a modern wastewater treatment plant in Mediouna, Morocco: (1) results of pretreatment, (2) tanks with primary and start of secondary stage, (3) installation of tertiary stage [Lukas Born]

(below) Water Treatment Plant in Lima, Carapongo [Ifak e.V.]

Identification of Driving Forces (Descriptors) Influencing Lima's Water System

The sustainable development of a city requires the sustainable management of its resources in order to ensure that the environment can be passed on to future generations in good condition [Belevi 2002]. To achieve this, an analysis of the environmental system, with its inherent problems and functions, must be conducted [Henseler et al. 1992]. To do so, the LiWa project has cooperated with ZIRN.[1] Both partners were able to identify thirteen descriptors. The descriptors are the main factors or driving forces that influence the development of Lima's water system by the year for which the scenario is developed, in this case by 2040 [LiWa 2012a]. The descriptors are:

A. Form of government
B. Corporate governance
C. Water tariffs
D. Demographics
E. Urban poverty
F. Water consumption
G. Network losses
H. Water resource management
I. Form of urban development
J. Coverage of water supply
K. Treatment and reuse of wastewater
L. Water resources
M. Climate (precipitation, risk, discharge)

Formulation of Five Scenarios Backed by Multiple Information Points

The combination of these descriptors led to the formulation of five consistent scenarios, by which Lima could develop in the future [LiWa 2012c]:

Scenario A: "Climate stress meets governance disaster" (worst case scenario: no improvement of the water system; the only changes to the current state are the treatment plants Taboada and La Chira; aggravated by climate stress; no support for improvement through the government; bad urban management)

Scenario B1: "Lone fighter catchment management" (increase of available amount of drinking water, but only through integrated river management; no cooperation between water authorities and the state's water company; water company is economically not working well; no government support; bad urban management)

Scenario B2: "Lone fighter private water company" (good, economically working private water company, but no cooperation with the river management; expansion of the wastewater treatment system; expansion of reuse of wastewater for irrigation; no government support; bad urban management)

Scenario C: "The opportunities of mesoscale actors" (a private water company is working economically well; increase of water infrastructure; increase of sewage treatment efficiency; but no government support; bad urban management)

Scenario D: "Climate resilience by governance" (good working government; good urban management; cooperation between water authorities and river management; water company is owned by the state and works economically well)

For each of these scenarios, time series for the mentioned individual descriptors A to M have been developed. These time series are the basis for the simulation with the LiWatool, which is based on a flow analysis of Lima's whole water system. Thus, a simulation using the LiWatool represents the main elements of the water system as:

- Water production
- Water supply
- Water consumption
- Wastewater discharges and treatment
- Water reuse

These main elements of the water system are linked and backed by additional elements, such as water and wastewater flows, pollutant fluxes, and energy fluxes [Schütze/ Robleto 2012; Schütze/ Robleto 2010]. Besides quantity, the quality of the water and energy fluxes are of further importance. In order to bring the economic side of the system to advantage, capital costs, operating costs, and tariffs set by SUNASS (Superintendencia Nacional de Servicios de Saneamiento) are incorporated within the model [Schütze et al. 2009]. The individual streams are described by algebraic equations.

Findings: Simulated Scenarios and Proposed Actions

Introduction

The first section of this chapter summarises different simulations that have been performed in the framework of this thesis. The goal of these different simulations was to find out how different solutions for Lima's water system can improve the situation in the future. But these approaches are just a small selection of possible solutions. These solutions and proposed actions are evaluated in the second section. The third section describes improvements of the LiWatool and applied methods.

The figures used in the following sections show how the water demand deviates in the future compared to the available amount of water. As a reference for the following scenarios of the first section, Figure 2 ↗ shows the future development of the demand compared to the availability of water for the current state of Lima's water system. The figure shows that demand will overrun the availability by the year 2021. It is important to mention at this point that improvements of the treatment plants Taboada and La Chira will be considered in every simulated scenario mentioned below, though the specific stages of these improvements differ in each scenario.

Simulated Scenarios

Simulation of the Sewage System with Projected Changes on the Plants of Taboada and La Chira

Lima's water authority, SEDAPAL, has invested a lot of time and money for the planning, development, and construction of the wastewater treatment plants Taboada and La Chira. Therefore, the following simulation [Figure 3 ↗] considers the effectiveness of these future project developments (Status 1). The basis for the simulation is also the time series for scenario A (climate stress meets governance disaster). The choice for this scenario was made

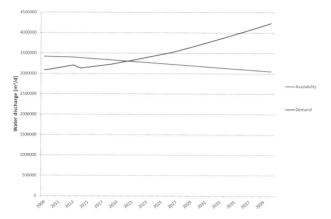

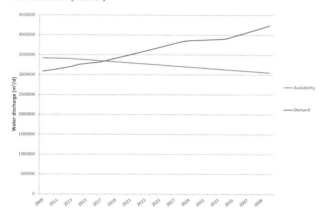

because only these measures are to be examined and therefore no other options for action are integrated. These are the preconditions: (1) the opening of the two treatment plants will—only for the use in LiWatool—be set at 2014; (2) the cleaning of the collected sewage is set at 100%; (3) the treatment of the collected sewage used here and in all future scenarios is, for simplicity, set to 100%, not 95%, as described in the scenarios essays of ZIRN.

The simulation shows that the use of treated wastewater in the year 2014 would increase from 31% to 80%. This is followed by a gradual increase until the year 2018. From this time onward, 100% of the treated wastewater from a secondary treatment stage can be used. Thus, the recycled water is then provided by the old treatment plants upgraded with secondary treatment stage at that time.

But the simulation also shows that a mere upgrade of La Taboada and La Chira does not improve the city's drinking water situation because the reuse of the then-treated water for irrigation and above all, the back-pumping to the respected green areas cannot be guaranteed. Here, a vicious circle starts: before the upgrade of the wastewater plants, untreated water was used for green space irrigation. If this wastewater is then pumped into the wastewater treatment plants, it cannot be used for irrigation anymore. Instead, this wastewater needs to be replaced by potable or river water, which will again increase the city's total water demand. Thus, the water demand would exceed the available water resources of Lima already in the year 2018.

Simulation of Lima's Sewage Disposal System with the Reuse of Treated Wastewater

The city has far too little green space per inhabitant. To increase the total green area, watering must be secured. An important step for this project is irrigation with treated wastewater. Irrigation with treated wastewater not only has ecological but also economic benefits. In order to reach the future goals of the WHO guidelines for the number of green areas per inhabitant, additional sewage treatment plants with a secondary, or even tertiary treatment stage should be constructed.

This simulation series is modelled with the time series for scenario B2 (lone fighter private water company). In order to increase the use of treated wastewater in this scenario, one of the two plants has to be expanded. With a complete extension of the La Chira wastewater treatment plant, over 38% of the collected sewage could be reused for irrigation. To achieve this, expanding the plant La Chira with an activated sludge method is suggested. An extension through ponds for a wastewater treatment plant of this size is too difficult to realise.

Figure 4 ↗ shows a very early exceedance of the availability of water resources by population demand. In order to counteract this exceedance, building a new sewage treatment plant with secondary treatment stage is proposed. The implementation of a new sewage-treatment plant is simulated in an additional run. Figure 5 ↗ shows the effect of the adjustment of the demand curve for scenario B2 (lone fighter private water company) with the expansion of La Chira and a new water treatment plant from 2028 onwards.

It should be explicitly stated that the construction of a new wastewater treatment plant in this case is a better solution than expanding the Taboada plant with a new cleaning stage. First, Taboada's location on the Pacific coast is unfavourable regarding the water reuse because the reuse of treated wastewater would incur high pumping costs. Second, from 2029 onwards, because capacity limit is reached for all treatment plants, increasing the capacity of the sewage treatment plant with a new one is advisable.

Simulation to Further Increase Drinking Water Sources

If the city of Lima fails to reuse treated wastewater or implement a change in consumption, growing water demand would have to be covered by an absolute increase in the amount of water. Cespedes [2012] has examined some possibilities for an increase in water amount in a report for SEDAPAL. Some of those projects to increase the discharge rate of the river Rímac include: the plant Huachipa and the projects Marca II and IV, the projects in the San Antonio reservoir, the reservoir Jacaybamba and the *Punrún Trasvase* (water tunnel) to the river Chillón. The following section examines which of the proposed measures should be implemented to meet the metropolitan region's water needs and how effective each measure would be.

The time series for this simulation is based on scenario B1 (lone fighter catchment management). The Taboada and La Chira wastewater treatment plants are considered in this case as well. However, since no other measures are being implemented towards the treatment and reuse of wastewater in this scenario, the reuse of secondary treated effluent remains at 31%.

Fig 4   Comparison Water Availability vs. Demand–*Scenario B2*: Lone fighter private water company [Author]

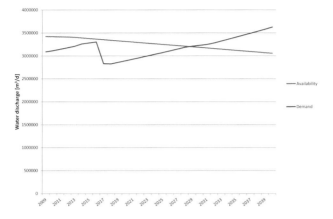

Fig. 5   Comparison Water Availability vs. Demand–*Scenario B2*: Lone fighter private water company + new waste-water treatment plant [Author]

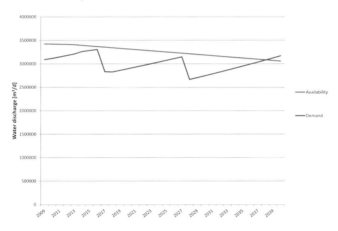

For these scenarios, it was always assumed that climate change will have a negative impact on the availability of drinking water. In this scenario, measures to increase water availability are simulated with and without the influence of climate change in order to illustrate the potential effect of climate change. When considering the scenario with the possible negative impact of climate change on the availability, for example by prolonged droughts, water availability will be reduced by a total amount of around 10% by 2040. Figure 6 ↗ shows the time course of availability and demand without climate change and Figure 7 ↗ shows the same plot taking climate change into account.

Integration of Various Measures in One Simulation

The simulations mentioned above are always limited to just one kind of measure. In order to show the potentials of an integrated water management, many different measures have been considered in one simulation. The basis of this simulation is the time series of scenario C (the opportunities of mesoscale actors). Its constituents are the following measures:

Fig. 6   Comparison Water Availability vs. Demand–*Scenario B1*: Without the influence of climate change [Author]

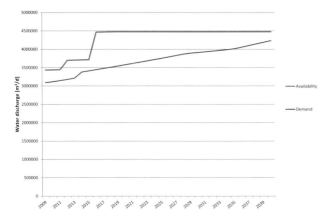

Fig. 7   Comparison Water Availability vs. Demand–*Scenario B1*: Lone fighter catchment management with the influence of climate change [Author]

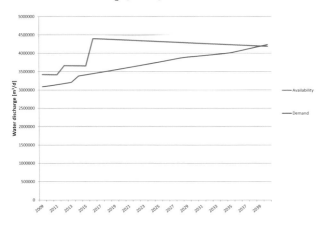

Fig. 8   Comparison Water Availability vs. *Demand–Scenario C*: The opportunities of mesoscale actors [Author]

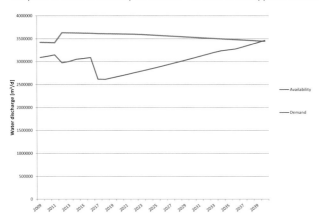

- Water-saving campaign in 2012 (reduction of overall water consumption by 10%)
- Increase of the capacity of the treatment plants by opening Huachipa I + II (increasing the capacity of the plant for the river Rímac to 25 m³/s (2012) and to 27.5 m³/s (2016))
- Increasing the amount of runoff available to river Rímac by 2.9 m³/s by Marca IV from 2012
- Increase the recycling of treated wastewater from 31% to 80% in 2014, further increases by 5% per year to the 100% mark in 2018
- Expanding the La Chira wastewater treatment plant with secondary treatment stage in 2017

Figure 8 ↗ shows the time variation of water availability and water demand in Lima between 2009 and 2040.

Critical Evaluation of Proposed Actions

General: Only an Integrated Water-management Plan Will Ensure Water Demand in 2040

Only the integrated combination of several measures will ensure water demand in 2040. Such an integrated water-management plan will increase the water availability and decrease the demand. This goal will not be achieved with the implementation of only isolated measures as shown in scenarios B1 or B2. The situation becomes even worse if no action is taken. Without further measures, water resources will be depleted by 2021, as shown in the simulation of scenario A in Figure 3 ↗.

Beside this more general conclusion, the following sections illustrate some more sectoral issues and further challenges that should be considered in planning a sustainable water household for Lima.

Development of More Green Areas

All of the solutions mentioned above assume a constant water demand for the irrigation of green areas. If the city wants to encourage the development of more green areas, this will lead to further water demand for irrigation as well. As the scenarios do not consider such a situation, other solutions to meet this additional water demand must be found.

Reconsidering the Location of Wastewater Treatment Plants

As already mentioned above, the Taboada and La Chira treatment facilities are in a rather unsuitable location to recycle reusable wastewater. Due to the direct location to the Pacific Ocean, the water must be pumped back into the city and to agricultural land, which requires a large amount of energy. With these high energy costs, the financial savings for the recycled water would again be neutralised. To avoid these costs and thus to use treated wastewater more efficiently, building sewage treatment plants closer to irrigated areas would be more suitable.

Water Quality

Water quality is an important issue. Regarding parameters like nitrogen or coliform bacteria, treatment plants with only a primary cleaning system do not perform as well as those with a secondary stage. There are no reliable input values for such parameters in the framework of the LiWatool. Therefore, it is not possible to come up with detailed comparison parameters in this thesis. Hence, future investigations will be necessary.

But there are other challenges regarding water quality: the biological oxygen demand (BOD_5) in the Pacific Ocean is of great importance for the sustainable water household of Lima as well. To keep this load at a satisfying level, the combination solution is the best and scenario B1 (lone fighter catchment management) is the worst option.

Measures to Keep Energy Costs Low

Although donor organisations can finance the high investment costs of water infrastructure, the country must continue to bear operating costs. And as energy costs rise, operating costs of the proposed measures rise as well. Such costs are a heavy burden for Peru at the moment. An analysis of the energy consumption of the entire water system and of proposed measures therefore is extremely important. With the help of LiWatool, the energy consumption of the individual components (derived from information from SEDAPAL [SEDAPAL 2009]) is calculated by multiplying a power factor by the amount of water processed. Therefore, the energy consumption for each scenario rises along with the growing population and its increasing water consumption. If water demand can no longer be covered, the energy consumption curve remains constant as no more water can be produced. The comparison of the energy consumption also shows that solutions with enhanced reuse and expanded wastewater treatment plants are the most energy-intensive.

Beyond the operating costs, the investment costs of individual measure also need to be compared. But for such comparisons, concrete details of the measures must be available. The calculation of the investment costs for wastewater treatment plants is especially complex and is strongly correlated to future location. A detailed calculation of all the investment costs of the proposed solutions is beyond the scope of this work.

The Integration of Mega-projects

A smooth implementation of major projects as water reservoirs or large wastewater treatment plants such as Marca II or IV require political will, a long process of planning and approval, and finally a huge investment of money and time before they start to function. The success of such mega-projects can only be guaranteed if agreements between the involved institutions on the rights and usage patterns are carefully negotiated. Such negotiations ought to take place as early as possible in the planning stage. This will prevent potential conflicts, for example between the energy and the water company. If such agreements were to succeed and new dams could be constructed, not only parts of the water problem could be solved, but the future energy demand of the region could be met as well.

Nevertheless, the construction of additional reservoirs will certainly have impact on the Andean ecosystem. A reservoir forms a barrier to fish migration and thus prevents spawning migrations and isolates individual fish populations.

Water-saving Campaigns and the Population's Participation

Additional measures such as water-saving campaigns can also lead to a decrease in water consumption. Although the implementation of such campaigns do not need a long time, they depend on political influences and can be cost-effective, thus needing proper preparation. The population itself carries an enormous stake in the success of such measures. Only when social groups with a large demand of water undergo a change in attitude and consume less water in the future, will water-saving campaigns have the desired success.

Regarding the poor segments of society, further water saving will not be possible. Already today, they realise how valuable water is and therefore consume very little. There is no more saving potential. Furthermore, even if they would save water, it wouldn't have a significant effect on the city's total consumption due to their small share of it.

Necessary Improvements of the LiWatool and Applied Methods[2]

Examining all important dimensions of Lima's water systems is beyond the scope of this work. Thus, the following section gives an idea how the LiWatool and simulation runs can be improved for future projects and some remaining questions and research topics are presented. The following are of interest:
- further examination of the quality of the treated wastewater under consideration of other factors such as coliform bacteria, nitrogen deposition, or BOD_5 load,
- improving the comparison of the different measures,
- deepening the knowledge on energy consumption,
- checking the impact of further combinations of measure as leakage reduction, water saving campaigns, or changed water prices if adjusted to the real water demand of the region,
- simulating shorter time steps (for example, monthly steps) in order to examine annual variations associated with glacial melt.
- checking the potentials, effectiveness, and risks of seawater desalination for Lima,
- extending the LiWatool to a more detailed level (e.g., district level). This may be of further interest as the results of this simulation are qualitative but not quantitative. In addition, more detailed investigations are necessary as water management measures are generally non-transferable and should be adapted to local conditions. With a more detailed model the following questions can be examined: (1) what are the preconditions for a more decentralised system for wastewater collection and treatment; (2) which districts of the city are more suitable for a decentralised sanitation, which ones for a central sewage system; (3) what is the cleaning performance of different cleaning systems.
- further elaboration of LiWatool's capacity to simulate the capacities of wastewater treatment plants if they do not run at full load. The model of the LiWatool, applied for this research, is only capable of simulating wastewater treatment plants operated at full load.
- further assessment of water dams and reservoirs with their impacts to the Andean region, to the water system of the whole city, and to the energy balance of Lima's water system. These questions are already being scrutinised in a further research carried out in conjunction with the LiWa project.
- simulating whether it is possible to sustain a stable and resilient water system with less resource-intensive projects as the mentioned mega-projects.

Conclusion and Outlook

This paper was used in the context of the LiWa project to illustrate the challenges of the current situation and to show possible and necessary contributions of different institutions on a path to avoid water scarcity for future generations of greater Lima. Furthermore, this research project was also important for the improvement of LiWatool itself.

This paper shows that the Lima metropolitan area has a very complicated water system with many factors influencing each other. Furthermore, the problem cannot be solved with one measure alone. Even if the city's future water demand could be solved by implementing isolated measures either with consequences for the whole city or only for isolated districts, considering the entire water system is recommended. Individual measures have different effects on individual districts. Therefore, it requires strong political will, not only to increase the water supply, but also to allow the poorer parts of the city to participate in such an increase. A simple increase in water supply would not solve the lagging water infrastructure in poorer neighbourhoods. Furthermore, it is important not only to increase the availability of water, but also the quality of the life of the inhabitants of Lima. That is why the lack of urban green space should also be considered when changing the water system.

Additionally, it should be explicitly mentioned that the simulations are carried out under the time series created by ZIRN in collaboration with the project partners of the LiWa project. As actual developments of the metropolis and changing climatic conditions cannot be predicted with certainty, the simulations with the LiWatool also have certain limitations. But nevertheless, scenario D mentioned above (climate resilience by governance) is at least one scenario considering climate change in a full range of other possible scenarios. Depending on further data availability regarding these issues, LiWatool could be a substantial support for the Government of Peru, the city of Lima, and the utility SEDAPAL to simulate other scenarios in order to tackle a wide range of possible events with the best possible solutions. Nevertheless, the development of possible solutions and measures should not be limited to the Lima metropolitan area, but should include other cities and the rural areas of Peru as well. An exclusive focus on Lima can foster centralisation tendencies and can support further migration to the metropolitan region.

The example of industrialised countries such as Germany shows that the development of a functioning water system and the improvement of water quality need time. However, time is a very critical factor in Lima. The pressure of climate change and the city's rapidly increasing population call for rapid action to adjust the water system to these developments. Therefore, all stakeholders should work together on an integrated solution assuring a sustainable water household with sufficient water availability for future generations and for a liveable city.

References

Alcázar, L./ Xu, L. C./ Zuluaga, A. M. (2000): *Institutions, Politics and Contracts—The Attempt to Privatize the Water and Sanitation Utility of Lima, Peru*. Policy Research Working Paper—The World Bank Development Research Group

Belevi, H. (2002): "Material flow analysis as a strategic planning tool for regional waste water and solid waste management". In: *GTZ&-BMZ&-ATV-DVWK workshop Globale Zukunft: Kreislaufwirtschaftskonzepte im kommunalen Abwaser- und Fäkalienmanagement*. 12. Europäisches Wasser-, Abwaser und Abfall-Symposium

Brussel, M./ Morales, J./ Sijmons, K./ Knippers, R./Feringa, W./ Turkstra, J./ Meijere, J./ Krol, B./ Westen, C. V./ Rossiter, D./ Strobl, R. / Sijmons, K. (2008): *Atlas Ambiental de Lima*, Lima

Cespedes J. (2012): "Plan maestro para Lima y Callao 2012-2040". (Unpublished) Recursos Hídricos, Interne Präsentation, LiWa-Projekttreffen Stuttgart, 22.05.12

Drehkopf, T.(2012): *Wasserver- und Abwasserentsorgung in Lima—Simulative Auswertung von Zukunftsszenarien*. Diplomarbeit. Hochschule Coburg für angewandte Wissenschaften

Henseler, G./ Scheidegger, R. / Brunner, P. H.: "Die Bestimmung von Stoffflüssen im Wasserhaushalt einer Region". In: *Vom Wasser*, 78, pp. 91–116

[INEI] Instituto Nacional de Estadistica e Informatica (2007): Censos Nacionales 2007: XI de Población y VI de Vivienda: Perfil Sociodemográfico de la Provincia de Lima

[INEI] Instituto Nacional de Estadistica e Informatica (2011): *Perú: Anuario de Estadísticas Ambientales 2011*. Lima

Kehl, O./ Wichern, M./ Schuetze, M./ Alex, J./ Paris, S./ Gregarek, D./ Leon, C./ Horn, H. (2007): *Entwicklung angepasster Wassertechnologien für Megastädte am Beispiel Lima Metropolitana*. Version: Februar 2007. http://www.lima-water.de/documents/kehletal_dwa2007.pdf, 07.05.2012.

LiWa (2012a): *Deskriptorenessays*. Interner Report, Januar 2012

LiWa (2012b): *Storylines "Lima 2040"* Version 1.1/ ZIRN. Interner Report, Januar 2012

Loschko, M. (2011): *Wasserversorgung in Lima - Heutige Situation und zukünftiges Niederschlagsdargebot der Region*. Diplomarbeit. Universität Stuttgart

Moscoso, J. C. (2011): *Estudio de Opciones de Tratamiento y Reuso de Aguas Residuales en Lima Metropolitana*. Lima

Oswald, P. (2007): *Ecosan—Eine nachhaltige Lösung für die Sanitärprobleme der Marginalsiedlungen Limas (Peru)?* Diplomarbeit. Technische Universität Dresden. http://www.lima-water.de/documents/poswald_tesis.pdf

Schütze, M./ Robleto, G. (2010): *Challenges of water and wastewater management in the desert megacity of Lima/ Peru - how can macromodelling help?* In: NOVATECH Proceedings (2010), *7th International Conference on Sustainable Techniques and Strategies in Urban Water Management*; Lyon; 28.06-01.07.2010.http://www.lima-water.de/documents/schuetzerobleto_novatech2010.pdf, 07.05.2012

Schütze, M./ Robleto, G. (2012): *Macromodelling. Version: 2012*. http://www.lima-water.de/en/pp3.html, 13.07.2012

Schütze, M./ Robleto, G./ Alex, J. (2009): "Macromodelling as a tool for water management in a megacity". In: *International Conference Megacities Leipzig: Risk, Vulnerability and Sustainable development*

[SEDAPAL] Servicio de Agua Potable y Alcantarillado de Lima (2009): *Memoria Anual 2009*. Lima

[SEDAPAL] Servicio de Agua Potable y Alcantarillado de Lima (2010): *Anuario Estadístico 2010*. Lima

Notes

1 ZIRN stands for "Interdisciplinary Research Unit on Risk Governance and Sustainable Technology Development of Stuttgart University" (www.zirn-info.de)

2 The LiWatool simulator has been further developed after the accomplishment of this diploma thesis. For more information see: Schütze, M.; Alex, J. (2014): A simulator for model-based participatory integrated urban water management; 13th International Conference on Urban Drainage, Surawak, Malaysia, 7-12 September 2014

Zarela Garcia Trujillo
Master's Thesis at National University of Engineering, Lima, Faculty of Environmental Engineering

Comparison and Evaluation of Three Aquatic Plants for Determining the Efficiency of Nutrient Removal in Domestic Wastewater Treatment

Abstract

Treatment systems with aquatic plants are efficient and less expensive alternatives to the treatment of wastewater in conventional wastewater treatment plants. They may also be suitable alternatives due to their ability to absorb organic substances by removing biodegradable and non-biodegradable microorganisms, as well as nutrients, metals, and pathogens.

The removal by aquatic plants (macrophyte systems) is attributed to sedimentation processes, absorption, and removal of suspended solids and organic matter. This research project presents a comparative study of the purification capacity of nutrients in wastewater by three floating aquatic plants: Azolla filiculoides, Eichhornia crassipes and Lemna Minor. These three plants have photosynthesising parts on the water surface and roots spreading down to the bottom of the water column. The purification performance of these aquatic plants was analysed in small ponds with wastewater in order to assess the applicability under certain criteria of such a system to a larger scale for water-treatment plants in Peru.

Before starting this research in Peru, an evaluation of the purification capacity of Azolla filiculoides was conducted in a treatment plant in Suderburg (Germany). These assessments were held from July to November 2009 using two systems: the first was a single tank system, the second a "continuous flow" system that consisted of three ponds of 30.2 dm^2 each. The next research step, implemented from February to June 2010, consisted of experiments with Lemna Minor and Eichhornia crassipes in the CITRAR treatment plant in Lima (Peru). CITRAR (Research Center on Wastewater Treatment) is an institute of Lima's National University of Engineering specialising in wastewater treatment. The aim was to analyse the capacity of these aquatic plants to improve the quality of the effluent. As in Germany, a single "batch" system of 36.0 dm^2 in the first phase and an additional control pond without plants were used. The second phase of this research was conducted in tanks filled with effluents. Enriched with aquatic plants (Lemna M. and Eichhornia C.), these effluents slowly flowed through shallow water levels. These continuous-flow systems were composed of three ponds using an additional filtering system before the experiment.

The primary objective of this work was to assess whether aquatic plants in decentralised water-treatment systems remove nutrients from wastewater, and to observe whether such plants could be used for conventional and more centrally organised wastewater treatment. As a result, this research has shown that up to 90% of the nutrients could be removed. Second, it was possible to determine that Eichhornia crassipes is the best plant for domestic water treatment.

Fig. 1   Continuous system for determining nutrient removal in Suderburg (Germany), 2009 [Author]

Fig. 2   With only 9 mm rainfall per year in Lima, water reuse is crucial [Lukas Born]

PLANNING AND ARCHITECTURE

Ngoc-Anh Nguyen

Master's Thesis at Brandenburg University of Technology-Cottbus, Faculty of Environmental Sciences and Process Engineering

Integration of Environmental Components and Urban Climate Management in Land-use Planning in Ho Chi Minh City, Vietnam

Abstract

Ho Chi Minh City, the largest city in Vietnam and an emerging megacity of Southeast Asia, is now experiencing a high demand for land due to residential development, transportation, and economic growth. The rapid urbanisation and dense population growth in the past twenty years have significantly affected the city's land use, and have had adverse effects on urban flooding, urban climate, and its vulnerability to climate change. Land-use planning, at the same time, is a key measure for adjusting and helping the city to adapt to the environmental consequences and climate change impacts through the integration of environmental components and urban climate management. The study included a literature review for the situation analysis, followed by in-depth, semi-structured interviews with the Ho Chi Minh City authorities to understand the challenges and potential for such integration. The results showed that planning authorities are facing challenges in incorporating environmental considerations due to a barrier of legislation, enforcement regime, and an absence of an integrated framework. The study also pointed out three relevant proposals that would support efforts, including environmental and climate issues in land-use planning: (1) a strong integrated framework regime for climate change strategies, with collaboration among authorities and planners with appropriate policies, management systems and norms; (2) the effective implementation of strategic environmental assessment for land-use planning; and (3) land-use zoning. While the framework regime and strategic environmental assessment require nationwide policy and enforcement as well as methodological tools, land-use zoning needs more careful management adjustment for acceptance and adoption at the city and local levels.

Introduction: HCMC between Rapid Growth and Vulnerability

Focus of Research

The general objectives of this research study are to analyse the existing urban planning system, statutory planning at different administrative levels for Ho Chi Minh City, and to examine the need for integrating environmental and climate considerations into land-use planning.

In order to understand the need of such integration, three aspects for review were identified: vulnerability to climate change, urban flooding with urban growth, and urban climate. Finally, the study aimed to identify the perspectives and readiness of local authorities to implement environmental and climate issues into land-use planning of HCMC through discussion on strengths and weaknesses, legislation support, institutional sectors, and tools availability.

HCMC's Enormous City Growth

Based on the 2009 population and housing census, Vietnam has a relatively low level of urbanisation—approximately 30%—when compared with other Southeast Asian countries. Urban growth in Vietnam is concentrated mostly in large urban centres, which are the two primary cities: Ha Noi and Ho Chi Minh City [UNFPA 2010]. Ho Chi Minh City (HCMC), which covers an area of 2,095 km² in Southeast Vietnam, is estimated to have close to ten million inhabitants. HCMC has experienced steady urban growth over the past twenty years since the Economic Reform (DoiMoi) in 1986, and the population of the city includes 7.5 million as of 2011 and more than two million unregistered and seasonal migrants [GSO 2011]. Ho Chi Minh City is now an emerging megacity in Southeast Asia, with the ambition of strong economic growth in the region. One of the challenges for the city is the high pressure for land consumption due to residential development, economic growth, and transportation. In order to accomplish these, there is an urgent need for policy measures and management approaches for a sustainable land-use plan and development.

In another aspect, like other large cities in Southeast Asia—especially those that are low lying and located in tropical coastal zones—HCMC has the highest vulnerability and experiences the highest impacts of climate change. The ongoing, dramatic urbanisation and population growth have made HCMC even more vulnerable. Thus, the considerations of the environment and climate for land-use planning aims for more than just raising awareness, but also for real policy measures and implementing actions.

It is expected that planning authorities will face challenges in incorporating environmental concerns into planning to reduce risks and impacts to the city in the era of rapid urbanisation and climate change. For HCMC's land-use planning, integrating environmental components and urban climate management are important to improve decision-making. This integration also provides important indicators for assessing urban land-use planning and developments. The recognition and perception of local authorities play an important role in implementing these concepts and practices for better and more sustainable land-use planning.

Urban Flooding and Urban Development

Since the nineteen-nineties, floods have occurred with increasing frequency, and urban flooding in HCMC is now one of the biggest concerns for urban planners and authorities [Ho 2008b]. First, urban flooding occurs in Ho Chi Minh City because the city is located on the precarious banks of the Sai Gon River and in the estuarial area of Dong Nai River system; 72% of this total area has ground elevations ranging from 1 to 2 m above sea level [Storch et al. 2011]. The flooding of the city is associated with monthly high tides, when the maximum high tide affected by the East Sea tide fluctuates around 1.5 m. Second, this semidiurnal tide, peaking coincidently with the heavy rain fall season, makes urban flooding for HCMC more serious during September and October [Labaeye et al. 2011].

Fig. 1 Changes in areas (ha) of selected land-use types from 1997 to 2006 [Ho Chi Minh City's Master Plan up to 2025]

Types	Actual in 1997	Actual 2006	2006 vs 1997	LUP 2025	2025 vs 2006
	Area (ha)	Area (ha)	Difference	Area (ha)	Difference
Residential land	20,464.28	33,743.03	13,278.75	66,433.46	32,690.43
Industrial land	2,988	9,657.70	6,669.70	12,455.78	2,798.08
Agricultural land	133,815.00	123,297.80	-10,517.20	83,709.80	-39,588.00
Surface water	35,672.00	34,833.82	-838.18	32,122.73	-2,711.09
Channels, lakes	2,250.00	843.00	-1,407.00	1,506.78	663.78

According to many scientific studies and reviews, urban flooding in Ho Chi Minh City is not yet the consequence of climate change or sea level rise, but rather merely the rapid urban development of the city [Ho 2008a; Luu 2012; Ngan 2012]. Since 1989, under the pressure of economic development and increasing population, HCMC has expanded by infilling of open spaces and redevelopment of existing buildings. The issue of most concern is "the rapid expansion into lower-lying and former wetland surroundings, primarily at the expense of urban greenscape and valuable multifunctional natural areas" [Labaeye et al. 2011]. It is estimated that the capacity of water retention of lakes, ponds, and wetland areas in the city has reduced approximately ten times between 2002 and 2009 [Luu 2012]. The increasing imperviousness of the city results in a series of problems, including: the reduced capacity of natural storage, retention, and recycling of precipitation; significant increases in surface runoff which over-handled by the drainage system; decreases in groundwater recharge, which then causes the land subsidence. Therefore, the urbanisation process is considered one of the strongest factors leading to urban flooding risk and exposure of Ho Chi Minh City.

From the master plan for 2025, agricultural land will be reduced from 123,000 ha in 2006 to 83,700 ha in 2025—a loss of approximately 40,000 ha—and similarly, approximately 3,000 ha of surface water will be lost [Figure 2 ↗]. With advanced construction technology, new development can be elevated up to 2.5 m above mean sea level (required by regulations), however, new settlement development in wetlands and the lowlands will dramatically decrease the valuable natural multifunction areas, especially the city's capacity to cope with frequent flooding events [Labaeye et al. 2011]. The current solutions—primarily engineering technical and not integrated—to tackle urban flooding have been criticised. There is definitely an urgent need for additional measures like strategic urban land-use planning, which can be a more economic and effective soft measure [Ho 2008b; Luu 2012].

HCMC's Vulnerability to Climate Change and Sea-level Rise

HCMC's urban area, which is built on flat and low-lying land, has been historically sensitive to climate effects. Currently, 72% of the entire densely populated urban area of HCMC lies on a mean sea level of 2 m or less [Storch et al. 2011]. The situation is even more dramatic in the southern part of the city—Can Gio, Nha Be, and District 7—where almost the entire area (98.8%) is in this difficult topographical situation. Here, the city is also expanding and thus is even more vulnerable to climate change. Generally, HCMC is flood prone, given its low-lying location, tropical climate, and high-tide effects. Thus, with the added impact of climate change, a sea level rise will cause unequivocally significant impacts on the city. In 2009, the Ministry of Environmental and Natural Resources published a report, *Climate Change, Sea Level Rise Scenarios for Vietnam*. In a high-emission scenario, sea level rises (SLR) are projected to be up to 33 cm in 2050 and 100 cm in 2100, and correspondingly, 23% of Ho Chi Minh City will be flooded in the 100-cm scenario [MONRE 2009]. A report from the Asian Development Bank states that the impact of extreme and regular climate and hydrodynamic conditions in 2050 could be extensive and far reaching in its effects on the city's economy [ADB 2010].

Methods: Qualitative Interviews and Literature Review

The literature analysis reviews and describes existing information and available studies related to the research topic. The paper explores the situation of land-use planning in HCMC, and then examines the current situation in terms of the risk and vulnerability of land-use planning in the context of rapid urbanisation and climate change, focusing on urban flooding. This content analysis thus emphasises the need for integrating environmental and climate issues for HCMC for better planning and decision-making.

Qualitative fieldwork, using common qualitative research techniques—including semi-structured and in-depth interviewing—provides the opportunity to build on knowledge from the literature analysis, by developing a series of broad questions put to stakeholders. The selected agencies and institutions are responsible for and related to HCMC's urban land-use planning. The study includes interviews of officers from the Department of Natural Resources and Environment (DONRE), the Department of Planning and Architecture (DPA), and the Southern Sub-Institute for Urban Rural Planning (SIUP). This series of interviews took place over a two-week period.

Findings: Challenges and Opportunities for the Integration of Environmental Components and Urban Climate Management in HCMC's Land-use Planning

In the first section of this chapter, the major challenges in integrating environmental components and urban climate management into HCMC's land-use planning will be presented. The second part focuses on tools for this urgently needed integration and on the opportunities for Ho Chi Minh City's future urban development if this goal is to be reached.

Challenges

HCMC's Land-use Planning within the Context of Other Spatial Plans

Land-use planning is the system of economic, technical, and political government measures for the most adequate, scientific, rational, and effective planning and management through allocation and management of land resources. One of the objectives of land-use planning is, on the one hand, to allocate land to foster socio-economic strategies identified in the *Vietnam Socio-economic Development Plan* [Ministry of Natural Resources and Environment 2004].

Fig. 2 Coordination chart for urban planning and land-use plan [Do and Tran 2011; Luu 2011]

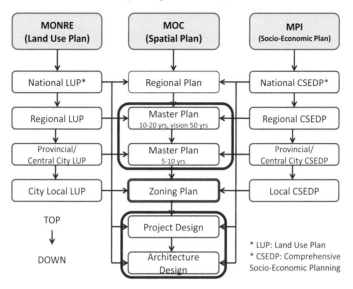

On the other hand, the land-use plan should also restrict land-use consumption. Reconciling these contradictory objectives is one of the challenging tasks of land-use planning. For local governments and spatial planning systems, there are three different planning systems relating to and influencing the land-use plan: the *Vietnam Socio-economic Development Plan* (Ministry of Planning and Investment-MPI), the *Spatial Plan* (Ministry of Construction-MOC), and *Land-use Plan* (as a sector plan, by Ministry of Natural Resources and Environment-MONRE). These plans are developed and controlled at different levels of local government management. Hence, the land-use plan for Ho Chi Minh City is affected by these three types of plans, which are practiced horizontally, as shown in Figure 1 ↗.

Too Little Emphasis on Climate Change in Land-use Plans

For the general discussion about the current situation and possibility of integrating environmental parameters in land-use planning, HCMC's current land-use plan is usually criticised for being too affected by socio-economic strategies in order to enhance the city's economic opportunities. As stated in regulations, spatial plans should first follow the directions and orientation laid out in the general socio-economic development plans, and secondly also follow the more concrete sector plans by transferring the then-defined goals into spatial implementation [Ministry of Natural Resources and Environment 2004]. The consideration of environmental protection and natural conservation of land resources are normally neglected. Most of the informants expressed that with the threat of environmental consequences and climate change impacts, the consideration for environment and urban climate in urban planning becomes increasingly relevant—not only for raising awareness amongst responsible authorities and planners, but also for the development of actions and adaptive responses.

Fig. 3 Summary of key legislative instruments and documents supporting the integration of environmental and climate-related in land-use planning [Vietlaw Database http://www.vietlaw.gov.vn/LAWNET]

Legislation No. and Date	Name of Legislation
No. 16/2003/QH11 26 November 2003	Law on Construction
No. 52/2005/QH11 29 November 2005	Law on Environmental Protection
No. 32/2009/QH12 17 June 2009	Law on Urban Planning
Decision No. 445/QD-TTg 07 April 2009	Revising the Vision of General Planning for Vietnam Urban Development up to 2025, vision to 2050
Decision No. 158/2008/QD-TTg 02 December 2008	Decision on Approval of the National Target Program to response to climate change
NTP-RCC 2008 27 July 2008 (Draft)	The National Target Program to Respond to Climate Change
Approved 14 December 2011 Launched 07 March 2011	The National Strategy for Natural Disaster Prevention, Response and Mitigation to 2020
2008	Vietnam General Technical Guidance on the Application of Strategic Environmental Assessment
Ministry of Construction, 2011	Technical Guidelines for Strategic Environmental Assessment (SEA) of Construction and Urban Planning
Circular No.01/2011/TT-BXD 27 January 2011 In effect 15 March 2011	Guiding the strategic environmental assessment in construction and urban plans
Decision 1547/QD-TTg 28 October 2008	The Irrigation Plan for Flood Control for the HCMC Area up to 2025
QD 936/QĐ-UBND 25 February 2012	Detailed Planning to Implement Flood Mitigation Program 2011–2015 for HCMC

Challenges in Policy and Legal Framework

Existing laws as a means to influence land-use planning: The legal foundation is the underpinning for encouraging and implementing the integration of environmental and climate protection into spatial planning. Hence, including environmental and climate issues into land-use planning could be accomplished through existing legislation that regulates the requirement of environmental protection in urban activities. Figure 3 ↗ summarises a number of existing decisions and plans with the theme of climate change and natural disaster prevention, response and mitigation, and the theme of urban flood control. These existing laws and strategies could be utilised to seriously influence land-use planning.

New laws: Not only should existing laws be obeyed, but in the case of Vietnam, new ones need to be established. Therefore, most of the respondents from DONRE and DPA expressed their positive attitude toward the government's efforts to establish new legislative instruments or legal tools to guide environmentally sustainable urban planning. Additionally, government representatives also confirmed that huge efforts are already now being made to base current plans on new policies that consider more environmental issues.

Missing information and instruction on new laws: Although impressed by updated legislative efforts, they expressed concerns about the effectiveness and enforcement of these policies. In particular, they are not yet clearly instructed by the government, and there is still a degree of reluctance as to how to handle new requirements. To overcome this unsatisfying situation, strategic support and capacity development of planning authorities is needed.

Weighing different interests: Another challenge for the integration of environmental parameters into land-use planning is the pressure from policies that support social and economic development strategies. According to an informant from the Division of Land-Use Planning, DONRE, "the consideration of environment into land-use planning seems to be difficult for many urban planners, as they set strong priorities on residential and industrial development". Although legislation supporting the consideration for environment and climate change does exist, contradictions still clearly exist and are challenging.

Thus, the study identified that land-use planning and environmental issues are currently reflected in the Vietnamese legislation system, and changes of legal instruments related to land-use planning are needed, including new regulations and the amendment of old ones. However, further efforts are still strongly required. They need to tackle the mechanism framework and create suitable tools for effective implementation and enforcement.

Challenges in Procedures, Policy and Management Frameworks, and Coordination

One requirement but two plans of two authorities: The first impression from the informants is that institutional fragmentation is one of the major constraints of the current land-use planning system in Ho Chi Minh City. The representative from the *Division of General Planning Management* expressed that, "the job of HCMC land-use planning seems to be conducted twofold by both MOC and DONRE". It is clearly acknowledged that there are conflicts and pressures between plans prepared by different government agencies due to differences in goals, interests, objectives, ambitions, approaches, and responsibilities. Most of the informants noted that there is lack of coordination, lack of a common base of information, lack of integrated multisector strategies, and confusion during implementation. For this reason, feedback from stakeholders emphasised that these shortcomings are the strongest barrier to integrating environmental issues into land-use planning.

Information gaps and non-correlating data: According to a stakeholder from the *Division of Research and Planning*, SIUP, "the land-use planning in HCMC ... is relatively messy in contrast to many other plans such as regional plan, city master plan, and sector plan". Additional feedback provided by DONRE officers revealed that barriers also occur within the vertical management system for land-use planning. For applying the land-use plan, the general plan included only broad guidance on where developments should be encouraged and enforced. Thus, the general plan lacked specifics on permissible land-use criteria.

Lack of capacities: The implementation and application of the plan is weak due to a lack of technical staff in key and management agencies. DPA's respondents highlighted that the level of specialised and professional knowledge are very uneven among different agencies, and within different departments within one agency. However, according to interviews with representatives from DPA, DONRE, and SIUP, most correspondents agreed that Vietnam has improved significantly in terms of human resource capacity in the planning field, to the extent of adopting new technology, practices from regional and international experiences.

Missing cooperation among different municipalities: The implementation and application of the plan also faces difficulties due to insufficient coordination of policies between districts and city governments. One of the reasons for this is the rather recent introduction of the *Law on Urban Planning* in 2009.

Land-use plan versus city master plan: As DONRE is responsible for the new land-use plan of HCMC for the fifteen-year period 2010–2025, there is the pressing need to adopt and follow the revised city master plan, which the Prime Minister approved in 2010 [Prime Minister of Vietnam 2010]. The informant from DONRE expressed concerns about the conflicts among these plans due to "the land-use need of different sectors or departments, pressure for land-use conversion, which are mostly planned or required in other previous plans". In order to improve this situation, DONRE will form a committee to prepare and review the land-use plan. This committee includes a variety of department agencies, such as the Department of Natural Resources and Environment, the Department of Construction, the Department of Transportation and Public Works, the Department of Agriculture and Rural Development, consultant agencies, and NGOs. Comprehensive understanding and communication among agencies should be achieved in order to:

- identify inappropriate or irrational issues in the existing land-use plan of the city master plan;
- adjust and fix both plans;
- identify zoning areas that have conflicts and need more research and consideration;
- develop a road map for research; and
- attain an appropriate development process.

The environmental issue as a vehicle to adjust and align different planning processes and levels: The urgent need to tackle climate-change issues produces not only problems but contains a potential as well—by including climate issues in development or land-use planning, the problematic fragmentation of institutions could be overcome as well. Of great help in that respect could be the *Vietnam National Target Program to Response to Climate Change* [Prime Minister of Vietnam 2008]. This national programme will support the improvement of staff capacities or the building of organisations and institutions dealing with policy issues on climate change. And this also would be a major boost for the issue discussed.

The implementation of the detailed *Flood Mitigation Program 2011–2015 for HCMC* could be utilised for the same purpose [Peoples Committee of HCMC 2012]. It can provide the basis for tackling missing connections and fragmentations referring to the institutional coordination. This requires a strong effort in developing documents, instructions, action plans, as well as establishing and consolidating the management and organisation systems of the programme.

Opportunities and Tools for the Integration of Environmental Components in Land-use Planning

The following sections will describe three relevant aspects that could support the inclusion of environmental and climate issues in land-use planning. The first option is to strengthen the new approach on land-use zoning, the second to introduce *Strategic Environmental Assessment* (SEA) as a new tool, and the third to build and develop capacities among the responsible planning authorities.

New Planning Instrument: Replacement of District Land-use Plans with Land-use Zoning

According to the conventional management structure for land-use and urban planning in Vietnam, the second level of planning and management, under the city level, is the district level. District land-use plans are applied within the district administrative management which can be an advantage in terms of management, corresponding to the precedent administrative framework and legislation system. However, district land-use plans are criticised for being inflexible, as urban development is multiconnected, always variable, and can reach far beyond administrative boundaries [Nguyen 2012].

Therefore, and as a pilot project, these district land-use plans are to be replaced with new land-use zoning. According to the *Law on Urban Planning* [National Assembly 2009], land-use zoning is made for areas within cities, towns, and new urban areas [Article 18]. Respondents from DPA and SIUP were very supportive of land-use zoning as an advanced approach that allows the combination of equality, economy, and environment. It not only provides opportunities for flexibility and rationality, but also includes more parameters for decision-making—such as geographical conditions, landscape and water integration, as well as equitable distribution of environmental resources. Therefore, this replacement shows that Vietnam is now approaching regional and international standards of urban practices, urban planning, and urban management [Quang 2012].

Representatives from DONRE, DPA, and SIUP provided many opinions and discussions regarding (1) the district land-use plan; (2) the zoning plan; and (3) the potential for implementing land-use zoning for the better integration of urban environment and climate parameters. There is a significant level of uncertainty as to whether the new land-use zoning can be carried out effectively, and about the fact that HCMC now has too many types of urban planning, namely: master plan, district plan, sector plans, et cetera. Authorities from DONRE are cautious, because after the revision of the master plan of HCMC was approved in late 2011, most of the districts promptly developed their land-use plans. In addition, these district plans are very limited in the environmental integration or assessment requirements. Therefore, authorities expressed deep concern that the consultancy, approval process, and procedure for urban developments would become even more complex and perpetual (e.g., new legislation, instructions and policies for technical standards and norms).

Several zoning plan projects have already been carried out in HCMC, with support from international expertise and experience. However, it is not advisable to apply land-use zoning to the whole area of HCMC in a targeted period of time. The resulting time pressure for completion, given the available resources and capabilities, can easily lead to mistakes that can be very costly and ineffective. In fact, pilot zoning plans need to be monitored in the process of establishing them, and evaluated in their results. Open feedback can then support the current development of district and detailed plans.

New Tool: Strategic Environmental Assessment (SEA)

Strategic Environmental Assessment (SEA) is a new multicriteria assessment for implementing environmental targets into strategic urban plan. Through SEA, a land-use plan can be achieved, escaping from the conventional thinking and assessment, which only focuses on the cost-benefit of the land value, and/or land conversion related to market money or development/economic growth. When asked whether or not SEA can support HCMC's land-use planning process with better environmental consideration, representatives from DONRE expressed a positive outlook: findings and recommendations from SEA can improve the land-use plan, and with its help DONRE will be more confident with their plan.

Sharing a similarly optimistic view, an informant from DPA highlighted that SEA will lead to a better quality of land-use plans by contributing scientific arguments into the planning process. Furthermore, when SEA is carried out effectively and started parallel to the planning process from the very beginning, it can help to adjust and improve the plan by considering environmental issues.

Additionally, it was mentioned that there are difficulties for authority agencies in proceeding or implementing SEA, as the related legal framework for SEA in Vietnam is still limited and incomplete. An officer from DPA, who is the only one trained and in charge of SEA for DPA, said: "Vietnam can adopt SEA practices and tools quickly through international training and experience sharing, however, the consistent legal framework and instructions are missing or not yet instructed toward authorities agencies comprehensively, causing lots of reluctance, confusion, delay, or even elusion". Moreover, she also expressed that the limited availability and accessibility of data/information is also a barrier for SEA practices. Nevertheless, all interviewed stakeholders strongly believed that SEA will become more respected and powerful by supporting the planning processes for Vietnam, and in particular for HCMC.

Capacity Development and Technology Transfer

As mentioned above, capacities within Vietnamese planning authorities have significantly improved. Nevertheless, they are a long way from reaching the necessary level of qualification and knowledge. Before this goal is fully reached, help from foreign agencies can temporarily bridge the remaining gap. An example of such a case was given in an interview with DONRE: the land-use plan of Ho Chi Minh City will be prepared by a consultant company through a comprehensive bidding process. DONRE will be responsible for controlling and managing the outcome of the land-use plan, making sure that the plan satisfies all expected requirements and objectives. This bidding process is believed to provide broad opportunities for other expertise and experiences from the market, showing diversified approaches and practices from different consultants.

Moreover, international assistance and support provide a strong benefit to Vietnamese capacity building and technology. There have been many international cooperation programmes and projects, which bring alliance partnerships and/or cooperation among international and local authority agencies, research institutions and universities, and even the private sector. This cooperation is important and necessary for Vietnam to share and transfer experiences, technologies, and best practices with developed countries. The Megacity Research Project on Ho Chi Minh City is such a successful example for cooperation between German and Vietnamese authorities. Here, research conducted by German experts in cooperation with Vietnamese authorities provides findings and recommendations that are helpful and meaningful for DONRE in preparing the current land-use plan for HCMC. According to DONRE, "it is expected that the results of the project will be the integration of environmental aspects into the urban planning for HCMC".

Summary and Conclusions

The Need for Environmental Integration into Land-use Planning for HCMC

Ho Chi Minh City, the largest and most populated city in Vietnam, has experienced significant urbanisation, which is an extreme case of land-use change over the last several decades. With the goal of becoming a leading economic-social centre in Vietnam and Southeast Asia, Ho Chi Minh City will thus expect even more rapid and dense urban expansion and city development.

Similar to other cities in the coastal tropical region in developing countries, Ho Chi Minh City has been suffering many adverse consequences of unstable rapid urbanisation—with urban flooding being one of the most significant warnings. Research studies strongly assert that this rapid growing has already caused urban flooding in the city during the past decade, and the city is more vulnerable to flooding due to ineffective urban planning than the impacts of local climate change. Moreover, in the future, climate change is more rapid than previously anticipated, thus the solutions for adaptation to climate change become even more urgent and important for authorities and planners. Besides, urban climate management is also a solid aspect that affects human comfort and the city's well-being. Beyond the technical solution for irrigation or a dyke system for the city as is now applied, an effective integrative spatial plan will be required for a more appropriate, low-cost, powerful, and sustainable solution regarding land use. The arguments emphasised the urgent need to move forward to integrate environmental factors and urban climate aspects into the HCMC land-use plan, otherwise delays would result in significant adverse economic and social consequences not only for the city, but also the region and the nation.

Challenges: Legislation and Enforcement, Climate Change Strategies and Frameworks

The perspectives from authority stakeholders showed the understanding and attention to the need for an effective land-use plan that should include strong environmental considerations in the context of dealing with current urban issues as well as global climate change. However, this study explored the many barriers to integrating environmental parameters and climate management in land-use plans. The complexity and inconsistency of the management regime to accomplish land-use plans are predicted to be the strongest obstacle. Moreover, the overlaying and overlapping of both horizontally and vertically planning processes cause reluctance and delay, or even complete standstill on the way to reaching more sustainable planning results.

Supportive legislation is expected to be updated in the context of improving HCMC's land-use plan which needs to address urban flooding, environmental protection, and climate change. However, the guidance and enforcement of the current regulations remain a concern to the responsible authorities and planners.

Tools and Opportunities: Strategic Environmental Assessment and Land-use Zoning

To foster the integration of environmental and climate parameters in HCMC's land-use plan, two tools were discussed: the Strategic Environmental Assessment (SEA) and land-use zoning.

SEA provides a strategic decision-support tool, offering the prospect of including and integrating environmental and sustainable issues in the preparation, design and implementation of the land-use plan. The implementation and application of SEA is a new moving forward approach for Vietnam. But using SEA for HCMC's land-use plans needs:

· a stronger enforcement of regulations, concrete frameworks and guidelines from the Ministry of Natural Resources and Environment;
· an improvement of capacities about SEA's approach and methodology; and
· improved availability of data.

Land-use zoning is expected to be a powerful tool to apply further environmental and urban climate consideration into down-scale land-use plan, which can provide more flexibility, involvement of more stakeholders and more planning transparency. However, the management arrangement between land-use zoning and the existing district land-use plan reflects a complex divergence, which requires a more careful decision and management roadmap. Pilot studies and application in different regions with diversified international cooperation can be a starting point, other than uniform application without proper management, observation and learning from results.

Conclusion

Ultimately, conflicts between plan designations for economic development and the protection of the environmental and human health always exist, and planners will have to be responsible and take positions for the disputing area management. It can be argued that cities can learn from their mistakes to improve. However, for Ho Chi Minh City's land-use plan, there are two points in focus: mistakes should not be too big to become inevitable and irreversible, and the same mistakes should not be repeated in HCMC or even in other Vietnamese cities. The approach to advanced technologies and international cooperation, together with well-trained technical personnel will be an advantage for HCMC to lead in applying environmental consideration in planning in Vietnam. Nevertheless, a strong paradigm shift has to occur in order to accomplish this adaptation.

Acknowledgement

I would like to thank the Ho Chi Minh City Department of Natural Resources and Environment, the Department of Planning and Architecture, and the Southern Sub-Institute for Urban Rural Planning for their support and informative interviews with the representatives. The situation analysis of this paper employed results of BMBF's Future-Megacities-Project "Integration Urban and Environmental Planning for Adaptation of Ho Chi Minh City to Climate Change".

References

Asian Development Bank (ADB) (2010): *Ho Chi Minh City–Adaptation to Climate Change: Summary report*. Mandaluyong City

Do, T.L./ Tran, T.L.A. (2011): "*Urban Development in Vietnam Challenges and Adaptation Program to Climate Change*". Presentation. Asian Cities Climate Change Resilience Network Workshop, Ha Noi, 18.11.2011. http://vietnamcityclimatechange.net/

General Statistics Office (2011): *Population and Employment Data*. http://www.gso.gov.vn, 01.06.2012

Ho, L.P. (2008a): *Influences of the Man-made Activities on Local Climate Changes in HCMC*. MS, Ho Chi Minh City Technological University. HCMC

Ho, L.P. (2008b): "Impacts of Climate Changes and Urbanization on Urban Inundation in Ho Chi Minh City". In: *11th International Conference on Urban Drainage*. Edinburgh

ICEM (2009): *Ho Chi Minh City–Adaptation to Climate Change Study Report. Volume 1: Executive Summary*. Ha Noi

Labaeye, A./ Brugmann, J./ Nguyen, V.P./ Bao, T./ Ly, K.T.T./ Nguyen, A.T./ Storch, H./ Schinkel, U. (2012): "Reality Check: Ho Chi Minh City, Vietnam". In: *Local Sustainability, Resilient Cities 2*, Volume 2, pp. 367-76.

Luu, D.C. (2012): "The role of urban planning in flooding mitigation and climate change adaptation for HCMC". In: *HCMC's Urban Planning Workshop, 16 March 2012*. Urban Planning Association. HCMC

Luu, D.H. (2011): *An Overview of Spatial Policy in Asian and European Countries, Vietnam Profile*. http://www.mlit.go.jp/international/spw/general/vietnam/index_e.html#g03, 06.04.2012

Ministry of Natural Resources and Environment (2004): *Decree 30/2004/TT-BTNMT, (guiding the elaboration, adjustment and evaluation of land-use planning and plans)*. 01. November 2004. Ha Noi

MONRE (2008): *National Target Programme To Respond To Climate Change*. Ministry of Natural Resources and Environment. Ha Noi

MONRE (2009): "Climate Change, Sea Level Rise Scenarios for Vietnam". Ministry of Natural Resources and Environment, Ha Noi National Assembly. In: *Law on Urban Planning*, Law No. 30/2009/QH12. Ha Noi

Ngan, A. (2012): *Flooding mitigation in HCMC: many, but no effective solutions*. http://m.tuoitre.vn/tin-tuc/Chinh-tri-Xa-hoi/Khoa-hoc-Moi-truong/Van-de-moi-truong/121895,Chong-ngap-tai-TP-HCM-Nhieu-giai-phap-nhung-hieu-qua-chua-cao.ttm, 16.05.2012

Nguyen, D.S. (2012): *Zoning, Planning, and Innovate Planning Approaches*. http://www.tonghoixaydungvn.org/default.aspx?Tab=121&Tinso=5757, 01.06.2012

People's Committee of Ho Chi Minh City (2012): *QD 936/QD-UBND, (Flood reduction programme 2011 to 2015 for HCMC)*. 25 February 2012. Ha Noi

Prime Minister of Vietnam (2010): *Decision 24/QD-TTg, (Regulation on general planning and construction issues for HCMC until 2025)*. 06 January 2010. Ha Noi

Prime Minister of Vietnam (2008): *NTP-RRC 2008 (national program to respond to climate change)*. 27 January 2008. Ha Noi

Quang, C. (2012,). *Changing Urban Planning Approach*. http://www.thesaigontimes.vn/Home/dothi/hatang/69270/Thay-doi-phuong-phap-quy-hoach-do-thi.html, 01.06.2012

Storch, H./ Downes, N.K. (2010): "Liveable and Resilient Ho Chi Minh City: Tackling the challenges of climate change, energy security and sustainable urban development". In: *Proceeding of REAL CORP 2010*, Vienna 18–20 May 2010.

Storch, H./ Downes, N./ Katzchner, L./ Nguyen, X.T. (2011): "Building Resilience to Climate Change Through Adaptive Land Use Planning in Ho Chi Minh City, Vietnam". In: *Resilient Cities Local Sustainability*, Vol.1, pp. 349–63

United Nations Population Fund in Vietnam (UNFPA) (2010): *Fact Sheet Urbanization in Vietnam: Evidence from the 2009 Census*. Ha Noi

Jakob Kopec
Bachelor's Thesis at TU Dortmund University, School of Spatial Planning

Land-use Change Detection and Analysis for Ho Chi Minh City

Abstract

This bachelor's thesis has been written in the framework of the Future Megacities' research project in Ho Chi Minh City (HCMC) "Integrative Urban and Environmental Planning Framework–Adaptation to Global Climate Change". The paper's purpose is to detect and analyse HCMC's land-use change for the periods 1989–2000, 2000–2002, and 2002–2005. For this, remote sensing techniques and methods on the basis of Landsat satellite imagery will be shown. The second important task is to describe and evaluate urban growth regarding well-known urban planning principles like the compact city [ARL 2005] or the city of short distances [Anas et al. 1998]. This will be done by means of urban density gradients, the jaggedness degree, centre-oriented entropy, and the fractal dimension developed by Dr. Nguyen Xuan Thinh. The outcome of the thesis shows the potential of the linkage between remote sensing techniques and geostatistical density metrics as a powerful and useful tool for sustainable spatial planning and modern land-use change monitoring.

Introduction: Keeping Land-use Data Updated in a Rapidly Growing Environment

Consequences of HCMC's Rapid Urbanisation for Land-use Data

In 2007, over the half of the world's population already lived in cities. Urbanisation and rural emigration are proceeding rapidly like never seen before. Every year, the urban population increases by about ninety million. While metropolitan regions in Europe have been developing for hundreds of years to become cities of a million people, agglomeration areas in Asia have become megacities in only a few decades. One of these megacities is Ho Chi Minh City in Vietnam, formerly known as Saigon. Today, more than nine million people live in Ho Chi Minh City, plus about two million unregistered inhabitants in informal settlements. Tropical climate conditions and annual storms cause the Saigon River to overflow, and the flooding does great damage to the city. In addition, the city's rapid expansion, in association with increasing impervious surfaces, makes the flooding problem worse. Every year, over 90,000 people move to Ho Chi Minh City in search of better living conditions, work, and better prospects [Thinh 2012]. This growth strains the city's planning department and administration in multiple ways. Due to strong migratory pressures, there is a high demand for building land. Due to the lack of available building space, new informal settlements emerge, consisting of rudimentary houses. Urban planning must face this constant development pressure by designating new settlement areas at the cost of losing valuable agricultural land. Due to fast-paced urban development, land-use data quickly becomes outdated. At this point, remote sensing provides methods for generating high resolution and consistent land-use data at any point in time. On the basis of classified land-cover types, urban development will be evaluated using urban form metrics.

Challenges to Applying Landsat Data for Ho Chi Minh City

NASA's Landsat program has existed for forty years now. Since the beginning in the early nineteen-seventies, seven platforms have been capturing images of the earth's surface [NASA 2013]. This continuity made it possible to detect land-use change and anthropogenic impacts on nature. Due to Vietnam's Doi Moi reforms and the revival of the economy in the late nineteen-eighties, four time points–1989, 2000, 2002, and 2005–were chosen for Ho Chi Minh City [Labbé 2010]. These images, taken by Landsat-5 and Landsat-7 platforms, have no or a very low cloud coverage, which is important, because electromagnetic waves cannot pass through clouds; even dust and haze have a significant negative effect on overall image quality. Especially in tropical regions, such as southern Vietnam, acquiring adequate images from passive satellite sensors is very difficult. Additionally, because the city's boundaries extend into overlapping areas of two Landsat images, it was necessary to combine two scenes to one image by a mosaic procedure for every time step. The mosaic operation shows the best results when both scenes were taken on the same date. Due to changing electromagnetic characteristics, the mosaic procedure is not recommended for images whose acquisition dates differ widely. In this case, the image classification must be computed for every Landsat scene separately. Unfortunately, there is still an area in the south-east of Ho Chi Minh City that is not covered by Landsat data. This is a conservation area next to the coast consisting of densely wooded mangrove forests that have remained constant for decades. A technical defect of the Scan Line Corrector, which has appeared since 2003, limits the quality of the images and leads to black stripes. The wider black stripes at the image borders can be fully or partially eliminated by updating missing information with Landsat data taken before failure. Because of the wide date difference and rapid urban growth, this solution is not recommended for the study area of Ho Chi Minh City.

Methods and Workflow of Landsat Data Processing

Workflow within Landsat Data Processing

The methodology of the scientific work on Landsat Data Processing can be divided into three parts:

Work Package 1: Data Acquisition and Processing

The data acquisition focuses on Landsat data that is available in raw format as digital grey values. Therefore, Landsat imagery must be calibrated in radiances and reflectances, measured by satellite sensors [see passage below on Level-1-Calibration in the chapter "Methods of Landsat Data Processing" ↗]. Due to the atmospheric conditions of Ho Chi Minh City's tropical climate, it is necessary to apply an atmospheric correction for satellite images. Furthermore, there al-

Fig. 1   Workflow structured in three work packages [Author]

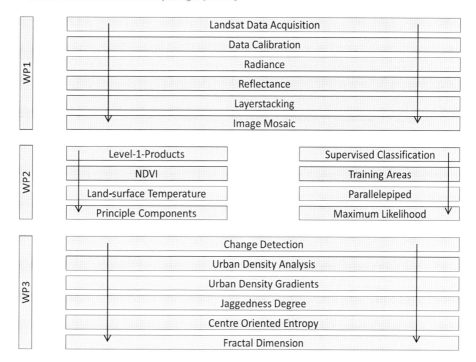

ways exist two Landsat scenes for each date, which have to be combined into one image. Layerstacking is a procedure for combining several bands of information into one geodatabase.

Work Package 2: Landsat Products and Supervised Classification

The second phase of the work includes supervised pixel-based image classification, for which the first step is to determine training areas for several land-cover types. Training areas consist of pixels representing a land-use class. These are set by the interpreter and depend on his local knowledge. The supervised pixel-based image classification is performed by the common parallelepiped and maximum likelihood decision rules. To optimise the classification, additional multispectral data products ought to be generated. One of the commonly used products is the Normalized Differenced Vegetation Index (NDVI), which indicates the photosynthetic activity of vegetation. In addition, the thermal infrared channel of Landsat imagery allows the calculation of surface temperatures. This product is suitable for detecting urban hot spots and shows the gap between different land uses. The aim of the principal component analysis is to reduce the spectral data with minimal loss of information. The determined principal components can be connected to the original spectral bands by layerstacking, which considerably improves the pixel-based classification.

Work Package 3: Change Detection and Analysis

This phase deals with the analysis of land-use changes, which is methodologically called change detection. It shows how the land cover has changed in the above-mentioned study periods. Furthermore, an evaluation of both urban growth and landscape change on the basis of spatial planning and landscape ecology criteria will be given. At this point, several urban density metrics will be used to describe and evaluate the city's expansion process.

Methods of Landsat Data Processing

Level-1-Calibration

Both, to enhance raw satellite data and improve the image-based land use classification and analysis, understanding the architecture of Landsat satellite imagery is important. Landsat-5 and Landsat-7 data consist of six spectral bands with a geometric resolution of 30 m and one thermal band. From Landsat-5 to Landsat-7, the thermal band's geometric resolution has been doubled from 120 m to 60 m. Furthermore, Landsat-7 has a panchromatic canal with a geometric resolution of 15 m, used to sharpen the imagery [Taubenstöck et al. 2010]. Landsat data is freely available from the web archives of the United States Geological Survey (USGS). The data is delivered in raw eight-bit coded tif-format as digital grey numbers. For scientific use and estimating further Landsat products, such as land-surface temperatures, calibrating these digital numbers back to radiances and reflectances measured by the satellite's sensors was necessary. Landsat data also need geometric and radiometric corrections or atmospheric enhancements to reduce image distortions.

The first step in calibration is to calculate the digital numbers reaching from 0 to 255 back to spectral radiances. There is a linear relation between digital numbers and radiances that can be expressed as follows [NASA 2013a]:

$$L_\lambda = gain * Q_{cal} + bias$$

where:

$$L_\lambda = spectral\ radiance\ of\ band\ \lambda\ [\ \frac{W}{m^2 * str * \mu m}\ ]$$

$$gain = rescaled\ gain,\ band\ related\ constant$$

$$bias = rescaled\ bias,\ band\ related\ constant$$

$$Q_{cal} = digital\ number\ of\ band\ \lambda$$

Gain and bias are band-related constants and can be found in the metadata file header included in the Landsat data package. For Landsat-7 imagery, the equation can be described as follows [Ibid.]:

$$L_c = \frac{LMAX_\lambda - LMIN_\lambda}{Q_{calmax} - Q_{calmin}} * (Q_{cal} - Q_{calmin}) + LMIN_\lambda$$

where:

$$L_\lambda = \text{spectral radiance of band } \lambda \ [\frac{W}{m^2 * str * \mu m}]$$

$$LMAX_\lambda = \text{spectral radiance scaled to } Q_{calmax} \ [\frac{W}{m^2 * str * \mu m}]$$

$$LMIN_\lambda = \text{spectral radiance scaled to } Q_{calmin} \ [\frac{W}{m^2 * str * \mu m}]$$

Q_{cal} = calibrated pixel expressed in digital number

Q_{calmax} = the maximum quantised calibrated pixel value (= 255)

Q_{calmin} = the minimum quantised calibrated pixel value (= 1)

$LMAX_\lambda$ and $LMIN_\lambda$ are the spectral radiances for each Landsat band. Maximum and minimum values are stored in the metadata file. To receive clear Landsat scenes free from noise and haze, a normalisation of solar irradiance needs to be performed. This step also provides a better in between-scene comparability of two or more images [Chander et al. 2009]. This combined atmospheric and surface reflectance can be estimated by the following computation [Ibid.]:

$$\rho_p = \frac{\pi * L * d^2}{ESUN_\lambda * \cos \theta_s}$$

where:

ρ_p = spectral reflectance of band λ

$$L_\lambda = \text{spectral radiance of band } \lambda \ [\frac{W}{m^2 * str * \mu m}]$$

d = distance between Sun and Earth [AE]

θ_s = solar zenith angle in degrees

$$ESUN_\lambda = \text{mean solar irradiance} \ [\frac{W}{m^2 * \mu m}]$$

The solar zenith angle is also listed in the meta-information. The earth-sun distance can be retrieved from interpolated values found in the Landsat user manual.

Normalised Differenced Vegetation Index

A common method of detecting vegetation in a study area is deriving a vegetation index. The normalised differenced vegetation index analyses the photosynthetic activity of vegetation, and thus is a good indicator of the vitality of vegetation or for its growth stadium. This index can also be used to differentiate between vegetation and plantless land covers, which is helpful for image classification.

The vegetation index is calculated by a Landsat band ratio. While the chlorophyll inside the leaf pigments of a plant absorbs nearly every visible red light, near-infrared light is almost entirely reflected [Köhl et al. 2006]. The normalised differenced vegetation index can be expressed with the following formula.

$$NDVI = \frac{Near\ Infrared - Visible\ Red}{Near\ Infrared + Visible\ Red}$$

In other words, for Landsat data:

$$NDVI = \frac{TM4 - TM3}{TM4 + TM3}$$

where:

TM3 = Landsat Thematic Mapper 3 (band 3, visible red)

TM4 = Landsat Thematic Mapper 4 (band 4, near-infrared)

The normalised differenced vegetation index is computed for every pixel of the satellite imagery and ranges from -1 (no vegetation) to +1 (dense and healthy vegetation). It is assumed that values above 0.5 represent natural vegetation; between 0.2 and 0.5 agricultural land use can be found and negative values correspond to water bodies due to the dearth of chlorophyll and sensitivity to water content.

As expected and visible in Figure 2 ↗, the mangrove forests in the south have very high NDVI values, while farmland, mostly the rice fields, appear in brown and yellow (0.2 < NDVI < 0.5). Where no vegetation exists, impervious surfaces are expected, noticeable as black areas that are assumed to be urban areas. Water bodies have a negative NDVI and are illustrated in blue colour.

Land-surface Temperature

Deriving land-surface temperatures is a useful tool for modern, ecological, and sustainable planning. Surface temperatures indicate urban hot spots and the density gradient between agglomerations and rural regions. Monitoring thermal processes is the first step in planning urban aeration actions for better living conditions in cities. Land-surface temperatures also indicate the type and material of land cover. Forests and water bodies radiate less heat than impervious surfaces, bare soils, or sands.

Land-surface temperatures in degrees Celsius are calculated from the sixth, thermal-infrared Landsat band as follows [Chander et al. 2009]:

Fig. 2 The normalised differenced vegetation index for Ho Chi Minh City in 2005 [Author]

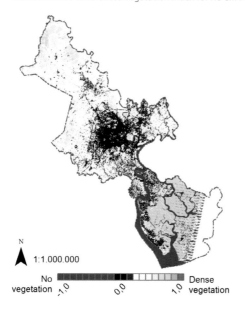

$$T_B = \frac{K2}{\ln \left(\dfrac{K1}{L_\lambda} + 1 \right)} - 272.15$$

where:

$$T_B = black\ body\ temperature\ [°C]$$

$$K2 = constant \left[\frac{W}{m^2 * str * \mu m} \right]$$

$$K1 = constant\ [K]$$

$$L_\lambda = spectral\ radiance\ of\ band\ \lambda \left[\frac{W}{m^2 * str * \mu m} \right]$$

T_B describes the temperature of a theoretic, ideal black body that fully absorbs incoming electromagnetic radiation. However, such black bodies do not really exist on the earth's surface. Therefore, T_B can be seen as an approximate value that needs to be adjusted. According to Boltzmann's law, the surface temperature of any object regarding its characteristic emissivity can be derived as follows [Tran Thi Van 2008]:

$$T_S = \frac{1}{\varepsilon^{1/4}} * T_B$$

where:

T_S = surface temperature according Boltzmann [°C]

T_B = black body temperature [°C]

ε = characteristic emissivity of an specific object

The emissivity of an ideal black body is 1. Due to different materials and structures of objects, the emissivity of real land-cover types is always less than 1. To calculate the surface temperature according to Boltzmann's law the specific emissivity of the concrete object must be known. Different emissivity values for land surface types exist; for example, the emissivity of concrete ranges between 0.942 and 0.966, while that of water ranges between 0.973 and 0.979 [Albertz 2007]. Because the Landsat imagery for Ho Chi Minh City is not homogeneous, but consists of many unique surface materials, it is difficult to choose one of the corresponding emissivities. For ε, an emissivity value of 0.95 is often assumed, representing the mean emissivity for all objects and materials in one Landsat scene. J.A. Sobrino describes a method for computing in situ emissivities depending on the vegetation proportion in a study area [2004]:

$$\varepsilon = \varepsilon_v * P_v + \varepsilon_s * (1 - P_v)$$

where:

ε = in situ emissivity

ε_v = mean emissivity of vegetation = 0.94

ε_s = mean emissivity of bare soil = 0.96

P_v = proportion of vegetation obtained
    from normalised differenced vegetation index

The default values for ε_v=0.94 and ε_s=0.96. The vegetation fraction can be obtained from the natural vegetation index as follows:

$$P_v = \left(\frac{NDVI - NDVI_{min}}{NDVI_{max} - NDVI_{min}} \right)^2$$

NDVI = NDVI obtained from Landsat TM4 and TM3

$NDVI_{max}$ = NDVI for land cover assumed to be vegetation = 0.5

$NDVI_{min}$ = NDVI for land cover assumed to be bare soil = 0.2

Fig. 3   Land-surface temperature for Ho Chi Minh City in 2005 [Author]

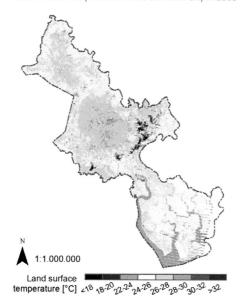

As visible in Figure 3 ↗, water bodies and forests have the lowest land-surface temperature between 18°C and 24°C. In contrast, farmland and especially dense urban areas have high land-surface temperatures of up to 32°C. Some cooler spaces exist within the city that can be assumed to be urban green areas. They are very important for aeration and climate mitigation. This Landsat scene contains some cloud formation, which is illustrated with temperatures below 0°C.

Principal Component Analysis

The principal component analysis is used to reveal correlations between all spectral Landsat bands. This method eliminates redundant bands and creates new uncorrelated band combinations, the so-called principle components, with a minimum loss of information. About 95% of the six bands' input information can be stored within the new generated principle components consisting of only three bands. By comparing the reflectance of each Landsat band, a multivariate attribute space is created. Deriving a regression analysis of the multivariate attribute space makes it possible to determine which Landsat bands correlate with each other [Glaser 1985]. A high correlation is given a value of above 0.8. The first step is generating the mean reflectance for each Landsat band obtained from the individual attribute space. These values can be drawn within a covariance matrix. As can be seen in the correlation matrix, reducing spectral information when a high correlation is given is reasonable. At least the Eigenvalues represent the amount of information the principal components store from all input bands.

This tool is very useful for compressing huge data volumes, and as a result, data processing is more efficient. Modern computer hardware enables this method to be applied to enhance the original Landsat spectral band with uncorrelated band information, by layer-stacking the principle components to the input files.

As sustainability is among the main topics of the Future Megacities research programme, another major question of this study is, what does a sustainable city looks like? Several urban planning principles like the compact city [ARL 2005] or the mono-centric city model exist for developing efficient urban structures. To measure whether cities tend to concentrate or sprawl, a variety of urban density metrics can be used. On the basis of vector data, the following enumerated metrics describe the spatial arrangement of urban land use in Ho Chi Minh City from a radial-concentric view. Due to the geometric resolution of 30 m, these metrics cannot display the real building type, but only the spatial distribution of settlement areas. Moreover, as this method is not a 3D-analysis, building heights as an indicator for density are not considered. Independently from administrative boundaries, urban land use will be analysed inside a circular study area with a radius of 20 km around the city centre. The urban compactness and structural efficiency will be compared to the most compact form of a circle.

Figure 4 ↗ illustrates the basic idea of the mentioned metrics. The grey areas are Ho Chi Minh City's settlement, detected by satellite remote sensing and extracted from land-use data. Other land use—e.g., water bodies or vegetation—is excluded from the analysis. Additionally, there is no differentiation between residential areas, industrial sites, or commercial areas—they are all combined into impervious surface, in this case called "settlement area". The investigation area concentrates on a circle with a radius of 20 km around Ho Chi Minh City's town hall. Therefore, the analysis even includes settlement areas outside the city's proper administrative boundary. In order to describe the spatial arrangement of settlement area and calculate the urban growth of the city for a long time lapse, the land-use data has been divided into buffer rings.

The first metric to describe the dynamics of urban growth is to calculate density gradients (D) within twenty buffer rings, each with the radius of 1,000 m around the city's town hall [Thinh 2004]:

$$D_i = \frac{s_i}{r_i} \text{ with } (i \in i_1, i_2 \dots i_n)$$

where:

D_i = proportion of settlement area in ring i [%]

s_i = settlement area in ring i [m²]

r_i = total area of ring i [m²]

n = number of ring zones = 20

This method makes it possible to detect both local growth centres between several years and also describes how the proportion of settlement area develops from the city centre to its outskirts.

The second metric, jaggedness degree (Z), is calculated via a perimeter-ratio between the boundary length of the urban area and the perimeter of its equivalent circle. The equivalent circle describes the optimal compact form with a given settlement area; this relation can be expressed as follows:

$$A_{settlement} = A_{equivalent\ circle} = \pi * r^2_{equivalent\ circle}$$

Figure 5 ↗ shows an excerpt from the study area of Ho Chi Minh City. The grey shapes form the settlement area of the town, intersected into equal buffer rings starting from the centre. Summing up all settlement areas, the city would fit inside the black equivalent circle. The jaggedness degree is defined as the perimeter of the settlement area divided by the equivalent circle's perimeter:

$$Z = \frac{P_{settlement}}{P_{equivalent\ circle}} = \frac{P_{settlement}}{2 * \pi * \sqrt{\dfrac{A_{settlement}}{\pi}}}$$

The jaggedness degree Z reaches 1 when $P_{settlement}$ equals $P_{equivalent\ circle}$. The more Z tends to 1, the denser and compacter the urban structure appears. In other words: the city would form a perfect circle if Z equals 1. Increasing Z-values mean a more fractured city form.

    The centre-oriented entropy measures the spatial distribution of urban structures according to the urban-density gradient and the distance to the city centre. The metric bases on a buffer analysis, where the first ring zone equals the equivalent circle. Around this one, twenty equal ring buffers will be created to reach the outer radius of 20 km [Figure 6 ↗]. The first step consists of calculating the relative proportion of settlement density in each ring [Thinh 2004]:

$$q_i = \frac{d_i}{d_o + d_1 + \ldots + d_n} \qquad i = 0\ (1)\ n$$

where:

q_i = relative proportion of settlement density in ring i

d_i = proportion of settlement area in ring i

d_o = proportion of settlement area in equivalent circle

n = number of ring zones = 20

To determine whether the urban structures concentrate around the city centre or are sprawled in the study area, the use of an entropy (H) measure is recommended [Ibid.]:

$$H = -\sum_{i=0}^{n} \frac{q_i * ln\ (q_i)}{ln\ (n+1)}$$

The entropy H ranges from 0 (most compact form) to 1 (extreme dispersion). When H equals 0, the city forms a perfect circle. If the relative proportion of settlement areas outside the equivalent circle grows, entropy is greater and consequently the city structure is less efficient.

The last metric, the radial-fractal dimension F, measures urban compactness depending on the distance between individual settlement areas and the city centre. For this reason, the settlement areas of each buffer ring are cumulated depending on the radius [Figure7 ↗], in this case associated with distance. If settlement areas develop in a circular way with increasing distance from the centre, it can be assumed:

$$S\,(r) = \pi\,r^2$$

where:

$$S\,(r) = \textit{cumulated settlement area within a distance r}$$
$$\textit{from city centre}$$

Because cities do not grow in a strictly circular manner, this relationship can be generalised as follows:

$$S\,(r) = \beta\,r^F \text{ with } 0 < F \leq 2$$

When F tends to 2, the city's growth can be rated as compact and radial-concentric. A fractal dimension around 1 indicates a linear structure, where a city develops along main roads, railways, or streams. F below 1 means that there is no radial city growth, but a very scattered spatial distribution of settlement areas. This is often the case in rural regions. In order to determine F, a logarithm function must be computed:

$$\ln\,(S(r)) = F\ln\,(r) + \ln\,(\beta)$$

The radial-fractal dimension F is the slope of the regression line through all points $(\ln(r), \ln(S(r_i)))$.

Fig. 4   (left) Ring buffer zones around the centre of a city [Author]

Fig. 5   (right) The equivalent circle for a given settlement area [Author]

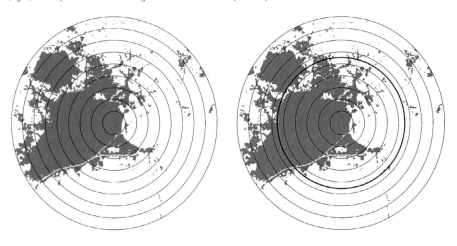

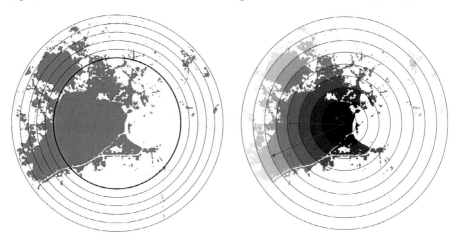

Findings: Precise Visualisation of Various Urban Growth Factors

Reasonably Accurate Data Available from Landsat Data Processing

The land cover of Ho Chi Ming City has been classified into urban area, vegetation, farmland, and water bodies for the four years 1989, 2000, 2002, and 2005. In comparison to the land-use database provided by the Ho Chi Minh City planning authority, the overall image-classification accuracy amounts to 77%. The detected urban areas even match 88%. This is an adequate result considering that the spatial analysis focuses on settlement areas. Unfortunately, the accuracy for natural vegetation is about 60% due to the difficult separation of vegetation and agricultural land use. This problem can be exemplarily shown for some industrial crops in Ho Chi Minh City. The north has large rubber plantations whose appearance and spectral characteristics are nearly identical to forests. Only their geometrical form and relative location to the river and settlements indicate agricultural use. Therefore, many plantations in the north have been incorrectly classified. The difference between the actual land cover (vegetation) and land use (cultivation area) dedicated in administration plans is one of the elemental problems in remote sensing. The land-cover analysis could be enhanced and would benefit from higher resoluted satellite imagery like ASTER (15 m) or GeoEYE (1.36 m). By using them, a more separated visibility of land use could be achieved [Figure 8 ↗].

Urban Growth Rate of 70% Almost Every Two Years

In Figure 11 ↗, the area and land-use change for every class for the above mentioned years are listed. The percentage relates to the area change between two sequential points of time. That only the urban area has developed constantly and with a high growth rate can be observed. From 1989 to 2005, the Ho Chi Minh City urban area grew by a factor of five. Even in the short periods between 2000, 2002, and 2005, the average urban growth is about 70%.

Fig. 8 Land cover classification for Ho Chi Minh City [Author]

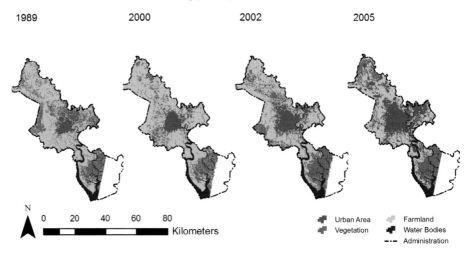

1989   2000   2002   2005

N

0   20   40   60   80
Kilometers

Urban Area   Farmland
Vegetation   Water Bodies
                    Administration

Fig. 9 Key figures of land-use change in Ho Chi Minh City from 1989 to 2005 [Author]

Land Cover	Area [km²]	Area [km²]	Change [%]	Area [km²]	Change [%]	Area [km²]	Change [%]
	1989	2000		2002		2005	
Urban area	102.9	174.5	69.5	291.0	66.8	522.1	79.4
Vegetation	485.2	289.7	-40.3	398.1	37.4	302.7	-24.0
Farmland	1066.2	1223.4	14.7	978.0	-20.1	809.6	-17.2
Water bodies	166.1	167.4	0.8	189.5	13.2	194.1	2.4

In 2005, the total settlement area of Ho Chi Minh City was 550 km². At this point, all types of impervious surfaces and infrastructure—for example, housing sites, rural regions, industrial use, airports—are taken together for the urban area.

Difficult Differentiation on Green and Water Areas

The problematic and difficult separation of farmland and vegetation can be seen in the results for the total area change listed in the same table. Farmland and vegetation have both increased and decreased over time. This is due to the classification process when the stadium of field crops changes during its growth or the different spectral characteristics before and after harvest. Since 2002, the area for agricultural use has constantly shrunk due to the ex-treme expansion of settlement areas. Water bodies have not changed considerably.

The technical limitations and reduced geometric resolution of Landsat data prevent the detection of detailed land-surface structures. This problem is apparent for some drainage systems in Ho Chi Minh City. The south of the core city is traversed by a network of canals that cannot be detected due to their small size. This extends to the mangrove forest next to the coast that consists of plenty of small bayous. Yet Landsat lacks the ability to capture these details. It is also noticeable that the city expands along major traffic and infrastruc-

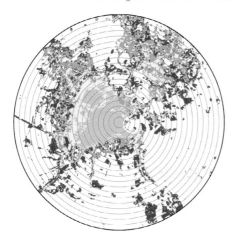

Fig. 11 Urban density gradients for Ho Chi Minh City for 1989, 2000, 2002, and 2005 [Author]

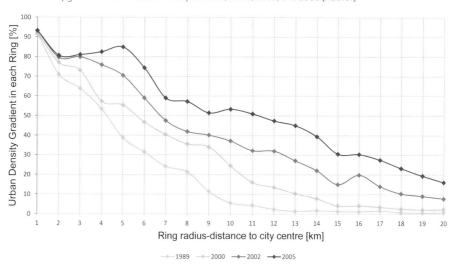

ture axes. This specific urban growth indicates the existence of major roads and traffic systems. Unfortunately, it is not possible to extract such structures with the given geometric resolution of 30 m.

Enormous Suburban Density

By computing density gradients in equidistant buffer zones around the city centre, it is possible to describe the dynamic of urban growth and localise these extremes. In this regard, this method is very useful to examine the growth in each ring zone in temporal progress. In 1989, the urban area proportion in each ring sank nearly exponentially with increasing distance to the city centre. Already in the tenth ring, settlements existed marginally with sinking proportions towards the last ring of the study area. Comparing the gradients for each year, some interesting developments can be recognised. In 2002, there was a significant rise in settlement density which led to suburbanisation processes. Within a distance of between 2 and 4 km around the city centre, a strong densification took place from 1989 to 2005, which is higher than in the immediate proximity of the first ring. The density in the city centre remained very high and unchanged. Because of the Saigon River and city parks, a higher density within the first buffer zones is not possible and even not recommended, because the core city zone benefits from the aeration of green spaces. The biggest increase in urban density proceeded in rings five and six, which doubled the urban proportion, and in the peripheral rings ten to thirteen where the settlement area even raised by 100% (!). That means that in 1989, the periphery of Ho Chi Minh City was nearly free of urban structures. As Figure 10 ↗ shows, Ho Chi Minh City has expanded westward in the first period from 1989 to 2002. From 2002 to 2005, the urban growth focused on the northern territories. The city's expansion southward seems to be very difficult due to the very wet ground that impedes opening up new building sites.

Suburban Development along Highways

The jaggedness degree is the quotient of the total settlement perimeter and the perimeter of the equivalent circle. The more the jaggedness degree tends to 1, the more compact the urban structure appears. From 1989 to 2000, the city's jaggedness degree increased from 28.71 to 23.05, like that of the German city of Dresden in the late nineteen-nineties (23.2), but not as compact as the settlement areas in Slovakia's capital Bratislava (11.8) [Meinel et al. 2003]. Since then, the jaggedness degree of Ho Chi Minh City has not changed noticeably. These high values are caused by the rise of many new settlements in the rural areas of Ho Chi Minh City. The jaggedness degree is mainly affected by the total settlement perimeter. Despite the constant increase of the equivalent circle, the jaggedness degree has remained nearly unchanged since 2000. This is because the growth rate of both the urban area and the settlement perimeter developed in balance. Nonetheless, the Ho Chi Minh City administration needs effective planning instruments to prevent the city's expansion into rural regions and to enhance urban densification where settlements already exist. The next metric is the entropy that describes the spatial disorder of urban structures. If the whole city completely takes up the equivalent circle, entropy equals zero. Low entropy means a compact structure. This metric is affected by the spatial distribution of settlements. The more urban structures concentrate around the city centre and the smaller the urban proportion in the outer rings, the more compact the city appears. In Ho Chi Minh City, new settlements especially arose in peripheral regions while there was less urban growth near the city centre. This is why entropy has been increasing since 1989 and will continue due to the development pressure in rural regions of Ho Chi Minh City. There was constant growth in the radial-fractal dimension—from 1.11 in 1989, to 1.62 in 2005—due to the past punctual densification of settlement-free areas. Nonetheless, it cannot be assumed that the city is expanding in a circular manner due to the limitations of the Saigon and Dong Nai River to the east as well as the very humid ground in the south of the City. A fractal dimension around value one indicates that urban areas develop along linear structures, such as main streets or highways. This spatial arrangement can especially be seen in the 1989-image-classification where the radial-fractal dimension is 1.11. These results show that there are many linear settlement areas formed along junctions between the city and the industrial sites in the east as well as along main roads directing to rural areas in the north and west.

Fig. 12 Key figures of urban density metrics for Ho Chi Minh City from 1989 to 2005 [Author]

	1989	2000	2002	2005
Settlement perimeter [km]	999.59	1117.55	1499.48	1781.79
Equivalent circle area [km²]	96.43	187.03	325.92	491.19
Equivalent circle radius [km]	5.54	7.72	10.19	12.50
Equivalent circle perimeter [km]	34.81	48.48	64.00	78.56
Jaggedness degree	28.71	23.05	23.43	22.68
Entropy	0.73	0.85	0.95	0.98
Radial-fractal dimension	1.11	1.35	1.56	1.62

Conclusion: Applied Processing of Landsat Data as a Powerful Urban-planning Tool

The combination of remote sensing techniques and geostatistical methods create a powerful analysis and monitoring system in modern urban planning. Remote sensing is not only applied in earth observation but also in landscape ecology and spatial research. Due to its free availability, its continuity and actuality, Landsat data is very suitable for land-use change monitoring in larger scales. Landsat provides a good compromise between required computing power for image processing and geometrical resolution. This is why Landsat imagery is often used to describe spatial patterns at the regional and national levels, but also allows performant analysis on Megacity scales. For the detection of detailed surfaces, satellite data with higher resolution is recommended. In tropical climate regions, radar imagery should be preferred over spectral image data, because active sensors are nearly insensitive to clouds. Against the background of sustainable urban master plans and spatial planning principles, the metrics demonstrated above represent vital methods for land-use monitoring and analysis in megacities and can be adapted to any other land-use data. On the basis of Landsat data, land-use change in Ho Chi Minh City was described. With the help of density metrics, urban growth could be detected and analysed. The combination of both methods provides a useful tool and can be applied to other megacities as an important step for establishing effective spatial control plans.

References

Albertz, J. (2007): *Einführung in die Fernerkundung - Grundlagen der Interpretation von Luft- und Satellitenbildern.* 3. Auflage. Darmstadt

Anas, A./ Arnott, R./ Small, K. A. (1998): "Urban spatial structure". In: *Journal of Economic Literature* (36), pp. 1426–64

ARL (Akademie für Raumforschung und Landesplanung) (2005): *Handwörterbuch der Raumordnung.* Hannover 2005

Chander, G./ Markham, B./ Helder, D.: (2009): "Summary of current radiometric calibration coefficients for Landsat MSS, TM, ETM+ and EO-1 ALI sensors". In: *Remote Sensing of Environment,* 113 (5), pp. 893–903

Köhl, M./ Magnussen, S./ Marchetti, M. (2006): *Sampling methods, remote sensing and GIS multiresource forest inventory.* Berlin

Labbé, D. (2010): *Facing the Urban Transition in Hanoi: Recent Urban Planning Issues and Initiatives.* Montréal: Institut national de la recherche scientifique

Meinel, G./ Winkler, M. (2003): "Spatial Analysis of Settlement and Open Land Trends in Urban Areas on Basis of RS Data–Studies of Five European Cities over a 50-year Period". In: Benes, T. (ed): *Geoinformation for European-wide Integration. Proceedings of the 22nd Symposium of the European Association of Remote Sensing Laboratories,* Prague, Czech Republic, 4–6 June 2002. Rotterdam: Millpress, pp. 539–46

NASA (2013a): *Landsat 7. Science Data User Handbook.* http://landsathandbook.gsfc.nasa.gov/data_prod/prog_sect11_3.html, 03.01.2013

NASA (2013b): *History. Landsat Programme.* http://landsat.gsfc.nasa.gov/?page_id=2281, 07.02.2013

Sobrino, J./ Jimenez, J./ Paolini, L. (2004): "Land Surface Temperature Retrieval from LANDSAT TM 5". In: *Remote Sensing of Environment,* 90 (4), pp. 434–40

Taubenböck, H./ Roth, A. (2010): "Fernerkundung im urbanen Kontext". In: Taubenböck, H./ Dech, S. (eds.): *Fernerkundung im urbanen Raum Erdbeobachtung auf dem Weg zur Planungspraxis.* Darmstadt

Thinh, N. X. (2012): *Strategien zum Hochwassermanagement in der Megastadt Ho Chi Minh City im Zeichen der rasanten Urbanisierung und des Klimawandels. Forschungskolloquium 05.07.2012. TU Dortmund*

Thinh, N. X. (2004): "Entwicklung von Maßen zur Charakterisierung und Bewertung der physischen und funktionalen Kompaktheit von Stadtregionen". In: *Photogrammetrie Fernerkundung Geoinformation* (3), pp. 221–32

Tran Thi Van/ Ha Duong Xuan Bao (2008): *Application of Geoinformatics to Urban Environmental Management in View of Urban Climatology: Case Study in Ho Chi Minh City, Vietnam* http://www.a-a-r-s.org/acrs/proceeding/ACRS2008/Papers/TS%2023.4.pdf, 07.02.2013

RABAT: Extensive use of plants in a tradtional part of Morocco's capital [Lukas Born]

Yassine Moustanjidi
Diploma Thesis at Technische Universität Berlin, Institute for Architecture

Multifunctional Urban Agriculture: An Urban Planning Model for the Megacities of Tomorrow. The Case of Casablanca

Abstract

What can be more exciting and thrilling than the story of Casablanca—the place where the image of modern and iconic Morocco has been drawn, with a lot of care and vigour, as a country ready in all aspects to step into a promising millennium?

However, Casablanca's unprecedented rapid urban and demographic growth since the beginning of the twentieth century, coupled with a chronic lack of integrative urban strategies, have led to an urban and ecological crisis in the city.

Casablanca is preparing for its 5.1 million inhabitants while still unable to solve its current problems; if Casablanca is the beating heart of the Moroccan economy, it is also the most polluted of its cities, the most congested, the densest ... in short, it is as problematic as unique in the Moroccan urban context. After a century of economic, urban, and industrial development, Casablanca now faces tremendous challenges that merge with the fast process of mega-urbanisation: housing crisis, social segregation, high unemployment rates, soaring demographic growth, permanent congestion, air and water pollution, a virtual absence of open and green spaces. When looking at these major challenges as well as the increasing risks of climate change that threaten the whole region, it becomes less and less evident that the economic factors would continue to be the only determinants of the city's spatial and urban configuration, meaning that other ecological and socio-demographic variables have to become equally important in the process of Casablanca's urban development.

Through an extensive investigation of the development trends of growing megacities and the challenges they face, particularly in developing countries, the current work takes Casablanca as a case study, and proposes approaches, methods, and tools to integrate a green and productive infrastructure based on urban agriculture as a multifunctional component of urban planning.

In this regard, this research tries to analyse and reposition urban agriculture in the discourse on sustainable urban development and the impacts of climate change, by proposing a new multifunctional model of urban management and redefining the role of green open spaces in the context of Casablanca.

The proposed design highlights the issue of inner-city brownfields and vacant spaces in Casablanca, and how they can be regenerated by hosting new and multifunctional facilities and uses. Through the redevelopment of a 25-ha inner-city railway brownfield into a productive urban park, the project proposes comprehensive solutions and ideas based on the concept of multifunctional urban agriculture, and integrates various economic, ecological, social, and technical aspects aiming at the establishment of a complex urban ecosystem, and a vertical and multifunctional intervention linking various urban sectors in the city.

Fig. 1 Multifunctional urban agriculture park project, Casablanca [Author]

Shabnam Teimourtash
Thesis at Technische Universität Berlin, Institute for Architecture

Climate-responsive Residential Buildings for Hashtgerd New Town Based on Traditional Residential Architecture of Iran's Arid Region

Abstract

The present work explores the issue of climate-responsive architecture—how architecture operates in relation to climate, and, in this regard, how the energy demand of buildings would be affected. A large part of the world's total energy consumption takes place in buildings. Reducing energy consumption in the building sector has been generating growing attention in Iran after the reformation of energy subsidies in recent years. Iran's massive population growth in the last thirty years has led to planning and the partial implementation of new settlements, such as thirty new towns. These plans are at a critical point concerning Iran's future energy consumption, which depends mainly on fossil fuels.

This thesis investigates the impacts of climate efficiency on reducing the energy demand of Iran's residential buildings on the basis of vernacular architecture. This topic will be considered in two aspects: on the one hand, it shows design features, which minimise the environmental stress; on the other hand, it investigates how available natural energy sources, such as wind and solar energy, could be used to improve housing comfort.

This work refers to the hot-dry region, which constitutes the Iran's largest climatic region. Thirty-eight case studies from five reference cities of this region have been analysed. In parallel, a detailed literature and interdisciplinary structured research was conducted. It includes issues that can directly or indirectly influence the energy demand of buildings. The results are illustrated with an example from one of the most developed new towns of Iran which is Hashtgerd New Town. The example represents the typical structure of a contemporary residential building in Iran. The methodical procedure is as follows:
- analysis of the existing climate classifications defining the research area;
- analysis of the trend of climate change and its impact on future architecture;
- identification and analysis of traditional residential buildings, including their setting in the urban fabric and technical and constructive issues, based on case studies and findings from the literature;
- comparison of the analysed aspects within the framework of contemporary residential buildings based on the example of Hashtgerd New Town;
- and a conclusion regarding energy-related measures and the development of new implementation guidelines considering the current economic and social conditions based on the example of Hashtgerd New Town.

The results show that traditional buildings can be acknowledged as a central resource for the development of climate-efficient measures for buildings in Iran, and that the application of design criteria of vernacular buildings reduces environmental stress, uses natural energy sources to provide housing comfort, and thus minimises the energy demand of buildings. The findings of this work can be used to develop new settlements in Iran's hot-dry regions.

Fig. 1   Traditional house in Yazd, Iran [Author]

Nadia Poor Rahim
Diploma Thesis at Technische Universität Berlin, Institute for Architecture

The Feasibility of a New Generation Office Building in Hashtgerd New Town: Modern, Efficient, and Environmentally Friendly

Abstract

Within the framework of the Future Megacities' Young Cities Project, a plan for a 7,800-m² vacant lot in a prominent location in the Shahre Javan pilot community of Hashtgerd New Town has been developed. The city is located in Iran's Alborz province, 65 km west of Tehran and 25 km from Karaj city.

According to the Hashtgerd New Town master plan, a commercial mixed-use was proposed for this plot. Finally, the "New Generation Office Building" was chosen as a pilot project. Based on an architectural design concept by Dr. F. Nasrollahi, the feasibility study for this office building tries to anticipate the problems and key characters of the draft with the aim of reducing energy consumption and the demand for resources.

The requirements for the implementation of the project—including BMBF's project objectives on energy-efficiency of buildings, reduction of energy consumption, and CO_2 emissions—have been studied under interdisciplinary scientific aspects, such as social science, urban planning, technology, ecology, economics, and project management. This comprehensive approach aims to adapt and adjust the building into the surrounding urban fabric. Planned and envisioned as part of a sustainable quarter, the key to successful project development for the building ultimately lies in the early identification of common interests and early involvement of stakeholders. Therefore, the social analysis has identified future inhabitants as either being part of the lower class or of the middle class with lower incomes. Income levels have been considered in order to offer spaces with affordable rental prices. The result of the target group analysis for the whole residential area has shown that a mixed commercial and office use for the focused single building is appealing to the entire spectrum of potential users.

The New Generation Office Building follows the modern requirements for office buildings, which should be environmentally safe, affordable, easy, and implemented without much technical effort. Backing the project development with social and ecological ideas and concepts will create a proper quality for the future daily office work. This contributes substantially to project sustainability. Apart from these issues, economic considerations play an important role in the concept of sustainability. Thus, a cost analysis for the building was also conducted, which showed that the idea for the New Generation Office Building and two other buildings is economically viable if the property purchase price is under 1.7 million euro or is provided at no cost by the New Town Development Corporation (NTDC), as proposed up to now. After all, the study has shown that the interdisciplinary objectives can be successfully translated into a legal and economic framework contributing to the attractiveness of the location.

Fig. 1   New Generation Office Building, Design by Farshad Nasrollahi [F. Nasrollahi]

MOBILITY AND TRANS-PORTATION

SHENZHEN: Urban landscape [Matias Ruiz Lorbacher]

Xiaoli Lin

Master's Thesis at Technische Universität Berlin, Urban Management Programme

Transit-Oriented Development (TOD) for Megacities: Is TOD an Effective Solution for a Megacity's Traffic Congestion? Case Study of Shenzhen, China

Abstract

Increased motorisation and its associated traffic congestions seem to be an unavoidable urbanisation challenge for megacities in the South. Regarding BMBF's research objective of enhancing energy-responsive and climate-efficient structures in the urban centres for future megacities, this paper aims to reveal the underlying complexity of promoting Transit-Oriented Development (TOD), which is an integrative approach to public transport planning and urban planning. This research was done in the framework of the FMC-project in Hefei.

Shenzhen (SZ), chosen as a case study, is a South Chinese coastal city at the border to Hong Kong and one of the five pioneer cities[1] under the central government's "open door" policies since the late nineteen-seventies [Zou 1996; Ding 2003]. The aim of the Open Door Policy was to apply a land-leasing mechanism to attract foreign direct investment to develop mainland China's economy. The land-leasing mechanism has fundamentally accelerated Shenzhen's land-use development in the past thirty years. Today, Shenzhen turns out to be one of China's biggest megacities with a population of 10,467,400 in 2011 [Guangdong Statistic Year Book 2012].

Shenzhen's growing integration with Hong Kong's economy has increased mobility demands, first between the two cities, and second, in Shenzhen's central districts of Futian and Luohu. As a response, a metro was opened in 2004 (metro phase I) connecting Shenzhen's central districts with a border crossing to Hong Kong. The Shenzhen municipality further continued its effort in improving its metro system by applying the concept of TOD in its metro-planning phase II since 2011. The main objectives of this policy were to increase the numbers of passengers using public transport and to create mixed land use around transit stations—such as metro, bus, or tram stations. The general means of reaching these goals are (1) the integration of the metro planning into the land-use management system, (2) cross-institutional cooperation, and (3) the application of supplementary planning instruments to the holistic transit planning framework. But these objectives were not fully reached in Shenzhen due to the municipality's lack of experience.

TOD strategies should consider the public-transport system as a holistic system, integrating all different mobility modes in its planning framework. In the case of Shenzhen, too little attention has been paid during implementation to date. To improve this, a good governance structure for Shenzhen's TOD planning legislation is needed, an efficient financial model has to be applied, and a participatory process within the TOD planning framework should be launched. In any event, TOD as a multisector approach that integrates land use with transport planning and enhances governance structures deserves more attention, especially in China's research institutions and universities. Therefore, a success story within China would be of great importance for further studies. Unfortunately, Shenzhen is not yet such a best practice example. Thus, greater efforts have to be made to further improve its performance.

Introduction: TOD in China and Shenzhen

TOD Planning Principles

Transit-Oriented Development (TOD) is a planning strategy for compressing motorisation growth and promoting mixed land use, usually in areas close to urban-transport stations. Improvement efforts include the enhancement of pedestrian mobility and other non-motorised modes [Cervero 2006]. This could be implemented through urban scale control, better street design, and parking management [TDM Encyclopaedia 2012]. As a comprehensive planning framework, TOD integrates land-use management systems [Goodwill/ Hendricks 2002]; travel demand management level [Bajracharya et al. 2005]; and affordable housing strategies [Belzer et al. 2004].

Urbanisation and Transit-construction Trends in China

China is one of the world's economically fastest growing countries, and its urban growth has been strongly driven by political decisions relating to economic and land-use reforms since the late nineteen-seventies [Anderson/ Ge 2004]. Land resources were leased to various developers through market mechanisms resulting in higher governmental revenues [Zhang/ Pearlman 2004]. Urban population increased tremendously in many cities and this transition caused a high mobility demand in metropolitan areas, which exceeded the public transport supply—a common challenge for many municipalities in China. Many Chinese megacities—such as Beijing, Shanghai, and Guangzhou—have launched ambitious plans for transit networks in order to ease the on-road traffic pressure. However, more efforts are needed in order to increase the number of passengers and decrease motorisation growth. Shenzhen's rapid expansion of its transit network is an example of the complexities of transit network planning under the TOD planning framework.

Case Study Shenzhen

Special Economic Zone and its Urban Expansion

Shenzhen Special Economic Zone (SSEZ)[2] is one of China's oldest economic zones, designated in 1980 by the Chinese central government in order to test a market-oriented economy [Mee 2003]. Special policies and physical infrastructure support from the central government

Fig. 1   Shenzhen Urban Density [Shenzhen Statistic Year Book 2009]

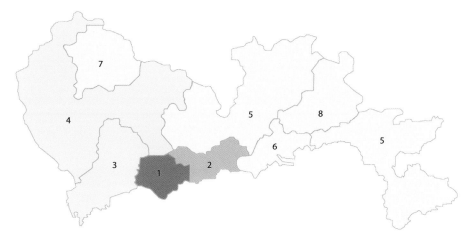

Shenzhen Administration Districts and its Populations

District Number	District Name	Land Area (sq.km)	Yearend Population (10 000pesons)	Population Density
1	Futian	78.66	120.61	15333.0791
2	Luohu	78.75	88.5	11238.0952
3	Nanshan	74.64	98.89	13248.9282
6	Yantian	185.11	22.77	1230.07941
4	Baoan	569.19	317.74	5582.31873
5	Longgang	682.85	180.02	2636.30373
7	Guang ming	155.44	41.59	2675.63047
8	Ping shan	167	21.1	1263.47305

Labels of Urban Density

> 50000	
45001-50000	
35001-40000	
30001-35000	
25001-30000	
20001-25000	
15001-20000	
10001-15000	
5001-10000	
<5000	

were applied in SSEZ to attract foreign direct investment [Bruton et al. 2005]. The Shenzhen urban landscape completely changed and its urban population increased from 314,100 in 1979 [Shenzhen Statistic Year Book 2009] to 10,467,400 in 2011 [Guangdong Statistic Year Book 2012]. Futian and Luohu are Shenzhen's two central districts with the highest urban density [Figure 1 ↗].

Ambitious Plans to Improve Shenzhen's Public Transportation System

Shenzhen is one of China's cities that has implemented an ambitious transit plan and intended to apply TOD strategies when planning its transit network. To date, Shenzhen's public transit system has been developed in two phases.

During Phase I, metro line 1 (east section) and metro line 4 (south section) with a total length of 22 km and twenty stations were opened in December 2004 [SZMC 2011]. These two lines connected Shenzhen's Luohu and Futian districts with the border checkpoints of Hong Kong [Liu Interview Nov. 2011]. The border separated mainland China's socialist system from the capitalist system of the former British colony of Hong Kong. However, this border did not separate the economic connectivity between both cities, which led to a large number of daily commuters.

During Phase II, the two lines of phase I were extended and another three lines were added. Now, these five lines have a total length of 178 km. Phase II was finished in June 2011. The daily passengers account for 446,000 [Shenzhen Government Online 2011]. During an ambitious Phase III (2011–2016), adding another 169.6 km to the existing network is intended [SZMC 2011].

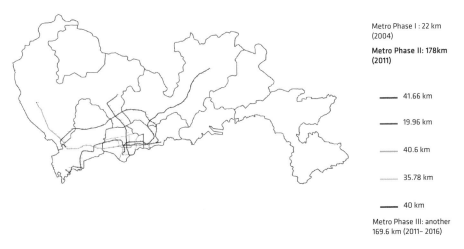

Metro Phase I : 22 km
(2004)

Metro Phase II: 178km
(2011)

—— 41.66 km

—— 19.96 km

—— 40.6 km

---- 35.78 km

—— 40 km

Metro Phase III: another
169.6 km (2011– 2016)

Focus and Objectives of Research

The research aims to reveal the effectiveness of public transportation improvement and motorisation mitigation in Shenzhen by applying TOD principles. Problems that can't be solved
by these principles will be studied in more detail in order to transfer the gained knowledge to
other Chinese cities.

These are the research objectives and questions:

1. What are the current barriers for Shenzhen's TOD approach in improving the population's
    accessibility to public transport (transit accessibility)?
2. Does better service of the public transit system lead to higher passenger numbers?
3. What additional planning instruments are needed for Shenzhen's TOD framework?
4. What experiences of Shenzhen's TOD approach could be transferred to other Chinese cities
    to support sustainable mobility concepts?

Methods: Interviews and Mapping

Literature Review

During the research, various methodologies were applied. A review of various books, academic
articles, official websites, and media news was conducted with a focus on sustainable urban
transport, new urbanism and TOD theory, land-use reform in China, and Shenzhen's TOD
planning.

Field Work Design

Stakeholder Interviews

Two semi-structured stakeholder interviews were conducted in Shenzhen regarding the public
sector's opinions of promoting TOD in Shenzhen. Interview partners were:

Fig. 3   Methodology instruments and integration [Author]

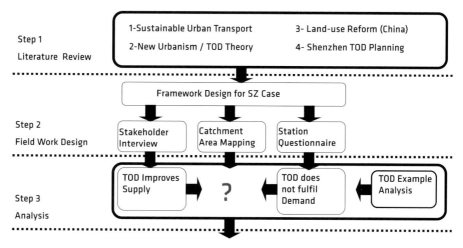

- Liu Longsheng, Director of the Rail Department of the Shenzhen Urban Planning and Land Resource Research Centre (SUPLR). This Centre is a sub-departmental unit of the Shenzhen government, which is responsible for transit network planning.
- Song Jiahua, Director of the Shenzhen Urban Transport Planning Centre Co. Ltd. (SUTPC). This consulting and design company supports the Shenzhen municipality in issues of transport research and management.

Questionnaires around Metro Stations

A survey, based on a structured questionnaire, was conducted in Futian district with thirty participants. Futian is the densest district in Shenzhen, both in population and transit network.

Mapping of Station-catchment Areas

A transit network catchment area is the geographical area in which people are able to reach public-transit service. It is commonly accepted as a circle area with a radius of about 500 m around public-transit stations. The method of station-catchment area mapping has been chosen for several transit stations in Futian district. The stations' catchment areas were set in relation with each respective sub-district density. The results of this comparison partially reflect the relationship between mobility demand and mobility supply.

Methodology-integration Process

Various methodologies have been integrated with each other during the analysis process [Figure 3 ↗].
    Step one: Materials about Shenzhen's transit planning have been collected through local newspapers and city planning documents. Books about TOD theory and international cases of sustainable urban transport have also been studied.

Step Two: Fieldwork instruments have been designed with three components: Semi-structured stakeholder interviews, station-catchment area measurements and questionnaires.

Step Three: Mobility supply and demand have been compared. The analysis of the fieldwork results has highlighted mismatches in travel demand and supply of Shenzhen's new planned transit lines. Additional effort is needed to improve the attractiveness of transit services in order to increase passenger numbers as well.

Findings: Challenges and Opportunities for Shenzhen's TOD Process

Based on the interviews and mapping activities, the most important findings and the gained knowledge regarding Shenzhen's TOD process are presented in the first three sections of this chapter. In the passages about transport and government issues, the text touches on some challenging and problematic insights and findings of TOD in Shenzhen. Based on these short problem descriptions, the text focuses on solutions and problem-solving strategies.

Categories of Shenzhen's TOD Zones

In order to understand Shenzhen's TOD processes and related projects, information was collected on the history of this issue and on different zones in which TOD projects have implemented.

Shenzhen's TOD concept was initiated around 2004–2005 by focusing on land-use reclassification along the planned transit network corridors of Phase II. It was organised by the Shenzhen Urban Planning Bureau (SUPB) with urban and transport planners. Vacant land and old factories were viewed as potential packages for TOD implementation due to their high capacity for future growth [Interview Song, Nov. 2011].

To come up with a plan on TOD, land use around transit stations was classified according to four criteria: current public-transport supply, future transport strategies, urban density, and future land development potentials. According to these criteria, four area types for different kinds of TOD were detected. By defining these areas, the team has focused especially on different walking distances to transit stations and on the degree of mixed land use [Figure 4 & Figure 5 ↗].

Differing Perceptions of the Concept of "Transit Accessibility"

Land-use reclassification is crucial for promoting TOD, but it does not indicate the transit station's accessibility level. Transit-station accessibility refers to the proximity of the transit station to the departure point (e.g., a private apartment building) and to the final destination (e.g., the office building). This distance has a strong influence on total travel time, which includes walking time to or from the station, waiting time for the service, and real travel time [Transport for London 2010]. It is an important factor that affects the choice between private car and public transport [Lindsey et al. 2010].

The representative of the public planning authority had a different perception of transit accessibility than normal citizens interviewed on the street. Planning authorities use different parameters to measure transit levels, such as network scale, length, and number of lines. The differing understanding among officials on Shenzhen's transit accessibility levels is further

Fig. 4 Guidance for TOD zones in Shenzhen City [Zhang et al. 2011]

Categories	Focus Functions	Walking Distance to Metro Station
Urban TOD (A) (Regional Level)	Direct Connection with urban artery Political cultural and economic activity centres	400–500 m to station centre
Urban TOD (B) (District Level)	Direct connection with urban artery Other activity complex centres	500–600 m to station centre
Neighbourhood TOD	Connection with secondary artery or neigh-bourhood street Located in community centres and well connected with other residential parcels and the city centre	600–1,000 m to station centre
Special Types of TOD	Special connection point for city develop-ment, such as airport and large scale transit centres	

Fig. 5 Guidance for TOD zones in Shenzhen City [Zhang et al. 2011]

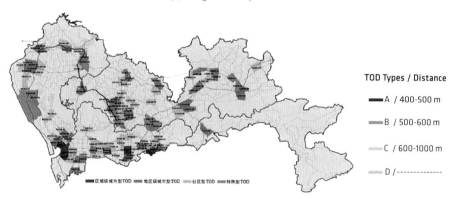

TOD Types / Distance

A / 400-500 m

B / 500-600 m

C / 600-1000 m

D / -------------

influenced by different definitions on the issue due to departmental cooperation gaps. The general hope is that, as long as the transit network crosses dense and congested areas and offers station access to the public, the more it will reduce the use of private cars [Interview Liu, 2011].

However, the questionnaire-based survey has shown that people's mobility choices depend not only on the availability or access of transit stations, but also on other factors such as total cost, total travel time for each trip, and other mobility availabilities. A transit station is just the prerequisite rather than a direct decisive factor for shifting people's mobility choice towards public transport.

Possible Solution

Bridging the gap of understanding on transit accessibility is necessary to improve transit service, make public transport more attractive, and reduce the gap between mobility demand and supply. This can be achieved by integrating participation processes into the planning process for further projects.

Fig. 6   Transit accessibility perception in Shenzhen [Author]

Target group	Interpretation of transit accessibility	Method
Director of Rail Department from Shenzhen Urban Planning & Land Resource Research Centre (SUPLR)	Network scale Length of lines Numbers of transit lines Numbers of connection points	Semi-Structured Interview
Director of Shenzhen Urban Transport Planning Centre co. Ltd (SUTPC)	Factor of accessibility: Financial budget / land resource availability	Semi-structured Interview
Public (30 participants)	Total cost Total travel time Convenience Other mobility choice	Questionnaire near the metro station

The Influence of the Land-leasing Mechanism

According to the TOD concept, urban infrastructure (e.g., metro or other transit lines) should play an active role in guiding urban agglomeration patterns. In other words, a high-density development should focus on transit corridors and junctions in order to catch potential passengers.

Shenzhen's metro lines do not play such an active role in guiding urban development along the transit corridors, as for example Copenhagen's Finger Plan. Instead, these metro lines act as passive mobility supply lines, even facing difficulties in inserting themselves into existing urban built-up areas. Urban land in Shenzhen has been intensively developed with high density and barely left space for transit network construction. This development was strongly driven by land-leasing mechanisms; several monofunctional urban clusters had been predefined by a formerly mandated master plan. Later, these areas were interconnected by road infrastructures.

Public transit network planning faces several conflicts, including: (1) extremely high travel demand between areas close to the Central Business District and other zones; (2) higher construction cost in the dense areas; and (3) many landholders like State Owned Enterprises (SOEs), who are not willing to cooperate with the Shenzhen municipality in providing land resources for the construction of public transit infrastructure. Transit network planning has to adjust the layout according to land resource allowance rather than real transport demand [Interview 2011, Song].

Possible Solution

Land-use management reform is needed to solve the conflict between different stakeholders for acquiring land resources for transit network. Responsibility and profit share should be well defined between different stakeholders and ideally could reach a certain level of agreement; furthermore, the agreements should be legalised within Shenzhen's urban-planning system.

Fig. 7   Shenzhen's urban land-use patterns expansion [Shenzhen Urban Planning Bureau 2005 cited in Hao et al. 2011]

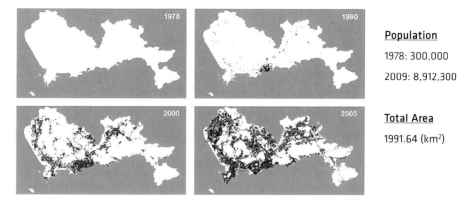

Population

1978: 300,000

2009: 8,912,300

Total Area

1991.64 (km²)

Fig. 8   Metro service evaluation—response in Futian district to the question: What do you think about the Shenzhen Metro Service? [Author]

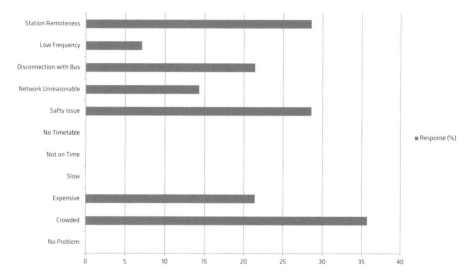

Transport Issues in Shenzhen's TOD

A questionnaire focusing on metro and bus service has been distributed in Shenzhen's central Futian district to thirty participants. Some of the results are shown in following section:

Metro Service: Mismatch between Urban Density and Available Metro Stations

Crowdedness seems to be the main problem of the metro service (36%), followed by stations' remoteness (28%) and "metro service's safety" (28%). Responses have also shown disappointment with bus service's disconnection to transit service (21%) [Figure 8 ↗].

To understand the "crowdedness" behind the transit planning, a mapping method to compare metro network's catchment areas (500 m) and the respective real urban density has been applied to Futian district. The result shows that the concentration of metro stations

Fig. 9 Comparison of Futian district's density with the catchment areas (500 m) of the metro network [Author/ Futian Government Online]

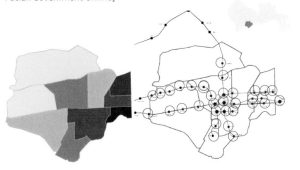

> 50000	
45001–50000	
35001–40000	
30001–35000	
25001–30000	
20001–25000	
15001–20000	
10001–15000	
5001–10000	
<5000	

does not reflect real urban density, which indirectly indicates a mismatch between mobility supply and real demand [Figure 9 ↗].

Possible Solution

Sufficient procedures for acquiring relevant data should be part of the TOD framework. It will help to improve the accuracy of the selection of transit stations. For example, the statistic planning bureau should cooperate with the police office because both authorities are involved in the collection of urban-density data. The statistic planning bureau is responsible for the data collection of Shenzhen's registered urban citizens, while the police office is more responsible for the data collection of Shenzhen's migrant workers. Both are important components of a more precise urban density analysis in order to choose an optimal location for metro stations according to the real travel demand and an affordable financial budget for construction.

Disconnection between Metro and Other Mobility Modes

The metro network needs to integrate with other mobility modes to create an efficient public transport system and meet different mobility demands. By integrating the metro network with the bus network, biking and walking facilities, more passengers could be attracted to public transportation. However, the new metro lines have weak connections with the current bus service due to different operational systems and companies.

Bus Service Companies as Competitors

Bus companies compete with transit companies as metro or BRT due to different operational systems. But although the three bus companies have divided the area into operational zones, in many cases they still compete with each other [Figure 10 ↗].

Pedestrians and Bikers as Losers in a Car-driven Urban Environment

Road connectivity and non-motorised transport modes are not well developed in Shenzhen. Pedestrians have to cross roads using over-bridge facilities or underground tunnels. Many mu-

Fig. 10 Shenzhen's bus companies and the respective operation zones [Shenzhen Urban Transport Planning Centre Co., Ltd]

Fig. 11 Bus-service evaluation responses in Futian district to the question: What do you think of the Shenzhen bus service? [Author]

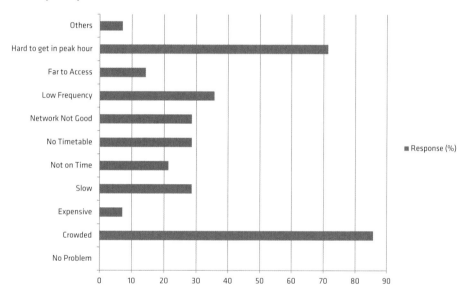

nicipal roads are occupied by illegal parking, which leads to many detours for pedestrians trying to access the public transport network, such as transit stations or bus stops. Biking routes have been blocked by many fences along the municipal roads, and the connectivity of biking facilities is not well developed in Shenzhen. Shenzhen has also prohibited motorbikes and considers them a factor in causing on-road accidents. The number of motorbikes has dropped tremendously in Shenzhen and they are almost non-existent in the city now [Figures 12 and 13 ↗].

Possible Solutions

Solution 1: A cross-sector agreement should be established between the various mobility service providers in terms of network connection and operation routes. In addition, profit share and operation modes should be finalised into the transport planning legislations.

Fig. 12   Shenzhen's modal split 1995–2005 [Shenzhen Urban Transport Planning Centre Co., Ltd]

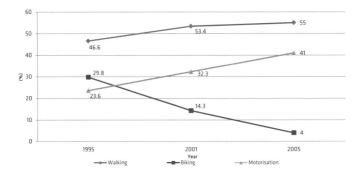

Fig. 13   Biking problems in Shenzhen–responses in Futian district to the question: What do you think is the problem of biking in Shenzhen? [Author]

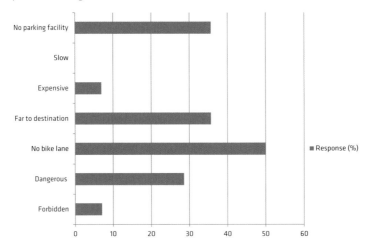

Solution 2: A pedestrian mobility improvement scheme should be developed in order to bridge the gap between infrastructure planning and real pedestrian mobility needs. Various slow mobility modes should be enhanced in order to bridge the gap of the "last mile" between transit stations and the final station; it is an important criterion for the comfortableness of the public-transport system in comparison with private cars.

TOD planning results are not simply the reclassification of existing land parcels around the transit station, but rather a pedestrian mobility enhancement strategy with the integration of all mobility modes. Regular surveys need to be conducted at the neighbourhood level to collect public opinion on mobility pattern and travel demand. A technical solution should be integrated with community planning results and facts.

Increasing Motorisation in Shenzhen Despite Opening of Public Transit Service

The opening of the Phase I transit service in 2004 (e.g., mainly the metro) and the further expansion could not curb rapid motorisation in Shenzhen's urban centres. Private vehicles have almost doubled from 647,069 in 2004 to 1,252,747 in 2008 [Figure 14 ↗].

Fig. 14 Vehicle numbers in Shenzhen 2004-2009 [Shenzhen Statistic Year Book 2009]

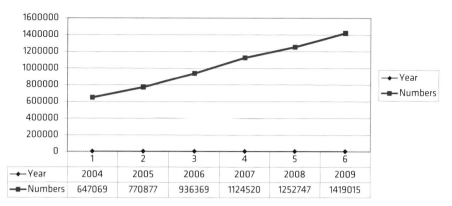

	1	2	3	4	5	6
◆Year	2004	2005	2006	2007	2008	2009
■Numbers	647069	770877	936369	1124520	1252747	1419015

Fig. 15 Private vehicle advantages—responses in Futian District to the question: What are the advantages of using private cars as compared to using public transport? [Author]

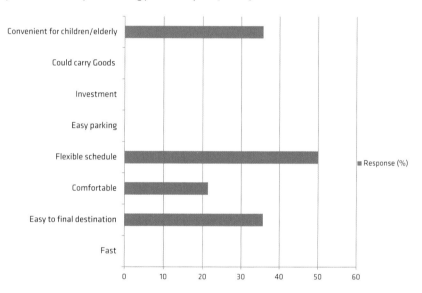

According to interview responses, the use of private vehicles is more preferred due to travel flexibility (50%), followed by convenience for elderly or children (35%), and the convenience level to each trip's final destination (35%) [Figure 15 ↗].

Possible Solution

Travel-demand management (TDM) is an important component of the effectiveness of the TOD approach [Bajracharya et al. 2005]. "Pull" and "Push" levels should work hand in hand in order to improve transit ridership and decrease reliance on private vehicles. But the Shenzhen municipality did not apply sufficient TDM schemes to reduce motorisation growth.

In order to increase the number of passengers and improve TOD outcomes, the Shenzhen municipality could learn from the government of Singapore by applying diverse TDM schemes

Fig. 16 Travel demand management: Comparison between Singapore and Shenzhen showing the TDM concepts in use [Author]

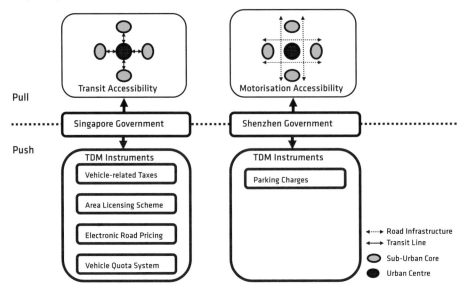

at the same time [Figure 16 ↗]. On the "Pull" level, Singapore has constructed main transit corridors leading to the centre. Here, bigger mass-rapid-transport trains (MRT) are in use. In addition, important satellite towns have their own, smaller, light-rail trains (LRT) feeding the main MRT lines [Cervero 2006].

On the "Push" level, the Singapore government was strongly involved in vehicle-compressing polices; several TDM schemes have been applied, such as vehicle related taxes, area licensing scheme, electronic road pricing and vehicle quota system, which have strongly limited the growth of vehicles in Singapore [Seik 2000; Goh 2002; Willoughby 2001]. However, Shenzhen has only considered a scheme to charge for parking during the metro-planning process.

Governance Issues in Shenzhen's TOD

Financial Restructuring Leads to Uncertainties

A sustainable financial mechanism plays an important role in TOD for a guaranteed transit network optimisation. Shenzhen transit planning relied heavily on governmental funding in phase I, but the municipality could not provide full financial support for further construction of the transit system. Therefore, a financial restructuring is underway, which leads to an uncertain future for Shenzhen's transit planning [Interview Song 2011].

Possible Solution

The direction of the improvement might be compared to the Hong Kong experiences on three levels: land-use policy level, transport-planning policy level, and financial resources level [Figure 17 ↗].

Fig. 17 Financial mechanism comparison of TOD-planning between Hong Kong and Shenzhen [Author]

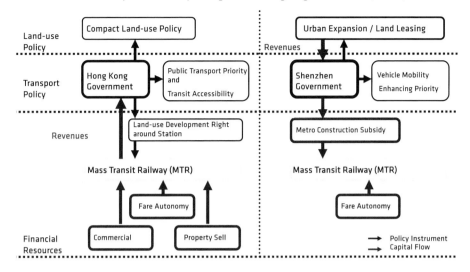

1. On the land-use policy level, Hong Kong has promoted a compact land-use policy [Lo et al. 2008], but Shenzhen has allocated its land resources through land-use rights to different land developers and state-owned enterprises.

2. On the transport-planning policy level: Hong Kong has applied a continuous policy to guarantee mass transit facility's a priority status [Lo et al. 2008]. However, Shenzhen has prioritised strategies to enhance vehicle mobility by expanding road infrastructures.

3. On the financial resources level: the Hong Kong government has granted land-use development around the metro stations to Hong Kong's successful and private rail and metro company, the Mass Transit Railway Corporation Ltd. (MTR), which plays the role of real estate operator as well as railway construction company. MTR has successfully managed metro construction costs without governmental subsidies by selling properties, face autonomy, and integration of commercial activities around the metro network [Lo et al. 2008; Tang 2009; Cullinane 2003; Cervero/ Murakami 2008; Tang et al. 2004]. However, Shenzhen's land resources have been distributed to different land-use developers; it could not provide a centralised development model as in Hong Kong. Thus, the financial resources of transit line operation in Shenzhen are far weaker than in Hong Kong.

Insufficient Adaptation of Shenzhen's TOD into the Legal Urban-planning System

The Singapore and Hong Kong TOD examples are not comparable to Shenzhen, due to the differences in political and city planning systems [Newman/ Kenworthy 1996]. The Hong Kong and Singapore governments are more strongly involved in urban planning legislation, and promote transit accessibility as well as motorisation restriction. Shenzhen's TOD results were not adapted into the Shenzhen City Comprehensive Plan (SZCCP)[3] and Shenzhen City Planning Norms and Standards (SZCPNS); those are important planning documents to guarantee a concrete planning outcome [Interview Song 2011].

Shenzhen's TOD approach has been limited to technical solutions instead of incorporating it into urban-planning legislation. Different departmental interests and conflicts have led to disagreement in implementing TOD results in the existing urban structure. Institutional incapacity for legislation formulation as well as adjustment of the existing planning regulations and mechanisms are the main barriers to future TOD implementation [Interview Song and Liu, Nov. 2011].

Possible Solution

Capacity building is important at both the technical and governance levels in Shenzhen. TOD implementation should be based on intensive cooperation across the various planning authorities. Therefore, an assigned independent authority should be responsible for monitoring the TOD planning process and for supporting the coordination of the TOD-planning approach among the various planning authorities. Shenzhen's city planning system needs flexibility in legislation formulation and policy introductions. Cooperation with Hong Kong and Singapore might be helpful for exchanging technical and institutional knowledge and improving capacities among personnel.

Gaps in Departmental Cooperation

Rapid-transit expansion came with many mistakes during the construction phase. For example, Shenzhen's urban-planning bureau focused on integrating the transit network within the urban spatial structure, while Shenzhen's railway department worked on solutions for specific transit stations regarding financial costs and technical requirements. These different perspectives led to suboptimal results in most cases. For example, the transit construction department may finalise the transit station according to the simplest solution, rather than following the plan from the urban planning department [Interview Liu, Nov. 2011].

Possible Solution

An assigned department should take responsibility for monitoring transit-network planning procedures in order to reduce the mismatches among the various planning authorities.

Conclusion: Shenzhen's TOD and its Transferability to Other Chinese Cities

Shenzhen's TOD attempt has shown its complexities in tackling cross-sector issues. Rapid transit network extension does not automatically increase transit ridership, indeed, the TOD approach needs to consider the following three aspects in its comprehensive planning framework: (1) integration with the land-use management system, (2) formulation of a comprehensive transport planning policy, and (3) integration with governance issues.

Land-use Management Level

Insufficient land-leasing mechanisms and a lack of land-resource availability have strong negative effects on the city's transit accessibility, leading to spatial constraints for public transport and non-motorised mobility.

On the land-resource availability level, the conflict between Shenzhen municipality and different land-use developers in acquiring land resources for transit construction is still unresolved, which leads to the remoteness of certain transit stations in Shenzhen.

Spatial constraints show as follows: first, in many parts, the city was subdivided into different monofunctional zones based on road infrastructure regulations. Thus, the daily commute demand (from home to work) between different zones is extremely high. Second, most of those parts are being developed into gated communities by various land-use developers. This leads to an insufficient integration of public-transport networks. For example, citizens have to walk very far to access a public-transport station due to the auto-oriented spatial scales and gated-community patterns.

A land-use system reform is urgently needed to enhance Shenzhen's TOD planning, which should address the cooperation scheme between the Shenzhen municipality and different stakeholders. This scheme should address the responsibilities and benefits shared between the Shenzhen municipality and various land-use developers during the transit network extension. This scheme should also provide guidelines for different road infrastructure planning institutions. Here, urban-planning patterns based on public transport mode and pedestrian mobility scale should be considered.

Recommendations for Improving Transport Planning

A holistic TOD approach is not a simple technical solution; rather it is a conceptual framework for improving the pedestrian mobility pattern. Shenzhen's transit-network extension has no direct influence on the motorisation growth trend. Transit ridership enhancement needs the upgrading of the physical transit facility as well as proper planning strategies and policies, which include a transit-accessibility enhancement scheme, a public-transit integration scheme, and a travel-demand management scheme.

Transit-accessibility Enhancement Scheme

On the macro level, an effective land-use reformulation scheme should be developed in order to guarantee sufficient land parcels for the construction of metro stations. On the medium level, an assigned independent institution should monitor transit accessibility level and coordinate the co-operation between various planning authorities during the transit-planning phase. At the micro level, a participatory approach during transit-network planning should be enhanced for gathering information of residents' mobility demand and behaviours.

Transit Integration with Other Mobility Schemes

Shenzhen's public-transport system needs to be an integrated system: for example, Shenzhen's TOD approach has shown that bus-service providers do not cooperate with the metro service provider. Therefore, while many buses take similar routes as the metro, most customers chose the metro service rather than buses, which leads to waste of energy and resources. Another example: when bus services are needed in certain areas to bridge the gap between metro stations and other destinations, it turns out that bus services are insufficient. These obstacles are frequently based on diverging institutional interests and profits. The cooperation between various mobility modes could improve the public transit network in general and meet different mobility patterns and needs.

Road connectivity should also be improved as well as non-motorised transport (NMT) planning. They are also important components of the entire public-transport system by improving the transit network's service and thereby especially influencing the mobility patterns on the "last mile". It will influence people's propensity in shifting their daily commuting choice from private cars to public transport.

Travel-demand Management Scheme

Without any doubt, transit facility upgrading is an important step for public-transit network improvement. However, in order to achieve an effective result in mitigating motorisation growth, a proper level of travel-demand management needs to be integrated into the TOD planning framework. And last but not least, Singapore's lessons should be learned and reformulated according to Shenzhen's local context.

Governance Issues in Shenzhen's TOD Approach

Integration of Shenzhen's TOD Legislation into its Urban-planning System

Even though Shenzhen's TOD approach has developed four types of TOD application categories in terms of land-use intensification, these results have been limited to a technical research level rather than being implemented into actual land-use planning practice. This happened due to non-functioning legal planning procedures that would consider TOD issues from the very beginning of the general urban-planning process and then on the levels of land-use planning and implementation. Therefore, Shenzhen's TOD needs to be legalised at a formal urban-planning level to have a larger scale of influence. Then, concepts of compact and mix-use, transit accessibility improvement, or motorisation restriction policies could be successfully applied. A legalised TOD planning process could smooth the conflicts between the various planning authorities during different levels of planning as well.

Sustainable Financial Scheme for Shenzhen's TOD

A sustainable financial mechanism for transit construction is fundamentally important to guarantee a sufficient transit network expansion. Examples for such mechanisms are a public private partnership model (PPP) for the development of urban infrastructure, or the additional integration of successful financial schemes and policies from Hong Kong.

Participatory Approach for Shenzhen's TOD

Promoting a participatory approach in Shenzhen's TOD planning is crucial for achieving effective outcomes in terms of transferring public values into transit network planning. Collecting information directly from citizens about their real mobility needs will contribute to a more sufficient transit-service supply. Furthermore, a deep understanding of influential factors for mobility choice could help the municipality to formulate a proper transport policy. None of these preconditions can be achieved without wide participation. In Shenzhen, the conventional top-down approach on urban planning should shift to a more bottom-up attitude for upgrading the urban infrastructure in the future.

References

Anderson, G./ Ge, Y. (2004): "Do economic reforms accelerate urban growth: the case of China". In: *Urban Studies*, 41 (11), pp. 2197–210

Bajracharya, B./ Khan, S. / Longland, M, (2005): *Regulatory and incentive mechanisms to implement transit oriented development (TOD) in South east Queensland.* http://www.reconnectingamerica.org/assets/Uploads/bestpractice017.pdf, 25.10. 2011

Bruton, M. J./ Bruton, S. G. / Li, Y. (2005): "Shenzhen: coping with uncertainties in planning". In: *Habitat International* 29, pp. 227–43.

Belzer, D./ Autler, G./ Espinosa, J. / Feigon, S. / Ohland, G. (2004): "The Transit-Oriented Development Drama and Its Actors". In: Hank, D./ Ohland, G. (2004): *The New Transit Town: Best Practices in Transit-oriented Development.* Washington

Cervero, R. (2006): *Public transport and sustainable urbanism: global lessons.* http://www.uctc.net/papers/806.pdf, 27.11.2011

Cervero, R./ Murakami, J. (2008): *Rail + Property development: A model of sustainable transit finance and urbanism.* http://www.its.berkeley.edu/publications/UCB/2008/VWP/UCB-ITS-VWP-2008-5.pdf, 23.10.2011

Cullinane, S. (2003): "Hong Kong's low car dependence: lessons and prospects". In: *Journal of Transport Geography* 11, pp. 25-35

Ding, C. (2003): "Land policy reform in China: assessment and prospects". In: *Land Use Policy*, 20 (2), pp.109–120

Goodwill, J./ Hendricks, S. J. (2002): *Building Transit Oriented Development in Established Communities.* http://www.nctr.usf.edu/pdf/473-135.pdf, 13.10.2011

Goh, M. (2002): "Congestion management and electronic road pricing in Singapore". In: *Journal of Transport Geography*, 10, pp. 29–38

Hao, P./ Sliuzas, R. / Geertman, S. (2011): "The development and redevelopment of urban village in Shenzhen". In: *Habitat International*, 35 (2), pp. 214–24

Lo, H. K./Tang, S. / Wang, D.Z.W. (2008): "Managing the accessibility on mass public transit: The case of Hong Kong". In: *Journal of Transport and Land Use* 1(2), pp. 23–49

Lindsey, M./ Schofer, J.L. / Cohen, P. D. / Gray, K. A. (2010): "Relationship between proximity to transit and ridership for journey-to-work trips in Chicago". In: *Transport Research Part A*, 44, pp. 697–709

Mee, K. N. (2003): "City profile Shenzhen". In: *Cities*, 20 (6), pp. 429–41

Newman, P./ Kenworthy, J. (1996): "The land use-transport connection an overview". In: *Land Use Policy*, 13 (1), pp. 1–22

Shao, Y./ Song, J. (2011): "Pearl River Delta Urban TOD Development Mode and Realization Methods Research". In: *Part Three: TOD, Green and Specific Topic of Transport Planning Research, 2006–2010 Excellent Article,* Shenzhen.

Shenzhen China (2009): *Shenzhen Statistic Year Book.* http://www.sz.gov.cn/tjj/tjsj/tjnj1/201012/t20101224_1620341.htm, 11. 11. 2011

Shenzhen Futian Government Online (2011): *Futian District the 6th national census publication.* http://www.szft.gov.cn/ft/zfbm/tj/ztlm/tjfx/201108/t20110801_304780.html, 20.01. 2012. http://www.szft.gov.cn/ft/zfbm/tj/ztlm/tjfx/201108/t20110801_304780.html, 20.01.2012

Shenzhen Government Online (2011): *Checkpoints and Transportation.* http://english.sz.gov.cn/economy/201107/t20110713_1676136.htm, 7.11. 2011

Shenzhen Urban Transport Planning Design Research Center Co. LTD (2010): *Land Use and Transport Coordination Development Research based on TOD Development Mode-Shenzhen as an Example.* http://www.sutpc.com/papershow.asp?id=196&Page=2, 03.01. 2012. http://www.sutpc.com/papershow.asp?id=196&Page=2, 03.01. 2012

Shenzhen Urban Transport Planning Design Research Center Ltd. (2011): *2006–2010 Excellent Articles (2011).* Shenzhen

Seik. F.T. (2000): "An advanced demand management instrument in urban transport: Electronic road pricing in Singapore". In: *Cities*, 17 (1), pp. 34–45

Statistics Bureau of Guangdong Province (2012): *Guangdong Statistic Year Book 2012* http://www.gdstats.gov.cn/tjnj/2012/table/4/04-05.html, 13.10.2011

SZMC Shenzhen Metro Group Co., Ltd (2011): *Stations and Maps.* http://www.szmc.net/cms/page?arg=en/stations, 7.11. 2011

SZMC Shenzhen Metro Group Co., Ltd (2011): *Group Company Profile.* http://www.szmc.net/cms/page?arg=en/about&code=49, 11.11.2011

Tang, B.S. (2009): *Public Interest, private rights and sustainable use of urban space.* http://www.bre.polyu.edu.hk/BRE_workshop/pdf/Public%20Interest,%20private%20rights_revised.pdf, 27.11.2011

Tang, B.S./ Chiang, Y.H. / Baldwin, A.N. / Yeung, C.W. (2004): *Study of the integrated Rail-Property development model in Hong Kong.* http://www.reconnectingamerica.org/assets/Uploads/mtrstudyrpmodel2004.pdf, 16.11.2011

Transport for London (2010): *Measuring Public Transport Accessibility Levels.* http://data.london.gov.uk/documents/PTAL-methodology.pdf, 27.11.2011

TDM Encyclopaedia (2012): *Transit-oriented Development–Using Public Transit to Create More Accessible and Livable Neighborhoods.* http://www.vtpi.org/tdm/tdm45.html, 27.11.2011

Willoughby, C. (2001): "Singapore's motorization policies 1960-2000". In: *Transport Policy,* 8, pp. 125–39

Xue, X./ Schmid, F. / Smith, R. A. (2002): "An introduction to China's rail transport Part 2: Urban rail transit systems, highway transport and the reform of China's railways". In: *Proceedings of the Institution of Mechanical Engineers, Part F: Journal of Rail and Rapid Transit,* 216, pp. 165–74

Zhang, X./ Tian, F. / Lu, G. / Shao, Y. (2011): "Shenzhen TOD Development Framework and Planning Strategy Research". In: *Part 3: TOD, Green and Specific Topic of Transport Planning Research, 2006–2010 Excellent Article.* Shenzhen.

Zhang, S./ Pearlman, K. (2004): "China's land use reforms: a review of journal literature". In: *Journal of Planning Literature,* 19 (1), pp. 16–60

Zhang, C./ Lin, Q. (2011): "For collaborative implementation of urban transports planning–Shenzhen Research and Practice". In: *Shenzhen Urban Transport Planning Design Research Center.* Shanghai.

Zou, D. (1996): "The open door policy and urban development in China". In: *HABITAT INTL* 20, (4), pp. 525–29

Notes

1 During the Open Door Policy of the late nineteen-seventies, China attracted foreign investments into Special Economic Zones. These zones where formed by the five pioneer cities of Shenzhen, Zhuhai, Shantou, Xiamen, Hainan. This policy started China's modernisation and industrial boom.

2 The Shenzhen Special Economic Zone (SSEZ) covers an area of 392 km² and includes the following four districts within Shenzhen city: Nanshan, Futian, Luohu, and Yantian.

3 The Shenzhen City Comprehensive Plan is a master plan developed by the municipality. The plan is rather general in guiding the direction and focus of Shenzhen's future urban development.

Tang, B.S./ Chiang, Y.H. / Baldwin, A.N. / Yeung, C.W. (2004): *Study of the integrated Rail-Property development model in Hong Kong.* http://www.reconnectingamerica.org/assets/Uploads/mtrstudyrpmodel2004.pdf, 16.11. 2011

Transport for London (2010): *Measuring Public Transport Accessibility Levels.* http://data.london.gov.uk/documents/PTAL-methodology.pdf, 27.11. 2011

TDM Encyclopaedia (2012): *Transit-oriented Development -Using Public Transit to Create More Accessible and Livable Neighborhoods.* http://www.vtpi.org/tdm/tdm45.html, 27.11.2011

Willoughby, C. (2001): "Singapore's motorization policies 1960-2000". In: *Transport Policy,* 8, pp. 125–39

Xue, X./ Schmid, F. / Smith, R. A. (2002): "An introduction to China's rail transport Part 2: Urban rail transit systems, highway transport and the reform of China's railways". In: *Proceedings of the Institution of Mechanical Engineers, Part F: Journal of Rail and Rapid Transit,* 216, pp. 165–74

Zhang, X./ Tian, F. / Lu, G. / Shao, Y. (2011): "Shenzhen TOD Development Framework and Planning Strategy Research". In: *Part 3: TOD, Green and Specific Topic of Transport Planning Research, 2006-2010 Excellent Article.* Shenzhen.

Zhang, S./ Pearlman, K. (2004): "China's land use reforms: a review of journal literature". In: *Journal of Planning Literature,* 19 (1), pp. 16–60

Zhang, C./ Lin, Q. (2011): "For collaborative implementation of urban transports planning - Shenzhen Research and Practice". In: *Shenzhen Urban Transport Planning Design Research Center.* Shangha.

Zou, D. (1996): "The open door policy and urban development in China". In: *HABITAT INTL* 20, (4), pp. 525–29

Manuel Fiechtner

Bachelor's Thesis at Freie Universität Berlin, Institute of Geographical Sciences

The Public Transportation System of Hefei, China: An Analysis

Abstract

In addition to the important megacities Beijing and Shanghai, there are a number of rapidly growing cities in the People's Republic of China. One of them is Hefei, the capital of the Anhui province with about 5.7 million inhabitants (2011), situated more than 300 km west of Shanghai. Especially since the beginning of the twenty-first century, Hefei is characterised by growth, expansion, and reconstruction. Due to this ongoing growth, traffic volume has undergone a massive increase, which has made huge investments in infrastructure necessary.

For Hefei, an extensive analysis of the current quality, major deficits, and an assessment of the effects and importance of the PT-system was missing. Therefore, this paper focuses on Hefei's public transportation system (PT-system), which is less developed than the infrastructure for individual transportation. In conjunction with other measures of the METRASYS project, an in-depth analysis can contribute to a reduction of climate-damaging individual traffic by assessing the potentials of Hefei's PT.

Methods from the empirical social research and analysis functions of Geographic Information Systems (GIS) were applied for this thesis. An explorative approach was used to retrieve information about Hefei's PT-system. Based on the fundamentals retrieved from interviews, additional GIS analyses were carried out. Through accessibility analyses and further GIS-analyses, the quality of Hefei's PT system was determined.

The bus system is the "backbone" of Hefei's PT system. It is especially dense in the inner city, but also makes vast areas of the city and the administrative district of Hefei accessible. The Bus Rapid Transit System is not really established yet, and the first metro lines will not start operating until 2014. Motorised individual transport has dominated Hefei's city traffic since the level of motorisation increased. Analyses of the coverage of bus stops prove that a large number of inhabited or residential areas have no bus stop available within a 300-m or 500-m radius. Hefei's bus system does not fulfil governmental standards and goals.

Hefei's eastern inner-city centre and the areas around important sub-centres have the best PT quality. These areas also have the best accessibility by foot to bus stops, accessibility within the PT to five selected sub-centres, and the highest density of supply of PT-service in Hefei. On the other hand, urban expansions (after 2001) or peripheral development areas like the Binhu-district have bad or non-existent PT-accessibility and altogether show poor quality of PT-supply.

It is unclear how long the growth process in Hefei will continue, how planned PT will be implemented and accepted or which other challenges in the urban and traffic planning Hefei will have to overcome, but the city will have to master a massive development of traffic infrastructure and implement major urban-planning projects.

Note: The described events and sources reflect the status as of the beginning of 2012.

Fig. 1   Research focus [Author]

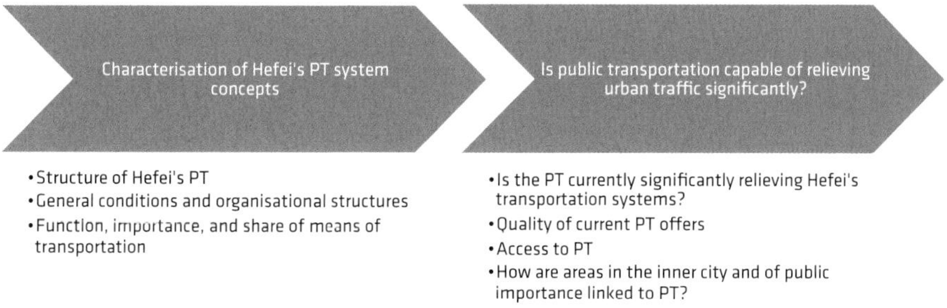

- Structure of Hefei's PT
- General conditions and organisational structures
- Function, importance, and share of means of transportation

- Is the PT currently significantly relieving Hefei's transportation systems?
- Quality of current PT offers
- Access to PT
- How are areas in the inner city and of public importance linked to PT?

Introduction: Challenges of Public Transport in Hefei and China

Hefei's Public Transport (PT)

The main focus of this paper is to analyse Hefei's public transportation system (PT-system) and assess the extent to which PT can contribute to relieving Hefei's traffic system. The particular focus is on Hefei's bus network. First, the efficacy of Hefei's current PT-system is described and rated. Based on analyses carried out with Geographic Information Systems (GIS), whether the PT-system is appropriately adjusted to Hefei's rapid development and to adapt to the changing demand is evaluated. Therefore, the city structure and development as well as its impact on the development of the PT-system are analysed.

PT in major cities has to offer mobility to all citizens, and to enable them to participate in the city's public life. Especially in times of global climate change and shortage of resources, PT is an alternative to automotive transportation and the backbone of urban transportation. Each day, PT allows thousands of citizens to reach the institutions of daily life. High-quality PT is an attractive alternative to motorised individual traffic and contributes to relieving cities from motorised individual traffic. Attractive and sustainable PT concepts contribute to environmentally friendly urban traffic and are essential for mobility concepts of major cities [Kirchhoff 2002; Gather et al. 2008; Nuhn/ Hesse 2006; Senate Department for Urban Development of Berlin 2011].

The focus of the following research is derived from these general conditions and theoretical basics in Figure 1 ↗.

Filling the Research Gap on Hefei's PT

A sustainable PT concept can function as a fundamental control system for the development of Hefei. By integrating measures of urban planning and traffic planning with traffic policies, it can also influence growth tendencies in the People's Republic of China at a regional level. As no further analyses focussing on PT quality were carried out in Hefei as part of the METRASYS project, this work evaluates a very important part of Hefei's transport system [Berberich 2010; Chu Jinlong et al. 2007; METRASYS 2010a; Eichhorst et al. 2010].

Public Transport in China and Hefei

Anhui's Capital: A Rapidly Growing Secondary City

The People's Republic of China (PR China) has a number of rapidly growing cities in addition to the important megacities Beijing and Shanghai. One is Hefei, capital of the Anhui province and the subject of this paper's research.

Especially since the beginning of the twenty-first century, Hefei is characterised by growth, expansion, and reconstruction. The city of Hefei currently has more than 5.7 million inhabitants and the Hefei administrative area has about eight million citizens (2011). Hefei is situated north of the Chao Lake between the Jangtsekiang and Huai rivers, more than 300 km west of Shanghai. It has historically grown as a monocentral city with a cultural, administrative, and economic centre in the historic old town (Circular Road). In the recent years, Hefei has experienced strong growth: Hefei grew by a factor of 2.5 during the last ten years. It is currently trying to dissolve the monocentral structure of the region and instead implement a polycentric structure with independent centres [Chu Jinlong et al. 2007; Yan Ping 2011].

Due to this ongoing growth, traffic volume has undergone a massive increase. This has made huge investments in infrastructure necessary. The degree of urbanisation in Hefei has reached such a stage that experts foresee a massive rise in traffic jams, housing shortages, and environmental pollution. As a result, the local government invested in road infrastructure, especially in the construction of elevated roads, but also residential buildings, and environmentally friendly urban construction projects [Yan Ping 2011].

This paper's focus is Hefei's PT-system, which currently consists of a bus network and the Bus Rapid Transit (BRT). The first metro lines are under construction.

Compared to streets and other infrastructure for individual transportation, the PT-system is less developed. In order to improve the quality of PT, investments are planned and in parts already decided. Currently, the major project is the construction of a new station, situated in a newly built quarter south of the city centre, which will serve as a multimodal connecting station. It will combine bus- and BRT-services, a metro-line, and regional train services [Yan Ping 2011; Hefei City Administration 2006].

An extensive analysis of the current quality, major deficits, and an assessment of the effects and importance of the PT-systems are still missing.

Urban Traffic and PT Quality in China

In recent years, China has experienced an increase in motorisation and is today one of the automobile industry's biggest growing markets. This led to huge investments in street infrastructure and automobile-centred urban and traffic planning, which still could not keep pace with the enduring fast development. Even though several elevated roads were constructed, there are still numerous traffic jams, which affect the PT—especially bus networks. In general, urban and traffic planning in Chinese megacities is more often characterised by high dynamics and investments rather than by gentle urban development, preservation of culturally valuable architecture, and sustainable planning. For example, the share of non-motorised individual traffic (especially the famous bicycle traffic) declined rapidly [Kenworthy/ Gang Hu 2002; Wei-Shiuen Ng et al. 2010; Pucher et al. 2007; Campanella 2008]. Due to these conflicts, the Chinese government determined the development of PT as a national priority in 2005 [Gwilliam 2010].

Yan Tang/ Kunzmann [2008] explain the strongly hierarchical Chinese planning processes, like the Five-Year-Plans and the guidelines of the Chinese State Council in detail. In China, various cities also compete with each other for investors. Regarding the development of traffic infrastructure, this can lead to heavy time pressure and radical methods, such as the compulsory change of residence and the eviction of settlements [Wei-Shiuen Ng et al. 2010].

PT in China: Bus and BRT Systems

In China, in addition to classic bus systems, PT consists of BRT approaches, heavy rail transportation, metro, other urban rail systems, and countless taxi entrepreneurs. The increasing demand for mass transportation systems is reflected in the huge investments into rail transportation, such as metros and city rail [Pucher et al. 2007; EASCS 2010]. Due to economic reforms, increasing motorisation, rising operating costs, and a rise in traffic jams, the share of bus systems has been declining since 1980 [Gwilliam 2010].

Kunming (end of the nineteen-nineties) and Beijing (at the Olympic summer games 2008) were the first Chinese cities that started (so-called) BRT systems [Darido 2006]. A BRT system is an innovative concept, applied in a number of emerging countries (in all BRIC countries except Russia) as cost-efficient and productive transportation mode. It includes various bus systems that are characterised by their efficiency, separated lanes, high capacity, and high speed [Wright/ Hook 2007]. China's BRT systems are used in the context of ecological and climate-political aspects and represent efficient and rapidly implementable options to solve urgent traffic problems [Eichhorst et al. 2010; Replogle/ Kodransky 2010].

PT Quality and Accessibility

For this paper, PT quality criteria described by Kirchhoff, like regional and temporal availability and accessibility, were used for the analysis. Described advantages of combined traffic modes in an intelligent PT-network structure also were applied [Kirchhoff 2002].

According to Schwarze [2005] and Spiekermann [2005], accessibility can be regarded as the main benefit of a PT-system. Most important features for passengers are the quality of connection and secure accessibility to the PT network that allows access to many activities within a given travel time [Schwarze 2005; Spiekermann 2005; Gather et al. 2008]. High accessibility is a local advantage for economical and private activities. In order to analyse accessibility, various indicators of accessibility can be determined and evaluated.

Using various calculation methods, specific parameters, such as space resistance and activity functions, are determined. One of the most commonly used indicators is the calculation of total travel time that is convenient for areas of various sizes [Gather et al. 2008; Krampe et al. 2010; Schwarze 2005; Spiekermann 2005; Prinz/ Herbst 2008].

Methods: Interviews and GIS Analyses

For this research, methods from empirical social research and analysis functions of GIS were applied. In order to retrieve information about the principles and organisation of Hefei's PT

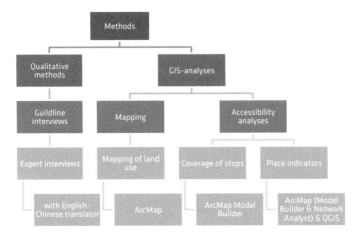

system, an explorative approach was used because little previous information was available. First, expert interviews were conducted. In the context of METRASYS, contacts to local experts were already established. The results of these interviews were the starting point for further analysis. Based on the fundamental knowledge retrieved from the interviews, additional GIS analyses were carried out. Hefei's PT system was evaluated based on the results of the GIS analyses. Figure 2 ⌐ gives an overview of the applied methods.

Expert Interviews

Expert interviews are semi-structured interviews and belong to the qualitative methods of social research. They are conducted using an interview guideline and are problem centred [Schlehe 2003; Meier Kruker/ Rauh 2005]. On the one hand, the guideline allows a structured and guided interview. Yet on the other hand, the interview guideline has to be flexible to enable the researcher to interact with the interviewee and react to new topics that come arise in the course of the interview [Lamnek 1995].

For this paper, four expert interviews of local experts were conducted with the support of an English-Chinese translator. The interview guide was pretested and adjusted. The interviewees were: Dr. Zhang Fengyan (Institute of Transportation Engineering of Hefei Academy of Urban Planning & Design); Luo Youbin (Hefei Urban Mass Transit Company); Zheng Rongbin (Operation and Management Dept. Hefei PT Group); and Dr. Yu Shi-jun & Dr. Zhu (Nanjing University of Science & Technology). With the interviewees' approval, all interviews were recorded. The audio recordings were then transcribed and analysed.

GIS Analyses

With GIS, geographic data can be recorded, processed, analysed, and presented. GIS is an important element of geographical science [Lange 2002]. In the following section, the theoretical fundamentals of the applied GIS methods are described.

The GIS analyses were carried out with the program ArcMap 10.0 and in part with QuantumGis (version 1.7). For the GIS analyses, data sets with current bus stops and the bus line routing were created. Furthermore METRASYS data sets on land use, the street network, and the water bodies of Hefei were used.

Survey of the Bus Network and Current Land Use

Hefei's bus network dataset (with bus line routing and bus stops) is the basis of most of the realised GIS analyses. Because no complete, official, and up-to-date data for the bus network was available for the project, the digitalisation of the bus line is based on the 2011 "tourist map of Hefei". In the context of the METRASYS project, current land use in Hefei was accessed [May 2011].

Coverage of PT-systems

The coverage of stops is a facility based indicator of accessibility and is an uncomplicated and easily realisable approximation for the accessibility of stops [Gather et al. 2008; Schwarze 2005].
For an initial analysis of Hefei's bus-stop coverage, buffer zones were created as polygons around bus stops and then blended with the land-use layer. Based on the areas not covered and the total area populated, the total areas for all populated and residential areas were calculated [Dehrendorf/ Heiss 2004]. As generally used in Germany and China (often as minimal standards), radii of 300 m and 500 m around the bus stops were chosen [Senate Department for Urban Development of Berlin 2007 & GB 50220-95, § 3.3.2].

GIS Analyses of Networks (GIS-Accessibility Analyses)

An analysis of networks is an important component of GIS analyses and is, for example, employed for the analysis and evaluation of traffic networks. These analyses are either implemented by independent analysis tools or by analysis functions, integrated into GIS systems. For this paper, the analysis tools of the ArcMap extension "Network-Analyst" were used. Optimal routes were calculated based on graph theory [Lange 2002].

GIS-Accessibility Analysis (Facility Indicators)

GIS-Accessibility analysis can be implemented either based on vector or raster data [Schürmann 2008; Schwarze 2005]. According to the chosen approach, the distance from the starting point to the network is considered to a varying extent [Prinz/ Herbst 2008]. In practice, isochrones (polylines or polygons with the same travel time or distance) are often used in vector-based accessibility analyses [Dulay/ Sloman 2006]. If raster-based accessibility analyses are implemented, they are predominantly applied as the result of interpolation of vector data [Schwarze 2005; Yigitcanlar et al. 2007]. Possible combined approaches have been described by Schürmann [2008] or Prinz/ Herbst [2008], based on Network Analyst in ArcMap. The real accessibility of stops often differs from the coverage of stops, because the distance covered by foot differs from the radius calculated as air-line distance (often used as the fastest vector-based accessibility analysis). Therefore, raster-based accessibility analyses are often more detailed and accurate.
As an approximation for the real accessibility of stops, this paper uses the sum of the footways along the street to the next station [Hochwimmer et al. 2009]. The determined distances are an approximation for the real footway to the next bus stop.

Fig. 3   Selected centres for the accessibility analysis of the bus network [Author]

Fig. 4   Criteria for the classification and assessment of areas of good quality in PT [Author]

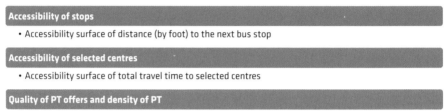

Accessibility of Selected Centres

According to the principles described in the prior chapter and based on data retrieved, an approximation of the quality of the connection of bus stops to selected centres in Hefei was ascertained. The calculated accessibility indicators are travel expense indicators [Schwarze 2005 and section above: "PT Quality and Accessibility"]. Because no utilisable information about time-tables was available at the time of this analysis, statistic data was used instead [Figure 4 ↗]. The bus stops served as starting points (Incidents) and five central centres (Facilities) were regarded as destinations [Figure 3 ↗].

Areas of Good Quality in Hefei's PT Network

In order to allow a combined evaluation of the quality of Hefei's PT network and infrastructure, an approach for the assessment of areas of high quality PT was developed. For each of the three quality criteria, one indicator was selected [Figure 5 ↗].

In order to obtain an indicator of the quality PT offers, a raster map of the supply density of the bus stops was calculated with the function "Kernel Density". The result was weighted by the number of bus lines. The raster size was determined as 100 m x 100 m (radius 1 km) because that way the results could be directly combined with the already calculated indicators [ESRI 2011a]. All three original data sets (raster format) were extracted and divided into three classes, according to two limiting values, and classified as an intermediate result [Figure 6↗].

The classification of the weighted bus stop density was based on the statistical method "Natural Breaks (Jenks)" [ESRI 2011b]. The classification of the other indicators is based on

Fig. 5 Illustrates the most important steps in the calculation of bus-stop accessibility and centre accessibility in GIS.

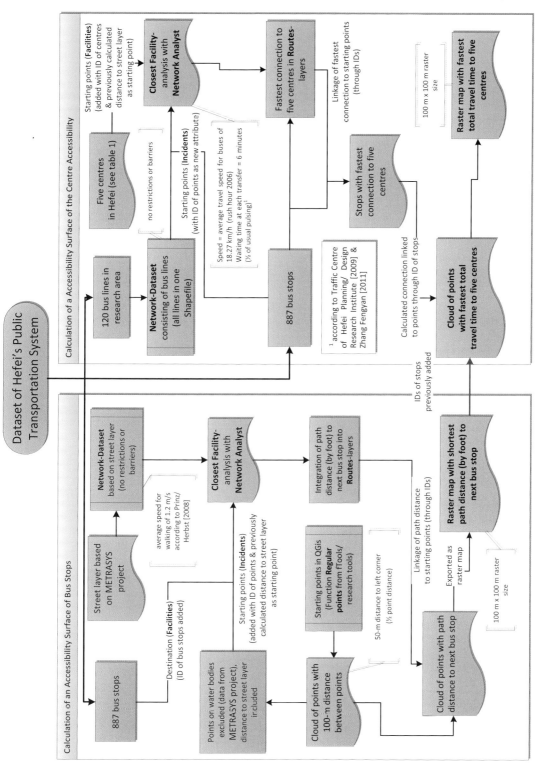

Fig. 6 Classification of intermediate results [Author]

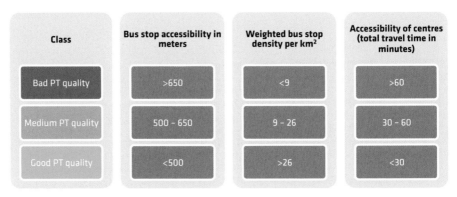

Class	Bus stop accessibility in meters	Weighted bus stop density per km²	Accessibility of centres (total travel time in minutes)
Bad PT quality	>650	<9	>60
Medium PT quality	500 – 650	9 – 26	30 – 60
Good PT quality	<500	>26	<30

Fig. 7 Classification of PT quality areas [Author]

Quality of PT areas	Classes
Very bad PT quality	3
Bad PT quality	4
Medium PT quality	5–7
Good PT quality	8
Very good PT quality	9

Hochwimmer et al. [2009] and Yigitcanlar et al. [2007]. Numbers from three (highest) to one (lowest) were allocated to the classification raster (based in the classification), summed up in a result file, and divided into the five classes shown in Figure 7 ⌝.

Findings: Good PT Quality in the Centre, Less in Suburbs

The results of land-use mapping show that major residential areas are concentrated within the Circular Roads as well as north, northwest, and east of the third Circular Road [Figure 8 ⌝]. The new expansions of the city are stamped by industry and trade areas. Only the Binhu district north of the Chao Lake and the areas south and east of the barrier lakes feature a dominant residential usage [Figure 8 ⌝]. The so-called 141-group, consisting of Hefei's city centre, the four new developing areas, and the new Binhu-district, is an approach to establish a decentralised metropolitan area of Hefei, with independent centres instead of the current mono-central urban structure [Figure 9 ⌝].

Properties of Hefei's PT system

In Hefei, PT has always been of great importance. Until the so-called great construction, which started in 2006 and describes the massive reconstruction of huge parts of Hefei, Hefei's PT was considered one of the best in China. Since then, the system has become less

Fig. 8 Map of current land use [Author]

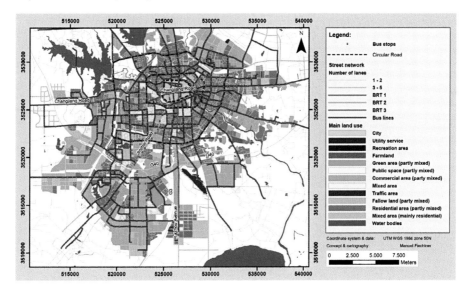

Fig. 9 Map of the 141-group [Author]

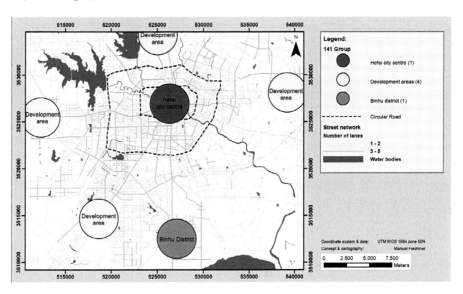

stable and reliable, whereby the attraction of the PT network has also declined [Zhang Fengyan 2011; Yu Shi-jun/ Dr. Zhu 2011]. During the twenty-first century, the share of PT in the modal split decreased due to the "great construction" (from 20% in 2006 to 17% in 2010), while the city's population increased from 2 to 3.1 million inhabitants [Ibid.]. Figure 8 ↗ also shows the PT network at the time of this research.

Means of PT in Hefei

Currently, Hefei's PT network consists of a conventional bus network and the first three lines of the BRT network. In addition, the first two lines of the metro network are currently under construction and therefore included in this analysis.

Bus Network

The backbone of Hefei's PT is the branched bus network. According to interviewees and other sources, more than 2,900 buses currently operate in 121 to 123 bus lines with an average passenger volume of 1.7 million passengers per day and 610 million passengers per year [2010]. In Hefei, as in other Chinese cities, bus traffic is important in traffic planning and organisation. It fulfils several tasks: it connects urban areas, supplies passengers to railroad lines and the BRT, and links the inner city to surrounding cities, villages, and other peripheral settlements [Hefei City Administration 2006; Municipal Planning Authority Hefei 2008].

BRT System

Currently, Hefei's BRT system is still under construction and consists of three lines (2011). Only one of them (BRT-3) is already operating in an acknowledged BRT corridor (on Changjiang). Because the BRT system is operating for a short time, no long-term experiences with BRT in Hefei were available. Nevertheless, initial problems have arisen. The previous implementation of the BRT concepts (2011) is viewed predominantly critically [Zhang Fengyan 2011; Zheng Rongbin 2011; Yu Shi-jun/ Dr. Zhu 2011]. There are no big differences between the BRT and conventional bus traffic in Hefei. The infrastructure and capacity of BRT buses is similar to conventional buses. Only few sections have specific bus lanes for BRT buses, which are mostly separated by cut-offs or road markings only. Thus BRT lines do not feature major advantages in speed. Only the BRT corridor on the Changjiang Road with the "central island style"-BRT stations currently fulfils BRT standards [Yu Shi-jun/ Dr. Zhu 2011; ITDP 2011; Zhang Fengyan 2011; Zheng Rongbin 2011].

Metro System

Although still under construction, the metro network already affects Hefei's PT system. Most current or future BRT lines fulfil the functions that the metro is to carry out in the future [Luo Youbin 2011; Planning and Design Institute Hefei/ US Energy Foundation 2009]. The metro is expected to improve connections with high passenger volume and link newly planned city districts to the inner city. Currently, the construction of up to twelve metro lines is planned by 2050 and the metro is expected to become the future backbone of PT. The first metro line is already under construction. The construction of a second metro line was planned to begin in 2011 but was delayed and started in 2012 [Luo Youbin 2011].

From the interviews, it became clear that BRT and metro systems have similar attributes, which clearly differ from the attributes of bus systems. The bus system's intended use is the allotment of large areas and the connection to BRT, metro, and railway [Zheng Rongbin 2011]. BRT and metro show similar efficiency parameters, yet the Chinese government favours the development of urban rail systems in combination with few BRT corridors [Yu Shi-jun/ Dr. Zhu 2011].

Fig. 10 Target values for the coverage of bus stops in Hefei [Altered illustration based on Municipal Planning Authority Hefei 2008]

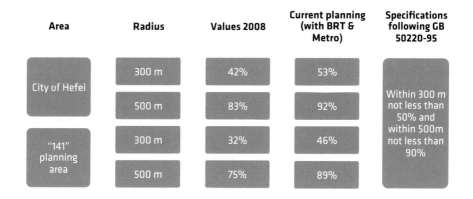

Area	Radius	Values 2008	Current planning (with BRT & Metro)	Specifications following GB 50220-95
City of Hefei	300 m	42%	53%	Within 300 m not less than 50% and within 500m not less than 90%
	500 m	83%	92%	
"141" planning area	300 m	32%	46%	
	500 m	75%	89%	

Fig. 11 Ascertained coverage of bus stops [Author]

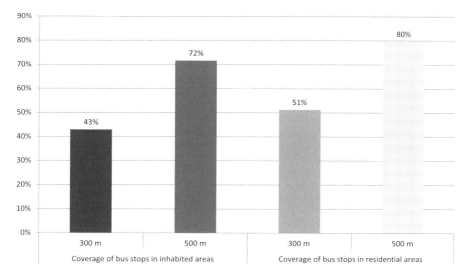

Coverage of Bus Stops

The analysis carried out to determine the coverage of bus stops in terms of radii around bus stops was described earlier in the section "GIS Analyses". In Hefei, compulsory specifications have to be met. Yet these specifications are supposed to be fulfilled only by the implementation of ongoing planning, not by the currently operating PT-system [Figures 10 and 11 ↗].

Based on the developed data sets, the current coverage of bus stops was calculated (see section "GIS-Analyses"↗). The utilisation of this calculation is illustrated in Figure 11 ↗. The research area consisted of the 141 group including Hefei's historical city centre in the middle of the map. Because the share of total population for each block was not available, it was assumed in this analysis that the population is evenly spread over the settlement areas. Figure 11 ↗ shows that the compulsory specifications where not fulfilled when the data was collected.

Fig. 12 Map of foot accessibility to the next bus [Author]

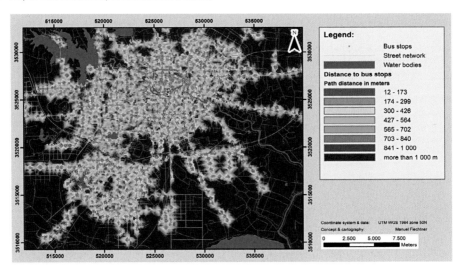

Accessibility of Bus Stops and Selected Centres, Supply Density

Areas close to bus stations naturally feature low footway distances, as reflected in Figure 12 ↗. In the inner city, footways are particularly short. City centres can be reached particularly fast from the eastern inner-city areas; from large areas (especially from the second or third Circular Road) even within an hour [Figure 13 ↗]. The longest total travel times were calculated for the areas southeast of the city airport. For the peripheral development area in the southwest, in the south, and in the east as well as for the Binhu-district and for the regions east of the airport, high total travel times to the centres of Hefei were calculated. Major parts of the regions with high total travel times are primarily used as industrial areas or are not developed yet [Figure 7 ↗].

Figure 14 ↗ shows the bus-stop density weighted by the number of bus lines as an expression of supply density. In the historic centre, alongside the road towards the main station and south of the historic centre, bus supply is extraordinarily dense. Municipal areas on the other hand usually have only single bus lines and are thus less densely allotted. The inner city clearly has a much denser bus network with many more bus routes; whereas, especially in urban expansions erected after 2001, supply is thin (e.g., the Binhu district).

PT Quality Areas

The final evaluation of Hefei's PT network shows that the area of the historic centre, the area around the main station, and the area east of Wanda Plaza have very good PT quality [Figure 15 ↗]. In general, the regions around the inner city's traffic axis, especially in the eastern part, are areas of good to very good PT. The new peripheral-development areas and major parts of the eastern and south Binhu-district are classified as areas of very bad PT.

In the analysis of PT quality, some defaults (fragments) occurred. In the coverage of bus stops, for example, fragments occurred especially near multi-lane streets. During the calculation of the fastest routes toward the centres, defaults occurred due to inaccurate steps in the calculation or classification. In Figure 15 ↗, these fragments are grey.

Fig. 13 Map of accessibility to centres through PT [Author]

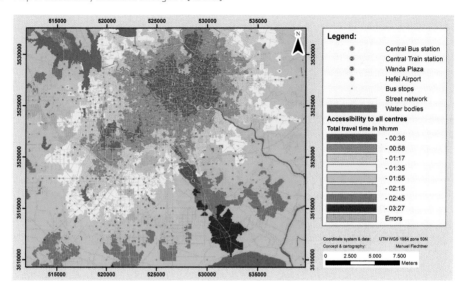

Fig. 14 Map of the bus network's density of supply [Author]

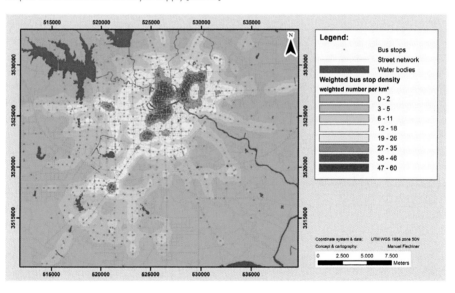

Fig. 15   Map of quality areas in PT [Author]

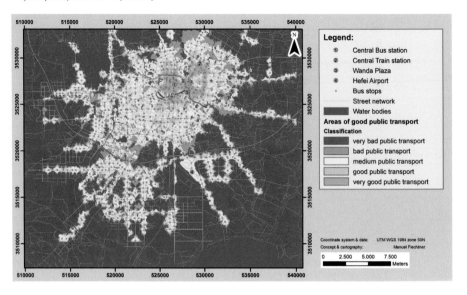

Conclusions: PT Development Must Speed up to Cope with Urban Growth

Like most parts of China, Hefei is currently affected by ongoing transformation and far-reaching processes of change, especially since the "great construction". In the next years, major infrastructural projects will give room to new paths in the development of PT and change traffic in Hefei. According to this analysis, those infrastructural projects, their realisation, and their impacts will be severe challenges for Hefei.

Currently, Hefei's PT-system has to be constantly adjusted to numerous construction sites, new traffic routes, and new urban areas. This makes an objective evaluation difficult. Nevertheless, the selected investigation and analyses allow a critical evaluation of Hefei's current PT-system.

How is Hefei's PT-system Characterised?

Hefei's PT-system currently includes conventional bus lines, the first lines of the BRT system, and taxis. The first metro lines are still under construction. The bus network is especially dense in the inner city, but also makes vast areas of the city and the administrative district of Hefei accessible. In contrast, the BRT system is not successfully implemented. In fact, the BRT system currently does not offer significant time savings for passengers and no relief to inner-city traffic. Likewise, the metro network can only influence city traffic in the future.

According to current planning, Hefei's PT network will undergo dramatic changes in the upcoming years with the implementation of BRT, metro, and due to new intermodal train stations. The metro can help break up Hefei's monocentral structure by offering better accessibility to new urban quarters. The new south railway station can enhance Hefei's decentralisation through faster access to the inner centre by intermodal orientation. During the transition period, fast direct connection will be served by BRT lines, which is planned to serve less densely populated areas once the construction of the metro network is finished. However, the implementation of these BRT-projects is still not fast enough.

Is the PT Capable of Significantly Relieving Urban Traffic?

The analyses show a dense and high to very high quality PT-system in the historic centre, major parts of the inner city (within the second Circular Road), and among the central traffic axes of the bus network. These inner-city areas feature high residential use and are publicly utilisable. However, outside the third Circular Road, the analyses show huge areas (mostly industrial areas) that are poorly covered by PT and poorly accessible by bus. Poorly accessible residential areas are also situated in the new Binhu-district.

Another result of the analyses is that in the research area standards for the access of inhabitants to the PT-system are most likely not fulfilled.

The eastern inner city, the region around the main station, the area around the Wanda Plaza, and the areas situated near the city hall and airport are easily accessible from areas around the selected centres. These are areas of very good PT quality. The urban expansions, therefore, are either poorly connected or not connected at all to the PT-system and have a very poor PT quality.

The hugely populated areas with very poor PT are a crucial gap in the network coverage of Hefei's PT system. The quality of the PT in not-yet-developed areas is an important indicator for further planning. Gaps in the allotment must be closed if the areas are to be developed.

According to this analysis, the PT-system merely offers a significant relief of traffic volume in the inner city (within the third Circular Road). In areas built since the great construction, PT-systems do not offer an adequate alternative to motorised individual traffic, and therefore cannot help to significantly reduce traffic volume in this area. In addition, the analysis shows that the adaption of the PT-system to the ever-changing challenges of Hefei as a dynamically growing city was not successfully managed. Establishing appropriate, sustainable, and competitive PT concepts in the face of rapid development and growth is extremely difficult and still a challenge for Hefei's PT concept development.

How to Fill the Gap between Sustainability and Construction Boom?

The aim of this paper was to analyse and evaluate Hefei's PT system in the context of the METRASYS project and to figure out whether the PT-system can significantly relieve the traffic network. Hefei's traffic sector in total faces severe current and future challenges. Its current PT-system is not able to solve these challenges completely. The dominating motorised individual transport, the daily traffic chaos, and the implementation of great urban planning projects affect Hefei like many other Chinese major cities. Therefore, future research, additional urban traffic planning and the adjustment of planned urban traffic projects will be necessary to generate adequate solutions.

It is unclear if Hefei can overcome future challenges in urban planning and traffic planning with many urgent problems still unsolved. If not, the scheduled growth process could be affected and aims like an attractive, polycentric, and liveable metropolitan region may not be reached. But the question about the reasonability of these further growth strategies for upcoming megacities, without significant aspects of sustainability, is necessary and has to be discussed in future of megacity research with more intensity.

One thing is for certain. In the near future, Hefei's PT-system will be characterised by great dynamics, the striving for improvement, and constant change—much like the rest of China in the twenty-first century.

References

Berberich, G. (2010): *Megastädte - die Welt von morgen nachhaltig gestalten*. Berlin, Bonn. http://www.ptdlr-klimaundumwelt.de/_media/Megacities_Shaping_of_a_sustainable_future.pdf, 01.04.2011

Campanella, T. J. (2008): *The congrete dragon. Chinas's urban revolution and what it means for the world*. New York

Chu Jinlong/ Xu Jiangang/ Gao Shu (2007): "Spatio-temporal Characteristics of Residential Land Growth in Hefei of Anhui Province, China". In: *Chinese Geographical Science*, 17 (2), pp. 135–42

Hefei City Administration (editors)(2006): "*City of Hefei Master Plan (2006–2020)*. (simplified version, Chinese). Hefei

Darido, G. (2006): *Bus Rapid Transit Developments in China: Perspectives from Research, Meetings, and Site Visits in April 2006*. FTA. Washington.

Dehrendorf, M./ Heiss, M. (2004): *Geo-Informationssysteme in der kommunalen Planungspraxis*. Halmstad

Dulay, N./ Sloman, M. (2006): *Time Contours. Using isochrone visualisation to describe transport network travel cost. Final Report*. London. http://www3.imperial.ac.uk/pls/portallive/docs/1/18619712.PDF, 10.12.2011

EASCS (2010): *Urban Rail Development in China: Prospects, Issues and Option*. World Bank. http://www-wds.worldbank.org/external/default/WDSContentServer/WDSP/IB/2010/07/21/000333037_20100721014805/Rendered/PDF/557720WP0P11791ort105jan100FINAL1EN.pdf , 02.01.2012

Eichhorst, U./ Sterk, W./ Böhler, S./ Wang-Helmreich, H. (2010): *Exploring Standardised Baselines for CDM and other Carbon Finance Mechanisms in Transport*. http://www.wupperinst.org/uploads/tx_wibeitrag/CITS_final_report.pdf, 10.05.2011

ESRI (2011a): *How Kernel Density works*. http://help.arcgis.com/en/arcgisdesktop/10.0/help/index.html#//009z00000011000000.htm, 10.12.2011

ESRI (2011b): *Classifying numerical fields for graduated symbology*. http://help.arcgis.com/en/arcgis-desktop/10.0/help/index.html#/na/00s50000001r000000/, 15.12.2011

Gather, M./ Kagermeier, A./ Lanzendorf, M. (2008): *Geographische Mobilitäts- und Verkehrsforschung*. Stuttgart

GB 50220-95: *Urban Traffic Planning and Design GB 50220-95 as amended and promulgated on 14.01.1995* (Chinese). http://www.upo.gov.cn/pages/zwgk/fgzc/bz/2460.shtml, 15.12.2011

Gwilliam, K. (2010): *Developing the Public Transport Sector in China*. siteresources.worldbank.org/INTCHINA/Resources/318862-1121421293578/transport_16July07-en.pdf, 05.10.2011

Municipal Planning Authority Hefei (2008): *Hefei overall draft Comprehensive Transportation Planning - Bus parts. Hefei City Comprehensive Transportation Planning (2007–2020)* (Chinese). Hefei

Hochwimmer, B./ Prinz, T. & Strobl, J. (2009): *Potenzialmodelle für zentrale Einrichtungen in Wien*. Salzburg. http://www.oeaw-giscience.org/download/Bericht_Potenzialmodelle_fuer_zentrale_Einrichtungen.pdf, 10.12.2011

ITDP (2011): *Hefei BRT*. http://www.chinabrt.org/en/cities/hefei.aspx, 01.02.2012

Kenworthy, J./ Gang Hu (2002): "Transport and Urban Form in Chinese Cities". In: *DISP* 151, 38, pp. 4–14

Kirchhoff, P. (2002): *Städtische Verkehrsplannung. Konzepte, Verfahren, Massnahmen*. Stuttgart, Leipzig, Wiesbaden

Kodukula, S. (2011): "Sustainable Transport and Bus Rapid Transit". In: *Fifth Asia Pacific Urban Forum* Bangkok, Thailand (22.06.11), pp. 1 - 38. http://www.unescap.org/apuf-5/bazzar/presentations/Bazaar1-and-2/3-Urb-Trans-GIZ/Transp-BRT-Kodukula.pdf, 02.02.2012

Krampe, S./ Prinz, T./ Herbst, S. (2010): "Erreichbarkeit und Angebotsbewertung im ÖPNV". In: Strobl, J./ Blaschke, T./ Griesebner, G. (editors)(2010): *Angewandte Geoinformatik 2010*, pp. 388-394. Berlin

Lamnek, S. (1995): *Qualitative Sozialforschung, Band 2: Methoden und Techniken*. Weinheim

Lange, N. d. (2002): *Geoinformatik in Theorie und Praxis*. Berlin, Heidelberg

Luo Youbin (2011): *Interview about Metro Planning of Hefei*. 13.05.2011. Hefei

Meier Kruker, V./ Rauh, J. (2005): *Arbeitsmethoden der Humangeographie*. Darmstadt

METRASYS (2010a): *Results*. http://www.metrasys.de/en/a_ergebnisse/index.html, 10.09.2011

Nuhn, H./ Hesse, M. (2006): *Verkehrsgeographie*. Paderborn

Planning and Design Institute Hefei/ US Energy Foundation (2009): "Hefei rapid transit network planning" (Chinese). Hefei. (unpublished)

Prinz, T./ Herbst, S. (2008): *Multikriterielle Modellierung der ÖV-Erreichbarkeit für die Stadt Wien*. www.wien.gv.at/stadtentwicklung/studien/pdf/b008000.pdf, 20.11.2011

Pucher, J./ Zhong-ren Peng/ Mittal, N./ Yi Zhu/ Korattyswaroopam, N. (2007): "Urban Transport Trends and Policies in China and India: Impacts of Rapid Economic Growth". In: *Transport Reviews*, 27 (4), pp. 379–410

Replogle, M./ Kodransky, M. (2010): "Urban Leaders Find Transportation Paths to Global Green Growth". In: *Sharing Urban Transport Solutions. 4, May 2010*, pp. 16–35

Schlehe, J. (2003): "Formen qualitativer ethnographischer Interviews". In: Beer, B. (editors): *Methoden und Technicken der Feldforschung*, pp. 71–93. Berlin

Schürmann, C. (2008): "ArcGIS Network Analyst: Erreichbarkeitsindikatoren auf der Basis von Rasterzellen für den Ostseeraum". In: *16. Treffen GIS-Anwendergruppe Küste (3.-4. November 2008)*. www.gis-kueste.de/2008/vortrag/gis_awtk_cs.pdf, 20.11.2011

Schwarze, B. (2005): *Erreichbarkeitsindikatoren in der Nahverkehrsplanung*. Dortmund. http://www.raumplanung.tu-dortmund.de/irpud/fileadmin/irpud/content/documents/publications/ap184.pdf, 10.11.2011

Senate Department for Urban Development of Berlin (editors)(2007): *Der Nahverkehrsplan – Berlin fährt vor!* Nahverkehrsplan des Landes Berlin 2006–2009. Berlin

Senate Department for Urban Development of Berlin (2011): *Stadtentwicklungsplan Verkehr (StEP Verkehr 2.0)*. Berlin

Spiekermann, K. (2005): *Erreichbarkeitsszenarien für die Metropolregion Rhein-Ruhr. Abschlussbericht*. Dortmund. http://www.spiekermann-wegener.com/pro/pdf/Erreichbarkeit_Rheinruhr.pdf, 10.12.2011

Traffic Center of Hefei Planning/ Design Research Institute (2009): "Hefei Traffic Data 2006 AS&P" (english translation). Unpublished project paper. Hefei

Wei-Shiuen Ng/ Schipper, L./ Yang Chen (2010): "China Motorization Trends. New Directions for Crowded Cities". In: *The Journal of Transport and Land Use*, 3 (3), pp. 5–25

Wright, L./ Hook, W. (2007): *Bus Rapid Transit Planning Guide*. New York. http://www.itdp.org/documents/Bus%20Rapid%20Transit%20Guide%20-%20complete%20guide.pdf, 05.03.2011

Yan Ping (2011): "Overviev of city planing of Hefei". Hefei City Planning Bureau. 05.04.11. Hefei. (not published)

Yan Tang/ Kunzmann, K. K. (2008): "The Evolution of Spatial Planning for Beijing". In: *Informationen zur Raumentwicklung*, 8, pp. 457–70

Yigitcanlar, T./ Sipe, N. G./ Evans, R./ Pitot, M. (2007): "A GIS-based land use and public transport accessibility indexing model". In: *Australian Planner*. 44 (3), pp. 30–37

Yu Shi-jun/ Dr. Zhu (2011): *Interview about PT-Planning in China and Hefei*. 18.05.2011. Nanjing

Zhang Fengyan (2011): *Interview about PT-system of Hefei*. 11.05.2011. Hefei

Zheng Rongbin (2011): *Interview about BRT System & Planning and Bus-network of Hefei*. 17.05.2011. Hefei

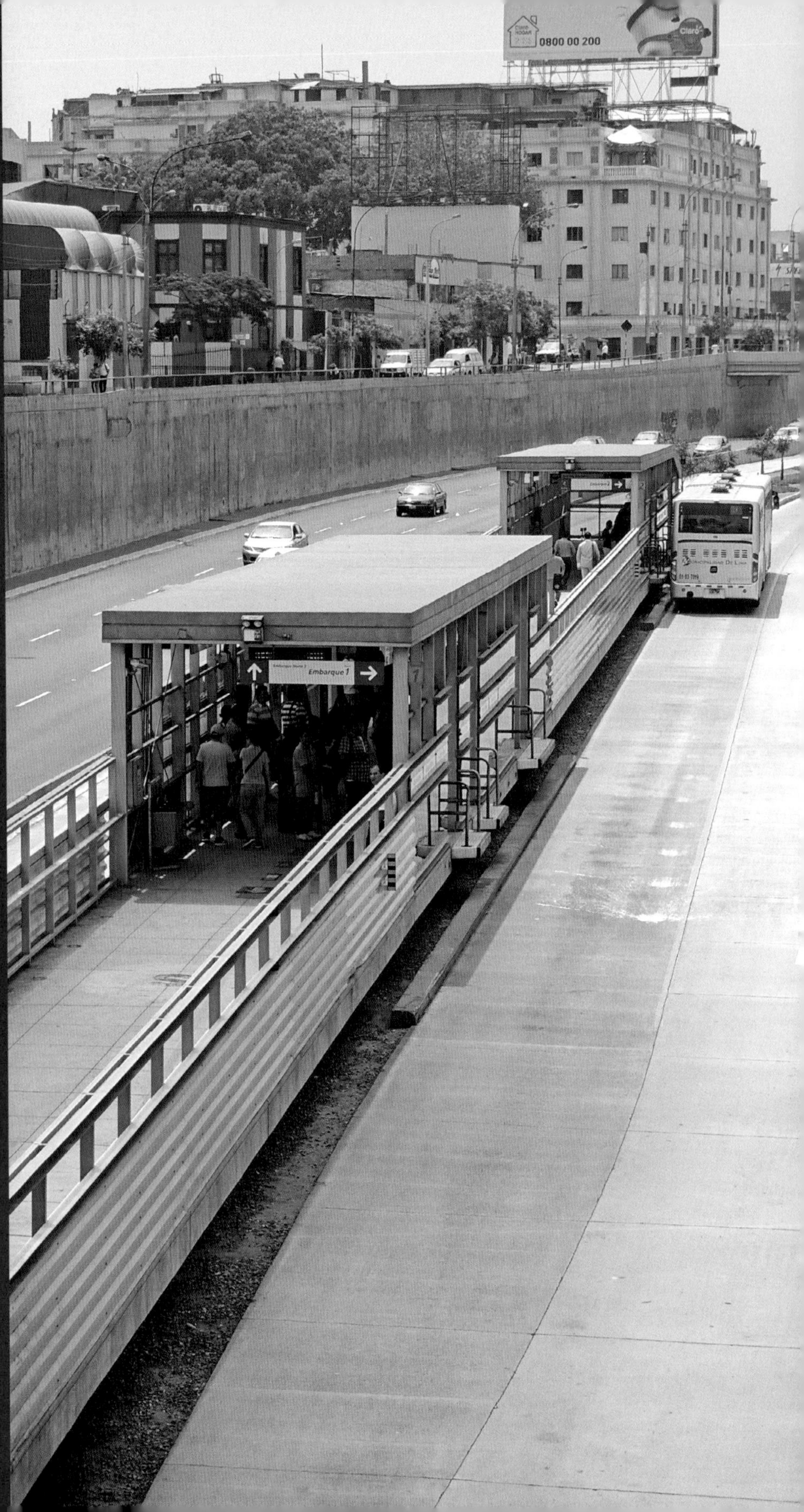

LIMA: Station of BRT system [Lukas Born]

Karsten Kozempel

Dissertation at Humboldt University Berlin, Department of Computer Science

Development and Evaluation of an Airborne Traffic Detection System[1]

Abstract

Caused by rising interest in traffic surveillance for simulations and decision management, many researchers focus on automatic vehicle detection systems to determine, for example, the traffic volume in cities. Vehicle counts and velocities of various car classes are the essential data basis for almost every traffic model and simulation. Especially for high traffic demands and congestions in megacities, conventional detection systems do not meet the demands. Thus, a more flexible detector has to be used—e.g., an airborne camera system. This paper presents such a system.

Vehicle detection was realised through the combination of a fast edge-based hypothesis generation and a more reliable hypothesis verification using a Support Vector Machine. Furthermore, a novel optical orientation algorithm based on road information was implemented in order to compensate the inertial measurement unit, which is essential to determine the sensor's orientation.

Due to image sizes of over twenty megapixels, first the region of interest had to be preselected using a street database. Afterwards, the first detection stage of the algorithm generates object hypotheses using specifically shaped edge filters. The second detection stage verifies them by extracting the SURF descriptor (Speeded-up Robust Features) of each hypothesis. A Support Vector Machine (SVM) is used to decide whether the object's descriptor represents a vehicle. How the verification stage improves the detection reliability by discarding false positives while preselection and hypothesis generation provide less computation time will be shown.

The second part shows an approach to measure and fuse optical orientation data of sensors during an airplane flight to acquire traffic data. This orientation data is necessary for geo-registration of any aerial images and extracted features. Since an inertial measurement unit (IMU) is a very costly component, alternative methods for orientation determination are considered. This chapter presents an approach achieved by fusing different optical information supported by a GPS sensor and a road network database with additional elevation information.

This work shows how road elements are extracted considering their colour hue, and how they are matched with the given database segments. To adjust rotation angles, a nonlinear simplex optimisation algorithm is used. Additionally, an interest-point tracking has been implemented to determine the relative orientation between adjacent images. Furthermore, the relative orientation is fused with the road orientation in a Kalman Filter to support outlier detection. The approach yields rotation errors of around 0.15 degrees for pitch and roll, which is sufficient for traffic surveillance purposes. Thus, the system's lower price, due to avoiding an IMU, can encourage more customer usage.

The innovation of this work refers to the combination of rapid preselection and more reliable verification of object hypotheses. Additionally, the automatic extraction of streets as landmarks for orientation determination and fusion with relative orientation parameters as stabilisation, which compensate the use of an inertial system, are novel.

Notes

1 This abstract is based on the original publication: Kozempel, K. (2012): *Entwicklung eines Systems zur Verkehrser-fassung aus Luftbildsequenzen - Luftgestützte Verkehrserfassung*. Südwestdeutscher Verlag für Hoch-schulschriften (5.5.2012). ISBN-10: 383813284X; ISBN-13: 978-3838132846

Fig. 1   Airborne Traffic Monitoring [Author]

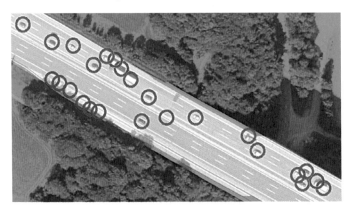

Fig. 2   Illustration of Airborne Imaging System [Author]

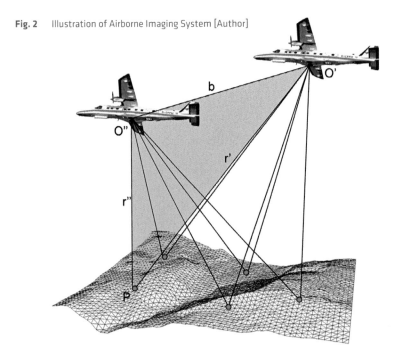

Steffen Bubeck

Diploma Thesis at University of Stuttgart, Institute for Energy Economics and the Rational Use of Energy (IER)

Perspectives for Gauteng's Transportation Sector: Potential Performance and Costs of Exemplary Transportation Infrastructure Extensions

Abstract

The international research project "EnerKey" has developed an integrated climate-protection concept for the province of Gauteng in South Africa. Within the project, numerous options for mitigating greenhouse gas (GHG) emissions and for increasing energy efficiency have been analysed. In this study, the option of enhancing the public-transport infrastructure was assessed.

Gauteng is the smallest province in South Africa in terms of area, yet the most populous. Gauteng's three larger municipalities—Johannesburg, Tshwane, and Ekurhuleni—together form a megacity of over eleven million inhabitants. The province provides the largest share of the country's economic strength (about one-third of the national GDP). Moreover, Gauteng's population growth and increasing prosperity have led to a steadily growing energy demand.

One major issue within the climate-protection concept is the transformation of the transport sector towards sustainability. This sector is responsible for one third of Gauteng's final energy consumption and about one quarter of its GHG emissions. Public transportation can make an important contribution towards sustainability in transport. In the past, an investment backlog led to limited quality in public transport, resulting in a dominance of minibus taxis and passenger cars. Countermeasures were already taken by the introduction of a bus rapid transit system (BRT) in Johannesburg (Rea Vaya) in 2009, and a rapid rail system for Gauteng (Gautrain) in 2010. An important area of research and also a practical question for decision-makers is the extent to which infrastructure enhancements can improve these innovative public-transport systems and reduce GHG emissions.

In this study, a trip-rate model was developed to assess the impact of infrastructure enhancements on the future transport performance of the Rea Vaya-BRT, the Gautrain, and a potential BRT system in Tshwane. The costs of these measures were also estimated in order to establish cost-potential curves. The estimated transport performance is then integrated into a reference forecast for 2007 to 2040, which includes the transport performance of all modes of transport (modal split), besides the BRT systems and the Gautrain. In this manner, the results are put into context, and the impact on transport-related well-to-wheel GHG emissions can be estimated.

The results show a significant potential for transport performance growth for the BRT systems at relatively low costs. Gautrain infrastructure investments also have the potential to increase passenger volumes significantly, but at much higher costs. Despite their potentials, however, both of these innovative public-transport systems will continue to have a low share of total transport demand until 2040. Thus, the positive impact on well-to-wheel GHG emissions reduction is negligible. Nevertheless, Gautrain and the BRT Systems can improve public-transport service in Gauteng in terms of reliability, availability, comfort, and safety.

Fig. 1   Station of Johannesburg's Rea Vaya [Ludger Eltrop]

PROJECTS IN BRIEF

On the following pages, all nine participating cities of the research programme on Future Megacities are presented. They were funded between 2008–2013. Details are collected about the context and challenges for the projects, their objectives, and approaches. A short overview of the most important outcomes and solutions is provided. More information on these solutions can be found in the Products and Tools Data Base at www.future-megacities.org.

Featured in this volume:
Adaptation Planning in Ho Chi Minh City (Vietnam)
Energy and Climate Protection in Gauteng (South Africa)
New Town Development in Tehran-Karaj Region (Iran)
Water Management in Lima (Peru)
Urban Agriculture in Casablanca (Morocco)
Transportation Management in Hefei (China)
Resource Efficiency in Urumqi (China)
Governance for Sustainability in Hyderabad (India)

Featured in other volumes:
Solid Waste Management in Addis Ababa (Ethiopia)

Note: The article about Shenzhen was written in the framework of the METRASYS project on Hefei.

Energy and Climate Protection in Gauteng (South Africa)

Context

Gauteng Province in South Africa is the most densely urbanised area in South Africa and covers an area of 18,178 km². The province consists of the three large metropolises: Johannesburg, Ekurhuleni, and Tshwane, as well as two other district municipalities. Most of the province is located at an average altitude of 1,500 m above sea level with high solar radiation levels. There has been a striking lack of energy-supply security over the last years, with frequent blackouts hindering Gauteng's aim to be competitive as a global city. The energy-supply system is dominated by electricity generated from coal. About one-third of the fuel for transport is also produced from coal. Gauteng's levels of energy consumption and gas emissions can be compared to that of developed countries like Germany. For the energy sector alone, the energy consumption in 2009 was 765 PJ and the total CO_2 emissions were 126 million tonnes (10.5 tonnes per person). Despite the high solar radiation, the share of renewable-energy use remains low. Due to low costs for electricity (relative to international costs), there are few incentives for energy-saving behaviour and a more energy-efficient policy implementation.

Objectives

The EnerKey project intends to contribute to a sustainable transformation of the Gauteng urban area by developing an integrated programme for an efficient, environmentally friendly and climate-protecting system of energy supply and utilisation. EnerKey supports this process by carrying out research and assisting stakeholders in the implementation and monitoring of projects, measures, and strategies. This includes the development and application of tools and instruments for energy and environmental planning. Providing training and education courses to staff and administration members of the municipalities will enable capacity building and dissemination of the results. The specific objectives are:

1. Assess the present values of energy consumption and GHG emissions of the energy system in Gauteng
2. Provide means to improve the energy performance in the building sector, especially in public buildings
3. Initiate a process to reduce energy consumption and related emissions from traffic and transport
4. Show viable options for using more renewable energy
5. Demonstrate, with a number of practical projects, that the implementation of sustainable projects makes sense and can be successful

Approach

The EnerKey project has a clear interdisciplinary and integrated approach by combining socio-economic and technical aspects, as well as by cooperating with partners from different departments of regional and municipal authorities, NGOs, the private sector, and universities. The project follows both a "top-down" and a "bottom-up" approach. In the short term, individual pilot projects are being initiated, for example, in schools, administrative buildings, and in the transport sector. These projects are developed and monitored with the help of decision support tools and models. In parallel, an integrated energy model approach is set up, resulting in the provision of measures and recommendations to improve urban development and the energy system in the region. The EnerKey project specifically undertakes measures for strengthening the Gauteng regional administration, to coordinate the municipal efforts in energy planning and in the development of pilot projects. Training and capacity building are undertaken to disseminate the results and findings.

Metrobus Station in Johannesburg [Carsten Zehner]

Solutions

- Gauteng Energy Office—the regional answer to energy challenges
- TIMES GECCO—A regional energy- and emission-cost optimisation model and training
- EnerKey Advisor Tool—assessing energy performance of buildings
- EnerKey Long Term Perspective Group—a government think-tank model
- Transport Emission Inventory—informed mobility planning
- Energy Technology Handbook—sustainable technologies for the future
- CDM—Emission Trade Evaluation Tool
- iEEECo—energy awareness activities for scholars and cost-efficient settlements for the poor
- African Sustainable House—a holistic dwelling approach
- EnerKey "Detectives"—education and installation of solar panels in schools
- EnerKey Environmental and Energy Atlas—Assessment of Renewable Energy options for the Gauteng Province

Contact

Project: EnerKey-Energy as a key element of an integrated climate protection concept for the city region of Gauteng
Ludger Eltrop | IER—University of Stuttgart
Email: ludger.eltrop@ier.uni-stuttgart.de
Harold Annegarn | University of Johannesburg
Email: hannegarn@gmail.com
Webpage: www.enerkey.info, www.enerkey.co.za, www.enerkey.de

Solid Waste Management in Addis Ababa (Ethiopia)

Context

Addis Ababa is one of the fastest-growing cities in Africa and also the main commercial, financial, industrial, and service-provision centre in Ethiopia. The city is presently facing a plethora of problems, including insufficient solid, and liquid-waste management. While an ever-increasing volume of waste is generated, the effectiveness of the solid waste collection and disposal systems is declining.

In Addis Ababa, around 80% of the solid waste produced is collected. The remaining waste is dumped on open spaces or drains. The city has separate systems available that handle solid wastes. The formal system managed by the city administration collects the waste from collection points and transfers it to the landfill site (secondary collection). The second system assembles groups of organised precollectors who collect the waste from households and bring it to the collection points (primary collection). The collection of recyclables is performed by so-called korales, who collect only a small percentage of recyclables directly from the households. Both the precollectors and the korales are physically, socially, and economically disadvantaged waste workers, whose work compensates for the lack of municipal services. Up to now, the recycling sector in Addis Ababa, particularly for organic waste, remains undeveloped.

This means that organic waste, which makes up more than 60% of the municipal solid waste, is simply collected and dumped in the landfill. The landfill gas generated by the organic waste is not collected either, thus contributing significantly to the greenhouse gas emissions of the city.

Objectives

The general objective of the IGNIS project is to demonstrate that waste, if it is understood and treated as a resource, can be a source for income generation and can contribute to global climate-protection, as well as to local environmental protection and sustainable development. Hence, the project aims to generate income from valorising municipal solid waste through establishing qualified, economically workable, and sustainable waste treatment. Furthermore, the project seeks to contribute directly to poverty reduction and improved sanitation, and, moreover, to reducing greenhouse gases from dumpsites, conserving raw materials, and improving energy and resource efficiency.

In this context, the project aims to provide an instrument that includes methods, practical approaches, and simulation tools to be applied to other emerging megacities, in order to assess the effects when introducing similar waste management and treatment methods.

Approach

The approach comprises different strategies that correlate with one another. An essential aspect of the project's approach is the generation of a reliable spatial, waste, and emission database for the scientific work and the calculations of various scenarios. Additionally, pilot projects have been implemented and will be developed further. The majority of these pilot projects are small-scale projects on a decentralised level (e.g., composting, anaerobic digestion, recycling). These pilot projects are analysed with a focus on technical, greenhouse gas, and emission-related, socio-economic, and occupational safety and health (OSH) related aspects. Furthermore, the scientific staff, the city administration, and the groups working on the pilot projects are given the opportunity to build capacities and become familiar with the technologies as well as with the concept of using waste as a resource.

The data collected and the results of the pilot project analyses are used for modelling, simulation, or up-scaling of the businesses. Scenario simulation will provide the possibility of showing the

Many of Addis Ababa's central districts contain village-like structures [Lukas Born]

effects, for example, on greenhouse gases and the socio-economy. IGNIS is not conceived as a specific, isolated solution for Addis Ababa. Rather, several aspects of the project—e.g., methods—pilot projects, results, and lessons learnt, are transferred to other fast-growing cities in order to learn from the specific requirements of those cities. As a result, the IGNIS approach will be modified and adapted accordingly.

Solutions
- Methodology for data collection on waste quantities and quality
- Model-based strategic planning for sustainable solid waste management
- Adapted occupational safety and health standards and solutions
- Market studies and business guidelines for entrepreneurs and for recycling products
- Business improvement options for a paper-recycling manufacturer

- Implementation projects for separate collection at source, biogas facility, charcoal briquettes from organic wastes, composting, school biogas-latrine
- Training modules for WEEE collection and dismantling
- Closing material cycles by means of using biogas sludge for erosion-prevention combined with energy crop production
- Obstacle-based transfer analysis methodology for technologies or methods

Contact
Project: IGNIS—Income generation & climate protection by valorising municipal solid wastes in a sustainable way in emerging mega-cities
Dieter Steinbach | AT-Verband Stuttgart
Email: dieter.steinbach@at-verband.de
Webpage: www.ignis.p-42.net

Urban Agriculture in Casablanca (Morocco)

Context

Casablanca, currently the largest and most populated urban region in Morocco, has grown within a mere century from a small settlement of 20,000 inhabitants to a metropolis of estimated 5.1 million by 2030. 22% of the national urban population live in Casablanca. 60% of industry in Morocco is concentrated in this agglomeration—creating rapid urban growth, accompanied by the development of deprived quarters (bidonvilles). In 1907, the city covered a small area of only fifty hectares. In 1997, the region "Greater Casablanca" was created comprising 121,412 ha and 8 prefectures. Thus, many previously rural communities with agricultural areas are being urbanised, thereby consuming valuable open space. As a resulting phenomenon of current development processes specific to megacities, Urban Agriculture (UA) as a spatial dimension is considered to present new hybrid and climate-sensitive forms between rural and urban space. An underlying hypothesis is that these reciprocal urban-rural linkages contain the potential for a qualified coexistence that could be the basis for forming sustainable climate-optimised, multifunctional urban and open spatial structures (productive landscapes) in order to make a long-term contribution to the sustainability of cities and the quality of life for their inhabitants. It is to be assumed that UA will only be able to coexist in the long term and in a qualitatively meaningful manner with other, economically stronger forms of land utilisation, when synergies between urban and agricultural uses arise.

Objectives

The project explores the existence of synergies between urban and agricultural uses and investigates how they might be developed. The project focuses on the possibilities of integrating peri-urban agricultural land into the urban development process.

It also analyses the extent to which UA can make a relevant contribution to a climate-optimised and sustainable urban development as an integrative factor in urban growth centres. It aims to answer the following research questions:

1. To what extent can UA play a significant role in adapting to the consequences of climate change, via climate protection, and via energy efficiency?
2. To what extent is UA an innovative strategy for sustainable land conservation of open urban areas?
3. To what extent can UA contribute to the struggle against poverty?
4. How can UA be integrated into urban development as a vital element in accordance with local conditions?

Approach

The parallel development of a theoretical basis, basic research, and applied research and implementation strategies characterises the project. The research team is bi-national, interdisciplinary, and transdisciplinary. The project pursues an open, process-oriented research approach subjected to follow-up adjustments.

According to the methodological approaches of the participating research disciplines, subsidiary research approaches follow different routes, comprising the normative, the descriptive/empirical, and the applied research orientation. The three most important methodological tools for the overall project are the spiral-shaped work approach, the integration of the subsidiary results, and the action-research approach via the pilot projects. The four topics urban development, agriculture, climate change and governance, and technical support were defined for the organisation of the working process and were studied in depth.

Decentral water treatment plant in Casablanca producing water for irrigation [Lukas Born]

Solutions

- Action Plan for integrating UA into the urban development process
- Design solutions for multifunctional space systems
- Models of regional and local climate, weather, water balance, air quality, and flooding as a basis for informed decision-making
- Experimental plants for industrial wastewater treatment and reuse
- Concepts for peri-urban tourism
- Approaches for healthy food production
- UA as an integrated element in informal settlements
- Awareness-raising (e.g., public campaign) and dissemination strategy

Contact

Project: Urban agriculture as integrative factor of climate-optimised urban development
Undine Giseke | Technische Universität Berlin, Chair of Landscape Architecture/ Open Space Planning (TU Berlin)
Email: undine.giseke@tu-berlin.de
Webpage: www.uac-m.org

New Town Development in the Tehran-Karaj Region (Iran)

Context

The enormous increases in population in threshold and developing countries in relation to rapid urbanisation, as well as rising living standards, pose significant challenges to the affected regions in terms of energy supply and climate protection. However, these rapidly growing regions also offer a great potential for shaping sustainable urban development. Particularly in Iran, these developments are strikingly manifest. The Tehran-Karaj region forms one of the fastest-growing urban agglomerations in the Middle East and is a major regional contributor to climate change. There is a demand for the construction of 1.5 million new housing units per year in a country that will be particularly affected by the effects of climate change. With the construction of new settlements, consumption of energy, commodities, and resources is rising dramatically. The related harmful climatic effects intensify global and regional risks.

Objectives

The Young Cities project is a German-Iranian applied research project that aims to develop solutions and strategies for a sustainable, energy-efficient, and resilient urban development in arid and semi-arid regions as a contribution to significant CO_2 reduction. The focus lies on contemporary, formally planned, mass housing, within the framework of the case study of Hashtgerd New Town in Tehran province. The project intends to decrease CO_2 emissions by reducing energy consumption within the principles of sustainable urban development. The aim is to help to reduce the consumption of other valuable environmental resources, primarily water, but also soil and air. These aspects are complemented by taking into account economic and social ambitions including social issues, efficient and flexible management, public participation, and environmentally conscious consumer behaviour, as well as by encouraging a positive local identity.

Approach

To implement the goals and objectives of the project, an integral, interdisciplinary approach to urban development was chosen, ranging across different levels and scales:

- Space—urban structure down to the sub-neighbourhood level
- Networks—infrastructure networks of energy, water, mobility
- Objects—buildings with a variety of different uses

The social and economic conditions of the project are addressed by the further dimension of cross-sector approaches. This part of the approach focuses on high-potential fields of action for sustainable development such as the following:

- Raising the qualification levels of construction workers for better construction quality, thus lowering energy demand of the buildings,
- The participation of the inhabitants and the raising of awareness on environmentally friendly behaviour.

The Young Cities project is committed to Action Research based on the method of "research through design": the verification of research hypotheses through planning, implementation, and realisation of pilot projects forms an integral part of the project. One area, thirty-five hectares in size, located in Hashtgerd New Town, 70 km west of Tehran, has been chosen as the central demonstration site for the development of an energy-efficient neighbourhood, called the "Shahre Javan Community".

Solutions

- Detailed master plan for a 35-ha pilot area; the Shahre Javan Community in Hashtgerd New Town
- "New Quality Building" with sixteen housing units, inaugurated in July 2010
- Manual for a climate-responsive and sustainable urban development

New neighbourhood under construction in Hashtgerd New Town [Lukas Born]

- Manual for integrated urban planning in semi-arid and arid regions
- Conceptual designs for energy-efficient residential and commercial buildings
- On-site vocational education and training for construction workers
- Public transport concept
- Wastewater concept
- Ecological assessment model
- Implementation of environmental compensation areas

Contact

Project: Young Cities–Developing energy-efficient urban fabric in the Tehran-Karaj region
Rudolf Schäfer | Technische Universität Berlin
School of Planning, Building, Environment
Email: rudolf.schaefer@tu-berlin.de
Webpage: www.youngcities.de

Resource Efficiency in Urumqi (China)

Context

Urumqi is the capital of China's North West Province, "Xinjiang Uygur Autonomous Region" (XUAR). With an initial population of 88,000 inhabitants in 1949, Urumqi is fast becoming the biggest economic growth node in Central Asia, with around 3.1 million inhabitants in the city and about 4.5 million in greater Urumqi. This rapid development is taking place in an ecologically highly sensitive (semi-)arid environment within a 50-km-wide irrigated green belt between the foothills of the glacial Tianshan Ridge (up to 5445 m a.s.l.) and the Junggar Basin (500–600 m a.s.l.) The cold winters are typically accompanied by extended periods of stable inversion layers, which lead to dramatic increased levels of air pollution. As the region is extremely mineral-rich (coal, oil, gas, ores), dynamic industrialisation and the rising wealth of the growing population, as well as the increasing volume of traffic, are further driving factors that have catapulted Urumqi onto the "blacklist" of the top five most air-polluted cities in the world [Blacksmith Report, 2007]. Both industrial and private household waste are increasing rapidly, not only in quantity but also in variety, without having led to specific adaptations in waste management.

Water is the most precious and socially sensitive resource in the region. A water provision gap starts to open up during the summer months and has to be gradually closed by the (over)exploitation of groundwater resources. Climate change is aggravating the situation, as the snowline rises, the period of snow coverage decreases, as does the period of permanent melted-ice water-runoff in spring.

Objectives

The project concentrates on energy efficiency, water resource efficiency and materials efficiency. Within the overall objective to promote a sustainability-oriented megacity development in semi-arid areas, the project aims to do the following:

- Lower energy consumption in private households, as well as in industrial areas, thereby lowering air pollution, CO_2 emissions, and resource extraction
- Promote the installation of renewable energy-based facilities
- Implement a GPR-based monitoring system, concentrating on soil moisture content as an indicator for climate change
- Design a realistic descriptive hydrological model and decision-making support system for Urumqi to allow political actors to be able to better predict future scenarios and their consequences on water availability and distribution
- Promote developments towards a circular economy on the level of industrial enterprises as well as industrial parks

Approach

The main focal points of the project are directed at the ecologically sensitive and closely interrelated core cycles (1) water, (2) materials, and (3) energy with three Sino-German task groups being assigned respectively. The Chinese teams are led by key political or scientific decision-makers who promote specific tasks based on high-ranking political contacts and who negotiate agreements, which has proven to be a helpful support for the project. Scientists, engineers, and other employees on the execution level proved to be important key partners within the development phase of products, processes, and the specification of advanced new ideas that contribute to greater resource efficiency in the respective fields of action. A cross-cutting exchange of ideas, concepts, and theoretical and practical solutions is being facilitated by various exchange activities.

Water resources in the mountains close to Urumqi [Carsten Zehner]

Solutions

- Construction of the first passive house in Western China
- Extra low-energy renovation of existing buildings
- Development of waste management software for enterprises in Midong Industrial Park that covers, classifies, and characterises all categories of waste
- Hydrological analyses and modelling, advice on efficient water use, and water information management for political decision-makers in Urumqi Region
- Mass and energy flow analysis in the Chinese PVC industry
- Capacity building for a soil moisture-based measurement methodology (Ground Penetrating Radar) as a basis for modelling climate change

Contact

Project: RECAST Urumqi—Meeting the resource efficiency challenge in a climate sensitive dryland megacity
Thomas Sterr | Ruprecht-Karls-Universität Heidelberg, Dept. of Geography
Email: thomas.sterr@geog.uni-heidelberg.de
Webpage: www.urumqi-drylandmegacity.uni-hd.de

References

Blacksmith Institute (2007): *The World's Worst Polluted Places—The Top Ten (of The Dirty Thirty)*, New York. In:
http://www.worstpolluted.org/reports/file/2007%20Report%20updated%202009.pdf (23.05.2014)

Transportation Management in Hefei (China)

Context

Growing urbanisation and the increasing size of metropolitan regions are a challenge, as well as an opportunity, for the economic development and the social balance of societies, particularly in rapidly developing countries like China. The dynamic evolution of Chinese cities poses special challenges for transport concepts. According to the recent census, five million people live in Hefei (capital of Anhui province, China), three million of whom live in the urban area. Meanwhile, the rapid rise of car ownership in Chinese cities significantly impacts people's lifestyles as well as the environment. Traffic congestion as a phenomenon has extended from first-tier cities to second-tier cities such as Hefei. The rapid growth of private car ownership has also led to the excessive rise in road construction that remains insufficient to keep up with traffic growth, while simultaneously consuming valuable land resources in Hefei. Traffic congestion is becoming ever more critical day by day and causes more delays, fuel consumption, air pollution, and CO_2 emissions. The rapidly growing demand for mobility and housing has created new challenges for urban administrative institutions, which have to deal with an unprecedented urban growth, thus leading to an urgent need for sustainable development.

Objectives

The main objectives of the METRASYS project are to contribute to climate protection through the development of sustainable transport in highly dynamic economic and urban regions. In particular, the project aims to provide decision-makers with the necessary means to effectively implement and guide sustainable transport in Hefei. Furthermore, special emphasis is placed on the general transferability of development approaches on traffic management for comparable megacities worldwide.

Approach

The project integrates different disciplines, e.g., spatial planning, transport science, engineering science, and political science, and addresses both planning and operational aspects of the transport sector, through deployment of a sophisticated geographic information system (GIS) and an advanced traffic-management system. This system also facilitates environmental evaluations and analyses with an emission and pollution dispersion model developed in this project. This, in turn, provides valuable feedback to the transport and urban planning process. Furthermore, the results are used to explore opportunities for climate finance, which provides additional incentives for sustainable transport development. This comprehensive approach was devised and has been implemented in close cooperation with relevant Chinese stakeholders. This contributes to a constructive and concrete stakeholder dialogue, bringing all relevant parties together, thereby addressing the challenges of sustainable mobility in a holistic manner. The project works in four main research areas related to energy-efficient future megacities:

1. Technology Development: Realisation of effective concepts and implementation of intelligent traffic management based on Floating Car Data (FCD) and video detection for intersection monitoring.
2. Model Development: Energy efficiency and reduction of greenhouse gas emissions by assessing the environmental impact of the traffic-management system and the planned urban traffic development through the validation and optimisation process using various models, such as traffic models, emission, and immission models.
3. Transport Planning: Capacity building and accompanying urban and transport planning for sustainable city development.

Besides high-rise buildings, there is still slow motion in Hefei's old city [Carsten Zehner]

4. Climate Finance: Identification of climate finance opportunities for sustainable low-carbon transport in Hefei.

Solutions

- Intelligent traffic management system based on floating-car data, video detection, and broadcasting with Digital Audio Broadcast (DAB)
- Model development for the assessment of environmental impacts of traffic as a basis for informed decision-making and climate-friendly transport planning strategies
- Guidelines and manuals for best practice in "traffic management", "transport planning", and "urban block design"
- Finance options for sustainable transport
- Strategic design proposal for pedestrian friendly cities

Contact

Project: METRASYS–Sustainable mobility for megacities
Alexander Sohr | German Aerospace Centre, Institute of Transportation Systems
Email: alexander.sohr@dlr.de
Webpage: www.metrasys.de

Governance for Sustainability in Hyderabad (India)

Context

Greater Hyderabad is predicted to reach a population of 10.5 million inhabitants by 2015. The rapid economic growth of the emerging megacity has facilitated higher living standards and modern lifestyles for the emerging middle class. This is, however, accompanied by escalating energy and resource consumption. Furthermore, long-standing problems remain unresolved. For example, approximately one-third of the population lives below the poverty line and continues to suffer from food, housing, education, and health problems. In addition to this, climate change is predicted to lead to extreme weather events, disastrous floods, strong heat waves, extreme droughts, and increasing water scarcity.

Given this natural, social, and economic context of Hyderabad, the question arises: what can be considered a reasonable response to the anticipated impact of climate change?

Objectives

The overall objective of the project is to develop a sustainable development framework for Hyderabad by prioritising mitigation and adaptation strategies for climate change and energy efficiency.

Focusing on the sectors of transport, food, land-use planning, and the provision of energy and water, the project pursues the following functional objectives:

1. To increase scientific knowledge and to generate a database concerning climate change, its mitigation and adaptation opportunities, as well as to ascertain the potential of energy efficiency through collaborative research.
2. To identify institutional and policy solutions to encourage the change of behaviour of relevant actors in order to address the problems (i.e. "getting the institutions right").
3. To design, propose, and implement demonstrable strategies for climate-change adaptation and mitigation, as well as for increased energy efficiency.
4. To ensure a wider adoption of these strategies by all relevant stakeholders and actors through appropriate communication, capacity building, advocacy, policy dialogues, and dissemination mechanisms.

Approach

The project aims to achieve climate-change adaptation and mitigation, as well as energy efficiency, through the design of appropriate policies that aim to change behaviour. Analysis of policies, of lifestyles in private households, of authorities for urban planning and administration, and of governance structures were conducted in tandem with a technical analysis in each of the focus fields: energy and water supply, food and health, and transport. The results of both analyses guided the conceptualisation of the pilot projects. The project applies a "discourse approach" to implement the necessary changes in the institutions and government organisations. The knowledge generated through the research and the implemented pilot projects that involve all the stakeholders and actors is embedded in local discourse and dialogue.

Eight pilot projects have been implemented and evaluated in the areas of urban planning, transport, food, and clean and efficient energy provision, as well as education for sustainable lifestyles. The management options that evolved through pilot projects have been transferred to relevant stakeholders in Hyderabad with the help of capacity-building measures. The consortium, involving partners from scientific, governmental, non-governmental, and private organisations, has formulated a Perspective Action Plan (PAP) for Hyderabad and proposed its adoption.

Problems of rural India effects Hyderabad's urban development as well [Carsten Zehner]

Solutions

- Climate Assessment Tool for Hyderabad (CATHY)
- Strategic Transport Planning Tool
- Street food-safety manual and on-site training to strengthen a climate-friendly urban food-supply system
- Collective action for fuel transition among the urban poor
- Cooperative and technical solutions to increase energy efficiency in irrigation
- Solar powered schools
- Education for sustainable lifestyles
- Community Radio

Contact

Project: Climate and energy in a complex transition process towards sustainable Hyderabad—mitigation and adaptation strategies by changing institutions, governance structures, lifestyles and consumption patterns
Konrad Hagedorn | Humboldt University Berlin, Department of Agricultural Economics
Email: k.hagedorn@agrar.hu-berlin.de
Webpage: www.sustainable-hyderabad.de

Adaptation Planning
in Ho Chi Minh City (Vietnam)

Context

The mega-urban region of Ho Chi Minh City (HCMC) in South Vietnam is one of the most dynamic examples of rapid urban development over the last two decades and, therefore, one of the regions most affected by climate change and risks in Vietnam. The urbanisation of Ho Chi Minh City has been intrinsically related to the process of industrialisation following the Doi Moi reforms of market liberalisation in 1987. Between 1986 and 2010, the population of HCMC almost doubled from 3.78 million inhabitants to the current level of 7.4 million inhabitants. In response to this high urbanisation pressure, HCMC's government was forced to repeatedly expand the urban boundary, leading to the establishment of six new urban districts. Due to HCMC's geographical location in a low altitude, intra-tropical coastal zone, northeast of the Mekong Delta and 50 km inland from the South China Sea, the city experiences significant annual variations of climatic and weather extremes. Together with its huge population, its economic assets, and the dominant role it plays in the national economy, the city is considered to be highly vulnerable to the impacts of climate change.

Objectives

The project aims to increase the resilience and adaptation capacities of HCMC in order to reduce the vulnerability of natural and human systems to the adverse effects of climate change. Hence, risks and vulnerabilities are assessed and sustainable adaptation measures are developed and incorporated into urban decision-making and planning processes. Consequently, the project seeks to establish a multi-layered, typological approach, which will be utilised to assess the sustainability of urban settlement developments. Furthermore, the project aims to develop adaptation strategies and measures which can be transferred to other affected regions.

Approach

The project follows an interdisciplinary approach by combining expertise in different fields related to the two overall topics which constitute the project structure: Action Field One focuses on environmental research; Action Field Two focuses on urban development.

The Urban Typology Framework provides important environmental and social information, which, in turn, is referred to the vulnerability assessment, based on strategic environmental assessment (SEA) as a basis for transferring scientifically known and documented problems of climate change into adapted planning systems (Action Field 1). Furthermore, the project aims to bring sustainable urban development strategies, in the context of climate change, into the mainstream urban system of HCMC. Based on the knowledge gained from the research, small-scale projects will be conducted with the Vietnamese partners to promote best-practice methods for further appropriate action (Action Field 2).

On the practical level, the instruments of zoning and building codes will be examined and recommendations will be made for their improvement with regard to sustainable urban development, energy efficiency, and resiliency to adverse climate changes. Furthermore, as the project follows an applied research approach, results are requested in terms of both implementation (practice) and research (theory). Both are complementary; thus, on the one hand, the implementation of measures will be an outcome of scientific research, and, on the other hand, research will be undertaken on the basis of the implementation of measures.

Especially HCMC's poor areas are vulnerable to flooding [Carsten Zehner]

Solutions

The following products are results of pilot projects implemented with different target groups:

- Urban Climate Map as a basis for planning decisions within the general land-use plan
- Urban Water Balance Modelling and Planning recommendations
- *Handbook for Decision-Makers: Land-Use Planning Recommendations—Adaptation Strategies for a Changing Climate in Ho Chi Minh City*
- *Urban Design Guidebook* as a tool for integrating climate change adaptation into planning and design decisions
- *Handbook for Green Housing* for disseminating good practices in urban design and architecture
- *Handbook for Community-Based Adaptation* as a guide for building resilient communities through local action

Contact

Project: Megacity research project TP. Ho Chi Minh
Michael Schmidt | Brandenburg University of Technology, Cottbus
Email: umweltplanung@tu-cottbus.de
Webpage: www.megacity-hcmc.org

Water Management in Lima (Peru)

Context

Lima, a desert city (9 mm annual precipitation), has a population of approximately 9.8 million and is growing at an annual rate of about 2%, largely due to the influx of poorer people from the provinces. This development puts additional pressure on informal settlements, which lack an appropriate supply of electricity, water, and sanitation. Consequently, the polarisation between rich and poor districts is increasing.

Water supply is mainly sourced from the Rímac River, which has an irregular flow due to the arid climate and due to significant seasonal rainfall variations in the Andean mountains. Furthermore, river flows from the Amazon catchment area are diverted in order to contribute to Lima's water supply while groundwater resources remain limited. The scarcity of water resources will further aggravate the situation, as Peru is the third-most sensitive country to impacts of climate change on precipitation and water availability [Rosenberger, 2006]. This is likely to intensify even more in the future due to the El Niño phenomenon.

At present, the water supply network covers 80.6% of the population of Lima, whilst about 77% of the population are connected to the public sewer network. At present, only about 17% of wastewater receives some form of treatment. New plants are under construction; however, they will only offer a limited degree of wastewater treatment. The major quantity of wastewater is simply discharged into the rivers or directly into the Pacific Ocean. Furthermore, the potential for water reuse has not yet been fully exploited. The water sector strongly interconnects with the energy system, not only in the inherent need for energy for water and wastewater pumping and treatment, but even more so for the joint use of reservoirs for water supply and for energy production.

Objectives

The Lima Water Project (LiWa) aims to improve sustainable planning and management of the water and sanitation system in Lima through informed decision-making and stakeholder participation. The project draws particular attention to the impacts of climate change and to the promotion of energy efficiency in water and sanitation systems. More specifically, the project intends to develop adequate and locally beneficial solutions for different problems and contexts that contribute to an overall favourable water-management concept.

Approach

The LiWa project focuses specifically on the development and application of fundamental procedures and tools for participatory decision-making, based on informed discussions. The project builds upon modelling and simulation of the entire water supply and sanitation system within the megacity system of Lima. Furthermore, the project integrates findings from global circulation models, regionalised to Peruvian river catchments. The project also develops and evaluates options for reorganising the water tariff system in order to meet economic, ecological, and social requirements. Additionally, urban planning aspects are considered by developing the ecological infrastructure strategy, which is based on the concepts of water-sensitive urban design. With this holistic project approach, key issues and challenges of climate-responsive and energy-efficient structures of water and wastewater management can be adequately addressed.

Hence, the following work packages are being addressed:

1. Integrated scenario development
2. Downscaling of climate models and water-balance modelling
3. Macro-modelling and simulation system

Irrigated park in central Lima [Lukas Born]

4. Participation and governance approach
5. Education and capacity building
6. Economic evaluation of water-pricing options
7. Integrated urban planning strategies and planning support

Solutions

- Simulator for macro-modelling of the urban water system for informed decision-making
- Simulation of Lima's future development, taking into account climate-change effects on the water system for long-term planning
- Round-table discussions as new forms of governance in the water sector
- Water-pricing options and improvement of tariff structure
- Integrated urban planning strategies and planning support
- E-Academy for education and capacity building

Contact

Project: Sustainable water and wastewater management in urban growth centres coping with climate change—concepts for Metropolitan Lima, Peru
Manfred Schütze | ifak e. V. Otto-von-Guericke-Universität Magdeburg
Email: manfred.schuetze@ifak.eu
Webpage: www.lima-water.de

References

Rosenberger, M. (2006): *Klimawandel in Peru – alle zwei Minuten ein Fußballfeld weniger.* Konrad-Adenauer-Stiftung, in: http://www.kas.de/wf/doc/kas_10909-1522-1-30. pdf?070523151027, (23.5.2014)

CASABLANCA: Different modes of traffic in the outskirts [Lukas Born]

Authors

Steffen Bubeck works at the Institute for Energy Economics and the Rational Use of Energy (IER) as part of the Graduate and Research School "Efficient use of Energy" Stuttgart (GREES). In 2012, he received a master's degree in technically oriented Business Administration from Universität Stuttgart. His current research focuses on cost-efficient potentials of expanding electrical end-use applications in Germany.

Email: steffen.bubeck@ier.uni-stuttgart.de

Manuel Fiechtner, born 1987, studied B. Sc. Geographical Sciences at the Freie Universität Berlin from 2008–2012 and started MSc in Urban and Regional Planning at Technische Universität Berlin in 2012. Since 2012, he has been working as a project assistant at the Berlin Senate Department for Urban Development and the Environment in an e-mobility research project. During his first study, he developed a special interest in public transportation, GIS, and megacities. As part of METRASYS project, he visited Hefei, China in May 2011 for his Bachelor's thesis.

Email: m.fiechtner87@mailbox.tu-berlin.de

Katharina Fricke has been studying geography, environmental physics, and political science in Heidelberg since 2002, supplemented by interdisciplinary environmental studies. She graduated from Ruprecht-Karls-Universität Heidelberg with a diploma degree in geography April 2008. During her PhD research, she was part of the task group "Water Resource Efficiency" of the multidisciplinary research project "RECAST Urumqi–Meeting the Resource Efficiency Challenge in a Climate Sensitive Dryland Megacity Environment", and finished her dissertation on the water resource challenge and adaptation measures in Urumqi Region in October 2012.

Email: katharina.fricke@geog.uni-heidelberg.de

Zarela Garcia Trujillo is a sanitary and environmental engineer. She has participated in research projects to obtain efficiency at wastewater treatment at CITRAR, Lima. She has worked in SEDAPAL, updating the register of water and sewer networks. Currently, she is working as a Technical Assistant in the execution of drinking water systems and sanitation, and a wastewater treatment plant.

Email: zarela.garcia@gmail.com

Christian Kimmich is an agricultural economist and Postdoc at the Swiss Federal Institute for Forest, Snow and Landscape Research within the domain of ETH Zürich. He conducted his PhD research at the Division of Resource Economics at Humboldt-Universität zu Berlin within the BMBF-funded emerging megacity programme on the sustainable provision of electricity for irrigation in agriculture from the perspective of evolutionary and institutional economics. He also worked on the regional governance of energetic biomass utilisation, food versus fuel conflicts at the Leibniz-Institute for Agricultural Engineering, and broader issues of ecological macroeconomics.

Email: christian.kimmich@wsl.ch

Jakob Kopec studied Spatial Planning at Technische Universität Dortmund. During his studies, he focused on geographic-information systems, remote sensing and geoinformatics, as well as on planning systems in the renewable energy sector. Since 2010, he has been working at the chair of "Spatial Information Management and Modelling" in Dortmund. He takes part in the BMBF research program "Megacity Research Project TP. Ho Chi Minh–Integrative Urban and Environmental Planning Framework–Adaptation to Global Climate Change" and in the BMWi research programme "Research for an environmentally friendly, reliable and affordable energy supply" in cooperation with the transmission network driver Amprion GmbH. He is also one of the founders of the cooperative "Die Energiegesellschafter eG".

Email: jakob.kopec@tu-dortmund.de

Karsten Kozempel graduated with an MSc in Information and Media Technologies from Brandenburgische Technische Universität Cottbus in 2007. From 2008, he worked as a PhD student for the German Aerospace Center and received his doctorate in computer science from Humboldt-Universität zu Berlin in 2012. Since 2011, he has worked as research staff member for the German Aerospace Center at the Institute for Transportation Systems. His research focuses on computer vision and photogrammetry for object detection and tracking, as well as situation detection and behaviour classification.
 Email: karsten.kozempel@dlr.de

Myriam Laux studied environmental engineering at Universität Stuttgart. She specialised in the field of water supply and sanitation, river and groundwater engineering. To gain more knowledge in hydrogeology she studied at the University of Waterloo, Canada from 2010 to 2011. To get some work experience in the field of river construction, she carried out an internship at WaterGroup Pty. Ltd in Sydney, Australia (2011–2012). She wrote her final thesis at ifak in Magdeburg in the LiWa programme on the Water Supply System of Lima and finished her studies in 2012. Since May 2013, she has been working for the engineering office Wald+Corbe.
 Email: myriamlaux@gmail.com

Xiaoli Lin graduated in 2008 from the Shenzhen University (China) with a bachelor's degree in Urban Planning. In 2010, she enrolled in the "Urban Management" master's programme at Technische Universität Berlin. In 2011, she worked as an internship in the megacity project METRASYS. Applying the research skills acquired from the METRASYS project, she conducted a research in Shenzhen about Transit-oriented Development for her master thesis.
 Email: linxiaoli@zedat.fu-berlin.de

Kara McElhinney is a 2012 graduate of the international master's programme "Water Resources Engineering & Management (WAREM)" at Universität Stuttgart in Germany. Her academic and professional interests include the integrated management of water resources in urban areas, interdisciplinary approaches to urban water infrastructure development, and urban design. A native of Boston MA, USA, Kara also holds a bachelor's degree in Mechanical Engineering from The Cooper Union for the Advancement of Science and Art in New York, NY. She currently works in Hamburg in the field of environmental consulting.
 Email: kara.mcelhinney@gmail.com

Yassine Moustanjidi is a Moroccan architect and urban designer; he holds a diploma in architecture from the National School of Architecture Rabat, an MSc in urban design from Tongji University, Shanghai, and Technische Universität Berlin. Yassine is a scientific research assistant within the chair of Landscape Architecture and Open Space Planning at Technische Universität Berlin. He is a PhD candidate with focus on the development of megacities and urban planning.
 Email: ymoustanjidi@gmail.com

Ngoc-Anh Nguyen received her bachelor's degree in Environmental Management from The University of Newcastle in Australia, and her master's degree in Urban Development Planning from Vietnamese German University in Vietnam. She has six years working experience in the non-profit sector. She is now working at the "International Union for Conservation of Nature".
 Email: ngocanh.na@gmail.com

Ntombifuthi Ntuli holds an MPhil in Energy Studies. She has worked in different spheres of the public sector. She spent eight years in Ekurhuleni Metropolitan Municipality working on Energy and Climate Change programmes. She spent three years at the Embassy of Denmark working as a Coordinator for the Business to Business Programme, where she facilitated business linkage between Danish and South African companies. She joined the National Department of Trade and Industry in January 2012. In her current role as Director: Renewable Energy Industries, she is responsible for facilitating the development of the local renewable energy industry.
 Email: ntombifuthi.ntuli@gmail.com

Nadia Poor Rahim obtained a bachelor's degree in architecture at the Art University of Isfahan/Iran and has a degree (Dipl.-Ing.) from Technische Universität Berlin. In parallel, she began a master's course in Real Estate Management. She worked in the Megacities Project "Young Cities|Iran" as a student assistant at the Department of Vocational Education of the TU Berlin. She recently started a new career as assistant researcher in a BMBF-funded project on Mobile Learning Unit.

Email: nadia.poorrahim@tu-berlin.de

Shabnam Teimourtash studied architecture and real estate management at Technische Universität Berlin. She wrote her PhD dissertation on energy and climate-efficient architecture within the framework of the Young Cities Project. She participated in DAAD's Scholarship Programme "Study and Research Scholarships of Today for the Megacities of Tomorrow".

Email: Shabnam.teimourtash@gmail.com

© 2014 by jovis Verlag GmbH
Texts by kind permission of the authors.
Pictures by kind permission of the photo-
graphers/holders of the picture rights.

Editors of the publications series:
Elke Pahl-Weber, Bernd Kochendörfer,
Lukas Born, Jan Müller, and Ulrike Assmann

Editor of this volume:
Lukas Born

Copyediting: Inez Templeton, Berlin
Design and setting: Tom Unverzagt, Leipzig
Lithography: Bild1Druck, Berlin
Printing and binding: GRASPO CZ, a.s., Zlín

Bibliographic information published by the
Deutsche Nationalbibliothek

The Deutsche Nationalbibliothek lists this publication in the Deutsche Nationalbibliografie;
detailed bibliographic data are available on the
Internet at http://dnb.d-nb.de

jovis Verlag GmbH
Kurfürstenstraße 15/16
10785 Berlin

www.jovis.de

jovis books are available worldwide in selected bookstores. Please contact your nearest
bookseller or visit www.jovis.de for information
concerning your local distribution.

ISBN 978-3-86859-279-5